ADVANCED ENGLISH VOCABULARY
Workbook One
REVISED EDITION

by Helen Barnard
Victoria University of Wellington

NEWBURY HOUSE PUBLISHERS, Cambridge
A division of Harper & Row, Publishers, Inc.
New York, Philadelphia, San Francisco, Washington
London, Mexico City, São Paulo, Singapore, Sydney

NEWBURY HOUSE PUBLISHERS
A division of Harper & Row, Publishers, Inc.

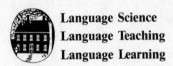

Language Science
Language Teaching
Language Learning

CAMBRIDGE, MASSACHUSETTS

ADVANCED ENGLISH VOCABULARY
Workbook 1

ISBN: 912066-19-9

Printed in the United States of America

First printing, October 1971
Revised Edition, first printing, October 1980
89   15 14 13

INTRODUCTION

The students for whom this course is intended fall into three main categories:

(a) Students in non-English speaking countries proceeding to non-English medium universities, who need the non-technical vocabulary which will enable them to read English textbooks and other material on their professional subjects (i.e. the physical sciences, mathematics, technology, and the social sciences*).

(b) Students in non-English speaking countries preparing to take professional courses at English-medium universities at home or abroad.

(c) Students of overseas origin in English speaking countries taking courses in English preparatory to entering universities or institutions in their host countries.

The students for whom the course was originally produced, and who served as an experimental group for the development and revision of the course material, belong to the third category. They were Colombo Plan students from various countries taking a three months' intensive English course at the English Language Institute in Wellington, preparatory to entering New Zealand universities and technical colleges. Some of the course material has also been used by groups of students in the Wellington Polytechnic, Canterbury University (Christchurch), the University of the South Pacific (Suva), and by a group of Peace Corps teachers assigned to teach the English needed for science and mathematics in Fijian schools.

The needs of the three groups of learners listed above identify the purpose of the course. Its purpose is to teach the vocabulary which will enable these students to read English books and periodicals on their subjects and understand what they hear in lectures and seminars where English is used. It aims to teach this vocabulary not merely by introducing it into the course material but by explaining it and making the students thoroughly familiar with it.

The course consists of five workbooks (each divided into sections) which can be covered in three months of intensive study, or spread out over a longer period. The workbooks are mainly self-instructional. A self-

*For present purposes, the 'social sciences' include economics, political science, anthropology, sociology, psychology and geography.

instructional course is essential for isolated students, and the workbooks are equally useful for pre-university classes. Individual learning activities for large classes can only be provided by workbooks, in the absence of expensive equipment. Even in a situation where classes are smaller it has been found that a "do-it-yourself" system produces better results, since it enables students to define their own objectives, program a sequence through which they can attain them, and establish them as navigators of their own progress.

The Basis of the Course

The course is based on a two thousand word vocabulary called the "second thousand" and "third thousand" word lists. A "first thousand" word list of 1,000 content words, together with about 275 structural words and phrases, is assumed to be known in advance. Words taught in each book are indexed at the back.

The first thousand word list takes into account the results of a previous study (especially M. West's 'Minimim Adequate' and 'General Service' lists, Basic English, Riewald's lists, and H. Bongers K list). The usefulness of each item was also checked, over a period of four years, by observation of overseas teachers at the English Language Institute (Wellington) who used the vocabulary for paraphrasing, speech making, teaching and defining words not in the vocabulary.

The second and third thousand word lists were compiled on the basis of counts of non-technical vocabulary in university science and social science textbooks prescribed in Osmania University, Hyderabad, India, and in Victoria University, Wellington. The glossary of "The Structure of Technical English" (A. J. Herbert, Longmans) was also consulted, and a few high frequency words included from counts of issues of "The New Scientist" and the Indian "Statesman." Technical words were excluded because these words form part of the subject matter of professional disciplines, and are therefore best taught through these disciplines.

How to Use the Course

Each of the thirty units of the course is divided into five subsections: (1) vocabulary, (2) word study, (3) dictation exercises and dictation passages, (4) reading passages, and (5) a short word-completion test on the section vocabulary, which can be corrected by the students.

INTRODUCTION (cont.)

The word-study subsections include explanation and definition of words, explanatory diagrams and drawings, programmed learning passages, and exercises on the structure and syntax when words present such problems. Students can complete the word-study tasks and exercises either alone or under the supervision of a teacher. The dictation exercises and dictations require the aid of a good speaker of English. When students have worked through the word-study and dictation subsections, they will have some familiarity with the section vocabulary which follows. The reading passages can then be read without recourse to a dictionary or any other aid, and therefore offer the experience of an achievement. If the reading passages are studied in class they can be used as a basis for oral or written exercises and tests. Samples of such exercises and tests are given at the end of the first workbook. Finally a short word-completion test (4) will help the students to assess their familiarity with the vocabulary of the section.

Vocabulary is taught in the workbooks by cumulative techniques, i.e. by explanation followed by planned *repetition* of the words in a variety of typical contexts. The main condition for the attainment of the objectives of the course is therefore the careful completion of *all* the tasks and exercises it contains.

Helen Barnard

Victoria University of Wellington
New Zealand

INSTRUCTIONS FOR STUDENTS

1. You learn the words in this course by reading them and hearing them and saying them again and again in natural situations and contexts. So you should do *every part* of the course carefully. *Do not leave out* anything. Follow all instructions carefully.

2. When you study the items in Word Study you will see blank spaces. Read each sentence softly to yourself, *including* the missing words. The blank spaces should be filled in with your mind's eye first, then with pen or pencil. Do not write the words mechanically, but think about the meaning of the sentence as you write.

3. After you have gone through the Word Study items once, turn to the vocabulary list at the beginning of the unit. Read through the list and put a mark (√) against the words you are sure that you know. If you do not feel sure about any word, turn back to the Word Study pages and study that word again. The reading passages and the little test at the end of the unit will also show you that there are some words you need to review (i.e. study again).

4. Notice that for the Dictation Exercises and Dictations you will need the help of someone who can speak English well.

5. You will find that you can read the Reading Passages without much difficulty, because you will be familiar with the vocabulary they contain. Try to understand the ideas and information in each passage. After reading a passage three or four times, write the *title* of the passage on a piece of paper and shut your book. Then try to write one or two paragraphs on the same topic (=subject), using ideas and sentences that you remember from your reading.

TABLE OF CONTENTS

UNIT I
1.1 Vocabulary   1
1.2 Word Study   2
1.3 Dictation Exercises and Dictation Passages   10
1.4 Reading Passages   13
1.5 Vocabulary Test   15

UNIT II
2.1 Vocabulary   17
2.2 Word Study   18
2.3 Dictation Exercises and Dictation Passages   25
2.4 Reading Passages   28
2.5 Vocabulary Test   30

UNIT III
3.1 Vocabulary   31
3.2 Word Study   33
3.3 Dictation Exercises and Dictation Passages   43
3.4 Reading Passages   46
3.5 Vocabulary Test   48

UNIT IV
4.1 Vocabulary   49
4.2 Word Study   50
4.3 Dictation Exercises and Dictation Passages   62
4.4 Reading Passages   65
4.5 Vocabulary Test   68

UNIT V
5.1 Vocabulary   69
5.2 Word Study   70
5.3 Dictation Exercises and Dictation Passages   81
5.4 Reading Passages   85
5.5 Vocabulary Test   88

UNIT VI
6.1 Vocabulary   89
6.2 Word Study   90
6.3 Dictation Exercises and Dictation Passages   100
6.4 Reading Passages   103
6.5 Vocabulary Test   105

UNIT   VII
  7.1   Vocabulary   107
  7.2   Word Study   108
  7.3   Dictation Exercises and Dictation Passages   117
  7.4   Reading Passages   119
  7.5   Vocabulary Test   122

UNIT   VIII
  8.1   Vocabulary   123
  8.2   Word Study   124
  8.3   Dictation Exercises and Dictation Passages   133
  8.4   Reading Passages   136
  8.5   Vocabulary Test   140

UNIT   IX
  9.1   Vocabulary   141
  9.2   Word Study   142
  9.3   Dictation Exercises and Dictation Passages   154
  9.4   Reading Passages   157
  9.5   Vocabulary Test   160

UNIT   X
 10.1   Vocabulary   161
 10.2   Word Study   162
 10.3   Dictation Exercises and Dictation Passages   173
 10.4   Reading Passages   175
 10.5   Vocabulary Test   177

Unit I

1.1 VOCABULARY

These are the words you will practice in this unit:

VERBS		
add		(+ noun plural)
add		(+ noun + to + noun)
allow	(al·low')	(+ noun + to + stem)
cool		
cool		(+ noun)
divide	(di·vide')	(+ noun)
divide		(+ noun + between + noun)
divide		(+ noun + by + noun)
divide		(+ noun + into + noun)
expand	(ex·pand')	
form		(+ noun)
heat		(+ noun)
multiply	(mul'ti·ply)	(+ noun + by + noun)

NOUNS			
addition	(ad·di'tion)	a million	(mil'lion)
accuracy	(ac'cu·ra·cy)	a multiple	(mul'ti·ple)
a bar		multiplication	(mul·ti·pli·ca'tion)
a basis	(ba'sis)	a quantity	(quan'ti·ty)
a century	(cen'tu·ry)	a set (of)	
(a) depth		a standard	(stand'ard)
a distance	(dis'tance)	a system	(sys'tem)
(a) division	(di·vi'sion)	(a) temperature	(tem'per·a·ture)
expansion	(ex·pan'sion)	a unit	(u'nit)
a fact		(a) value	(val'ue)
a figure	(fig'ure)	(a) width	
(a) height			
(a) length			

ADJECTIVES			
accurate	(ac'cu·rate)	metric	(met'ric)
based on		necessary	(nec'es·sary)
basic	(ba'sic)	official	(of·fi'cial)
complete	(com·plete')	perfect	(per'fect)
cool		special	(spe'cial)
equal to	(e'qual)	standard	(stand'ard)
familiar with	(fa·mil'iar)	sure	

ADVERBS	
accurately	(ac'cu·rate·ly)
nearly	(near'ly)
nowadays	(now'a·days)
probably	(prob'a·bly)

PHRASES	
for example	(ex·am'ple)
instead of	(in·stead')

1

Unit I

1.2 WORD STUDY

INSTRUCTIONS: Study the following words and the uses of them:

a distance   If we draw a straight line between two points or places, and measure the line, that length is the *distance between* the two points or places.

Examples: In America and England the d_____e b_____n two towns is measured in miles; in France and Germany the d_____e is measured in kilometers. The d_____ b_____ Boston and New York City is 225 miles. The _____ _____ my house and school is not great. My house is on a hill and can be seen from a _____ of three miles.

a century
pl. centuries   Time can be measured in seconds, minutes, hours, days, weeks, months and years. Beginning with the year of Christ's birth (called A. D. 1), time is also measured in *centuries*. The word *century* comes from the Latin word *centum*, which means 100. A century is a h_____d years.

Examples: This c_____y began in 1900 and will end in 1999. We live in the tw_____th c_____y. Columbus sailed to America in 1492. He sailed to America in the _____ _____ .

a quantity
pl. quantities   A *quantity* is the weight of a thing which can be measured, or the volume of a thing (the space it takes) which can be measured. Measures themselves (a gram, a pint, etc.) can also be called *quantities*. In mathematics, a quantity can also mean a number.

Examples: The smallest qu_____y of flour which you can buy at a grocery store in some countries is three pounds. The smallest _____ of flour which you can buy at a _____ store in the United States is one pound. The _____ of milk which this bottle will hold is one pint. Why did you buy such a large _____of oil? Twenty-four tons of coal is a large _____ .

a standard
standard
a bar   In some countries there is *a bar* (a long piece of metal) which is kept in the offices of the government. Its length is one yard. It is the *standard* yard. It is a standard of measurement. When people in the United States measure things, they must use a measure which is a copy of the st_____d yard (the metal bar) which is kept by the government in Washington, D. C. A measure should not be too long or too short. It should have the right length. To test its length we use a st_____d.

A st_____ is something which is used as a test of other things of the same kind. When we take something as a s_____, this means that we try to copy it, we use it to measure other things, or we use it to test the goodness or completeness of other things of the same kind. A s_____ may also mean an idea (used as a test) of what is best, or what people should do.

Examples: A yard is a _____ of measurement, and all persons who sell things measured by the yard must use a measure which is a careful copy of a _____ yard. The _____ yard is a metal bar kept in the offices of the government.

To pass a geography examination, a student must know something. The teachers or examiners fix a _____ by telling the students what they must know to pass the examination. The _____ of the examination is fixed by the things which students must know if they want to pass. In a mathematics examination, some questions may be easy and some may be more difficult. The difficulty of the questions tests the students and fixes a _____ which they try to reach.

Mrs. Brown cleans her kitchen floor twice a day. She has high st_____s of cleanliness. Madox Ford was not a great painter but he had a _____ . He took a long time over his paintings and threw away those which did not come up to his _____ .

(a) value   (a) The *value* of a thing may mean the money for which it can be bought or sold, or the things for which it can be exchanged. (A countable or uncountable noun.)
(b) The value of a thing may mean, not the money which is paid for it, but the money which *should*

2

1.2 WORD STUDY

be given for it. (An uncountable noun.)

(c) The value of a thing may mean its usefulness, or anything which makes people need it or want it. (An uncountable noun.)

Examples (The first meaning): In the next few years the value of land will go up, but the value of clothes and furniture may fall. The present value of your car is only 1000 dollars.
(The second meaning): I gave 40 dollars for this washing machine, but its real value is about 80 dollars. He sold his house for more than its real v____e.
(The third meaning): Walking has great v_____ for people who want to keep healthy. I stopped studying French ten years ago; so these books no longer have any _____ for me. I found his lectures of real _____.

a set (of)   We speak of a *set* of cups and saucers, a set of teeth, a set of chessmen (used for playing chess), a set of furniture, a set of rules, a set of problems. A set of things is a number of things of the same kind, which are kept together because they are alike, or which are used together, or which are thought of together.

Examples: She has bought a new s__ __ chairs for the dining room. I have lost two of my chessmen, so I must get another _____. I have never met such a stupid _____ _____ people in my whole life. Please do this _____ _____ problems for homework. Before you use this machine there is a _____ _____ rules which you must study.

complete   A thing is *complete* if it has all its parts.

Examples: This exercise is not complete; you have only written eight sentences; you have not finished it. This set of playing cards is not c_____e; the king and queen of hearts are not here. He has a _____ set of Shakespeare's plays in his library. People say that a family is not _____ without children.

official   We say that something is *official* when it is said, done, made or fixed by a government or by people who have the power to make rules or fix standards or tell us important things.

Examples: Every modern nation has o_____l standards of measurement. Some people say that the queen has given birth to a son, but the news is not yet _____. The President of the United States made an _____ speech on the television yesterday.

perfect   A thing is *perfect* when it is complete and has no fault, when it is the best of its own kind.

Examples: It is very difficult to draw a p_____t circle. Your work is good, but no one can call it _____. They found a _____ place for their holiday. She is a _____ wife.

necessary   Look at the spelling of this word and remember it! A *necessary* thing is one which is needed for living or for doing what we want to do.

Examples: Food, air, and clothes are necessary for life. To cook food, heat is nec_____y. To make accurate measurements, standard measures are n____ssary. If you want to study at a university in England, America, or New Zealand, it is nec_____y to know English. If you want to visit some countries, it is n____ssary to have a passport. When you make a cake, you must use the n_____y quantities of flour, sugar, eggs, and butter or oil. Before you go to school, it may not be n_____ to pass an examination, but in most countries it is _____ to pass an examination before you go to a university. In New Zealand, if you are over 21, it is not _____ for you to pass an examination to go to a university.

cool   In the summer, when we feel a *cool* wind on our faces, we enjoy it. We also enjoy a cool drink when we feel hot. In the hot weather we sit under a tree or go indoors: we try to keep c____. It is c____er in the evening than it is in the middle of the day. C____ winds and c____ places are often pleasant; cold winds and cold places are not pleasant. It is often pleasant to feel c____, but it is not pleasant to feel cold.

1.2 WORD STUDY

A wind feels c___l when it has less heat than the hot air around us. A person's body gets c___l or cooler when it loses some heat. So we can say that things or people are cool when they have less heat than the air or other things around them; the day is cool when it is not so hot as other days at a given time of year; things or people get cool when they lose heat.

cool
cool

When a thing *cools*, it becomes cooler or colder. When you cool something, you make it cooler or colder.

Examples: I must wait till the milk cools before I drink it. When you take a cake out of the oven you should leave it to c___l. Water takes longer to _____ than land.

You can c____ the milk by putting it in the refrigerator. The winds from the sea _____ the air in the afternoon.

allow
familiar with
special

New students who come to the university must get to know the buildings and classrooms well. They must become *familiar with* them. Soon they will want to use the university library; so they must learn the library rules. The library makes *special* rules and asks every student to keep them. All the old students are f_____r w___ these rules. New students must also become f_____ w_____ them. It is nec_____y to know these rules.

Students *are allowed to* (= have permission to) take books out of the library. They are a_____ed to take three books at a time. They are not a_____d __ keep a book for more than two weeks. They can also take magazines away to read. They are not _____ ____ keep a magazine for _____ _____ two weeks. In the library magazines are called **periodicals**. Every student will find books and periodicals about his or her special subjects. They will also find books about their sp_____l interests.

What do we mean by a student's special interests? We mean a student's interests which other people may not have. People's interests are different.

Each department in the university has rules of its own which are different from those of other departments; in other words, each department has special rules. The sp_____l rules of the library are made by the head librarian only for the library; other departments of the university do not have the same rules.

Most schools have s_____ classrooms for geography. In these classrooms you will find maps and other things useful for learning geography, though they are not useful for other subjects.

In some universities there is a _____ room for the teachers. This is a room used only by the teachers, not by everyone who comes to study or work at a university.

basic
based on
a basis
allowed to
not allowed to

We all learned arithmetic when we were at school. In some ways arithmetic is like a building. When people start to make a building, they put some very strong bricks or stones at the bottom and on top of these they put other bricks until the building is com_____e. In the same way, in arithmetic there are some rules which come first, and all the other rules must be built on them. These first rules are called the *basic* rules; basic really means **at the bottom**, or **underneath**. In arithmetic the rules of addition and equality are b___c; all the other rules are built on them, or *based on* them. The rules of addition and equality are the *basis* of work in arithmetic.

The rules and laws of a good government are based on the needs of the people. People are not all__ed __ break these laws, because if they do, they will give trouble to others. The rules of a good library are _____ _____ the needs of the students and teachers who use it. Students are not _____ _____ break these rules, because if they do, they will give trouble to all the other people who use the library.

4

1.2 WORD STUDY

add
add
equal to
instead of
a figure
a million

Tom likes to do arithmetic. Today he wants to *add* two numbers. He wants to add four to six. He _____s four to six and gets the correct result, which is ten. He writes: 6 + 4 = 10 This means "six added to four is equal to ten." When we do arithmetic we write + *instead of* **added to**. We write = instead of (in place of) *is equal to*. When we write numbers, we use *figures* instead of words. We write 6 (which is a f___re) in_____d of six. We write 4 in_____ of four.

When we do arithmetic, what do we write instead of thirty-six? _____

What do we write instead of a hundred and fifty-nine? _____

Add seven to ten. What is this equal to? Write the sum in figures and give the result. _____

Write these numbers in figures
(a) Forty-nine   _____

(b) Seven thousand   _____

(c) Eighteen million   _____

We can add six to itself. We can write 6 + 6. What is 6 + 6 equal to? It is _____ _____12.
6 + 6 = 12

How many sixes are there here? There are **two** sixes. When we add six to itself, or when we add two sixes together, we *multiply* six by two. When we do arithmetic, we write x instead of multiplied by. Six multiplied by two is equal to twelve. Write this in figures: _____

When we mu___ply six by a hundred, this means that we add six to itself until we have a hundred sixes. When we do this we write   6 x 100 = 600.

Now write the following in figures and give the result in figures.
(a) Eight multiplied by four is equal to _____ _____ .

(b) Thirteen multiplied by three is equal to _____ _____ .

(c) Three hundred and six multiplied by ten is equal to _____ _____ .

(d) Five million multiplied by a thousand is equal to _____ _____ .
     (Remember that there are six 0's in a million and three 0's in a thousand.)

divide
divide
divide
divide
division

Look at the spelling of this word, DIVIDE.

The first part of this word is DI-
DI- is the short form of DIS- (Latin).

One meaning of DI- and DIS- is "into two parts" or "into parts."

When we *divide* a cake or a loaf of bread or an apple, we cut it or break it into parts.
Here is a cake. We will cut it into three parts.

Now the cake is divided into three.
Many things can be divided. A cake can be divided into three parts, or divided **among** three people. A house can be di___ed into two apartments, or di___ed between two families. A big field can be di___ed into a number of smaller fields. When half the people in a country fight against the other half, the country is di___ed. A family may also be di___ed, when a husband leaves his wife or when there is a quarrel. These are unhappy *divisions*.

Now we will think about division in arithmetic. Can a number be di___ed? Yes. Here are 10 apples.

We will divide these apples **equally** among five children. This means that we must give an equal number of apples to each child.

To do this, we will do arithmetic. Instead of writing "ten divided into five parts," or "ten divided by five," we will write: 10 ÷ 5

5

1.2 WORD STUDY

What is this equal to? $10 \div 5 = 2$

If you look at the apples again, you will see that this is correct.

There are five children, and each child gets two apples. The apples are now d____ed equally among ____ children. We d_____d the number of apples by five to get this result. So numbers can be _____ ed.

Write these problems in figures and give the result.

(a) Divide eight by two   _____

(b) Divide a hundred by five   _____

(c) Divide two million by four   _____

(d) Divide a hundred and eighty by nine   _____

(e) Divide ninety-one by thirteen   _____

addition
multiplication
division

The work of adding is called *addition*.

The work of multiplying is called *multiplication*.

The work of dividing is called *division*. The result of dividing is also sometimes called division or a division.

How many divisions are there in this line?

Here are some problems. How will you do them: by addition, by division, or by multiplication? Cross out the two answers which are wrong.

1. $6 \div 2$
   (a) by addition   (b) by division   (c) by multiplication.

2. 24×8
   (a) by addition   (b) by division   (c) by multiplication.

3. $6 + 3 + 24$
   (a) by addition   (b) by division   (c) by multiplication.

How will you do the following problems: by addition, by division, or by multiplication? Cross out the two answers which are wrong.

1. Tom is 6 years old and Tom's brother is twice as old as Tom. How old is his brother?
   (a) by addition   (b) by division   (c) by multiplication.

2. I have 44 books for 11 students. If I give an equal number of books to each student, how many will one student get?
   (a) by addition   (b) by division   (c) by multiplication.

3. I went to the store to buy my groceries. I spent 20 cents on salt, 50 cents on rice, 90 cents on butter, and 55 cents on eggs. How much did I spend?
   (a) by addition   (b) by division   (c) by multiplication.

a multiple

What is the *multiple* of a number? It is that number multiplied by another.

4 is a m_____ple of 2, because $4 = 2 \times 2$.
6 is a m_____le of 3, because $6 = 2 \times 3$.
4 is not a m_____e of 3, because 4 cannot be divided by 3; 3 cannot be multiplied by another number to make 4.

Questions: (Answer Yes or No)
Is 12 a multiple of 3?
Is 12 a multiple of 5?
Is 25 a multiple of 5?
Is 40 a multiple of 13?
Is 40 a multiple of 8?

1.2 WORD STUDY

Finish these sentences:

32 is a m_____e of _____
 9 is a m_____ of _____
21 is a m_____ of _____
100 is a m_____ of _____

accurate
accurately
accuracy
inaccurate

The word *accurate* is derived from the Latin word **cura**, which means **care**. Accurate work is work which is careful and correct. The word accurate gives us the idea of keeping **close to a standard**, for example, a standard of measurement, of pronunciation, of grammar, or of truth.

Look at this sentence: **Ten is a multiple of three.**

Is this sentence acc____te? It is grammatically acc____te, because it is a _____e by the standards of grammar. It is also spelled *accurately*. But it is not mathematically a_____e, because it is not a_____e by the standards of mathematics.

Look at this sentence: **Eights is a multiple of the four.**

Is it accurate or *inaccurate*? Is it a_____ by mathematical standards? Is it a_____ by grammatical standards?

When we write essays or exercises for our teachers or for ourselves, we must try to be sure that our work is _____ in every way; in its grammar, in its facts, and in its spelling. High standards of *accuracy* are necessary for any students who wish to do their work well.

probably
sure

Mr. Brown says that he is *sure* that the morning train for New York leaves at 9 o'clock. He says this because he has just looked at the railroad timetable and found the time of the train, or because he uses that train every week. He **knows** the time of the train; so if anyone asks him he can say he is sure about it. If he is **not sure**, this means that he does **not really know** the time of the train. A man is s_____ about something when he knows it, or when he has the best reasons for thinking it.

If Mr. Brown says that he will *probably* catch the train, he means that he thinks he will catch it, because he has a very good chance of catching it. If the train leaves after ten minutes, and if it takes him eight minutes to reach the station, and if he goes now, he will pr____ly catch the train. He cannot be s_____, because something may stop him. His hat may blow off, or the train may leave two minutes early, or his watch may be wrong. If he wants to be s_____, he must give himself more time—15 minutes or 20 minutes. But he will pr_____ly catch it.

If I say it will pr_____ rain this afternoon, I mean that I have good reasons for saying this. There are dark clouds in the sky and someone on the radio said that rain might come in the afternoon. There is a good chance that it will rain, though no one can be quite sure that it will rain.

We say that something will probably happen when there is a good chance (an 80% or 90% chance) that it will happen, and when there are good reasons for thinking this, though we cannot be sure.

Notice the three positions (places) of probably in a sentence.

(a) Probably it will rain this afternoon.   (Probably is used at the beginning of the sentence.)
(b) It will probably rain this afternoon.   (Probably is used just before the "meaningful" verb.)
(c) He is probably ill.   (Probably is used after **is, are, was, were.**)

Examples:

Probably he will catch the train.
He will probably catch the train.
He has probably caught the train.
He is probably ill.
Probably he is ill.
Your tickets are probably at the office.
He probably forgot to tell her.
Your grocer probably sells potatoes.
Probably your grocer sells potatoes.

1.2 WORD STUDY

Exercise on PROBABLY

In the following sentences use probably in its second or third position (i.e., **not** at the beginning of the sentence). Rewrite each sentence.

1. *Example:* He knows the address.
    Write: He probably knows the address.

2. The present value of your car is 1500 dollars.

    _____

3. The President of the United States will make an official speech tomorrow.

    _____

4. It will be necessary to take your passport.

    _____

5. The distance is greater than ten miles.

    _____

6. He spends all his money on cigarettes.

    _____

7. He has learned multiplication at school.

    _____

8. These figures are not accurate.

    _____

9. You can buy a cool drink in the cafeteria.

    _____

10. They will allow you to use the special library.

    _____

length
width
height
depth
distance
temperature

In the following exercise, use one of the words given in each blank space, to make a meaningful sentence.

1. The _____ of this dress is 60 inches.

2. The _____ of this ruler is 1 inch.

3. The _____ of this room is 30° Celsius.

4. The _____ between New York City and San Francisco is 3200 miles.

5. The _____ of the well is 50 feet.

6. The _____ of Mount Everest is 27,000 feet.

7. His _____ is just over 6 feet.

8. Her _____ is 99° Fahrenheit.

9. The _____ between the points is 5 centimeters.

10. The l____h of the table is 1.5 meters, its w___h is 1 meter, and its _____ is .75 meters.

11. The patient's _____ was 102° F.

12. The _____ of the lake at this point is 10 meters.

13. The _____ of cloth sold by the yard is usually 36, 48, or 54 inches.

14. The _____ of the sea is greatest in the Pacific Ocean.

15. At a _____ of 20,000 feet a mountain climber needs oxygen, because the air is so thin.

nearly (= almost) There are *nearly* 600 students in the college. = There are just under 600 students in the college. My work is nearly finished. = There is very little to do before my work is finished.

1.2 WORD STUDY

He nearly fell into the river = He was in great danger of falling into the river (but did not fall in).

He comes here nearly every day = There are only a few days when he does not come here.

(Notice that *nearly* makes a difference to the meaning of a **verb**, or an **adverb**, or an **adjective**, or a **number**, and always comes **just before** that verb, or adverb, or adjective, or number.)

Exercise

Rewrite the following sentences, using nearly before a verb, adverb, adjective, or number, to give a meaningful sentence.

1. He died of hunger.

   _____

2. He is always at home.

   _____

3. The distance between the two stations is four miles.

   _____

4. The baby is asleep.

   _____

5. I forgot to bring my umbrella.

   _____

6. Breakfast is ready.

   _____

7. The house is complete; only the windows have to be put in.

   _____

8. The planet Mercury travels at 30 miles a second.

   _____

9. In 1960 there were twice as many people in the world as there were in 1900.

   _____

10. He goes to New York every week.

    _____

probably
nearly
sure

1. Mr. Adams: Tom's very late.
   Mrs. Adams: Yes, he's nearly 40 minutes late.
   Mr. Adams: Probably he won't come now.
   Mrs. Adams: No, I don't think he'll come now.
   Mr. Adams: Are you sure?
   Mrs. Adams: Of course I'm sure.

2. Mr. Smith: Is Bob in?
   Mrs. Jones: No, he's not.
   Mr. Smith: Where do you think he is?
   Mrs. Jones: He's probably at the movie.
   Mr. Smith: Why do you think so?
   Mrs. Jones: Because he goes there nearly every night.

Unit I
1.3 DICTATION EXERCISES AND DICTATION PASSAGES

A 1. The passage *Heat and Expansion* will now be read to you. When you hear the first adjective in the list below, write the noun which follows it and the article (if there is one) which comes before it. Do the same with the next adjective you hear, and so on. Be *very careful* to give the ending of the noun (singular or plural) correctly. When you have finished, the teacher will check the answers with you.

   (a) metal   (e) special
   (b) other   (f) cold
   (c) hot   (g) each
   (d) little

2. When the teacher tells you to begin, underline the following words or phrases in the passage *Heat and Expansion*. Underline each word or phrase only once. You must underline the *same word*, with the *same ending* (e.g., singular or plural). This is a race.

this fact	the ends	remember	expand	special
noise	the rails	meet	expands	closer
a railroad	spaces	probably	for example	heated

3. The teacher will read the words given below in a *different* order from the order in which they are given here. You must number the words in the order in which you *hear* them. For example, if you hear *special* first, you must quickly write 1 beside that word, and if you hear *easily* next, you must write 2 beside it. You must give all your attention to this, because the teacher will not read slowly.

	metal	expands	the wheels
the rails	special	together	
easily	buy	probably	

4. Practice the sounds at the ends of these words:

ends	sounds	winds	expands
lends			hands
sends			
friends			
spends			

5. Close your books. Now take the passage *Heat and Expansion* as dictation. Write on paper everything you hear spoken.

B 1. The passage *Winds* will now be read to you. Below you will see a list of verbs, given in the *stem* form. (The *stem* form is the basic form of the verb.) As soon as you hear each verb, write the form of the verb *which you hear.* This may be the stem form or another form. When you have finished, the teacher will check the answers with you.

   (a) take   (f) blow
   (b) get   (g) take
   (c) explain   (h) blow
   (d) enjoy   (i) have
   (e) keep   (j) cool

2. When the teacher tells you to begin, underline the following words or phrases in the passage *Winds*. (Look at the instructions in the first set of exercises.) This is a race.

water	slowly	cooler	explains
the land	quickly	across	lose
by the sea	longer	because	the other way

1.3 DICTATION EXERCISES AND DICTATION PASSAGES

3. Number the following words in the order in which you hear them. For example, if you hear *longer* first, you must write 1 beside that word, and if you hear *enjoy* next, you must write 2 beside it. You must give all your attention to this, because the teacher will not read slowly.

	quickly	enjoy	cooler	
the seashore	explains	blow	cool
	longer	across	lose

4. Practice the vowel sound in these words.

a race	a way	a rail	a train	a railroad
a space	a day	fail	rain	explains
a place	say		grain	again

5. The passage *Winds* will now be given as dictation.

DICTATION PASSAGES

(a) Heat and Expansion

The metal lid of a jam jar expands when it is heated. Probably you remember this fact when you buy a jar which you cannot open easily. Other things also expand when they are heated. The rails on a railroad, for example, expand on a hot day. Sometimes we see little spaces between the ends of the rails. When the wheels of a train pass over these spaces, they make a special kind of noise. On a cold day the ends of two rails do not meet, but on a hot day each rail expands and the ends get closer together.

(b) Winds

Water takes longer to heat than land and longer to cool. The earth gets hot quickly but the sea gets hot slowly. This explains why people enjoy sitting by the sea on a very hot day. In the daytime the sea water takes longer to get hot and so it keeps cooler. The winds from the sea are also cool. They blow across the seashore, taking the place of the warm air over the land. At night the cool winds blow the other way because the land has less heat to lose than the sea and cools more quickly.

Unit I
1.4 READING PASSAGES

(a)   UNITS

What are *units*? They are the fixed quantities we use to measure different things. For example, in the United States the units of length are the inch, the foot, the yard, and the mile. We use these units to measure lengths and distances. In France and most other countries the units of length are the centimeter, the meter, and the kilometer. The kilometer is a multiple of the meter and the centimeter is a division of the meter. Together the United States units form a *system*; together the French units form another system. A system is a set of things, ideas, or rules related in a special way.

The French system of measurement is called the metric system. It is easy to remember because its basic rules are multiplication by ten and division by ten. To change a unit into a larger or smaller unit we multiply or divide by ten, by a hundred, by a thousand, or by a million. Can you write a thousand in figures? Can you write a million in figures?

Here is a table of the most important units in the metric system.

Unit		Rule
a kilometer	=	1000 times the basic unit
a meter	=	the basic unit
a centimeter	=	$\frac{1}{100}$ of the basic unit
a millimeter	=	$\frac{1}{1000}$ of the basic unit
a micrometer	=	$\frac{1}{1,000,000}$ of the basic unit

In this system the meter is the basic unit; it is the basis of all the others. All the other units in the metric system are based on the meter. They are either multiples of the meter or parts of it.

It is not necessary for you to remember the names of all the units in this system. But you must remember the meter, the kilometer, and the centimeter, because these units are used very often.

What do we know about the history of units of measurement? In early times, English units were based on parts of the human body. The inch was probably based on the width of a man's thumb. The foot was based on the length of a man's foot. (We can be sure about this, because of the name.) The mile was probably 1000 steps; each step was 5 feet. The word *mile* comes from *mille*, which is the Latin word for a thousand. The word *million* also comes from *mille*, and means 1000 x 1000.

(b)   STANDARDS OF MEASUREMENT

Most units are *standard* measures; in other words, they are accurate copies of official measures which are carefully kept by governments. Probably the units we use are not perfect copies, because if you think carefully you will see that no one can make a perfect copy of anything. But they must be as accurate as we can make them. They are fixed by the laws of each country. No person is allowed to use a yard measure or a meter measure which is different from the government standard.

You can see why this is necessary. When a woman buys cloth she needs to be sure that a yard is really a yard, and when she buys a pound of sugar she wants a complete pound, not a quantity which is nearly (a little less than) a pound. She wants *value for her money*, as people say. If her yard is really a yard, this means that the shopkeeper's measure is copied accurately from the standard measure kept by the government.

In the thirteenth century, King Edward I of England had a standard yard made from an iron bar, and he fixed the foot as one third (1/3) of this length. The units used in England were later fixed by the Board of Trade, which was a government department. The yard and the pound, fixed by the Board of Trade, were kept at their offices. These were called the Imperial Standards. The Board also kept copies of them. Other copies were kept at the Royal Mint (where money is made), at the Houses of Parliament, at the Royal

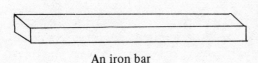

An iron bar

1.4 READING PASSAGES

Society (a society of scientists), and at Greenwich Observatory, which fixed standards of time. Why did the Royal Mint and Greenwich Observatory need copies of the Imperial Standards? You can think out the answer to this question.

A standard must not change. The Imperial Standard Yard was never allowed to get hotter or colder. It was always kept at the same temperature. But a yard does not measure temperature; it measures length. Then why must it be kept at the same temperature? You can answer this question. The Standard Yard was made of metal, and most metals _____ when they are heated. A standard of length must not change its _____.

(c) STORIES AND THEIR ACCURACY

Many stories about famous people are not based on facts. They are like some of the stories which people tell about their friends, which are passed from a friend to a friend's friend and so on. A story which is passed from mouth to mouth in this way may be better in the end than it was in the beginning, but probably it will end up as a very different story. Each storyteller adds something or leaves something out or changes something, so by the time the story is written in a book it is a long way from any basis in fact.

A man who tells a story does not always try to be accurate. He may not believe that facts are necessary in a story. He may want to make people laugh or make them cry; he may even want to make them think.

A good story is often told in many different languages. It may live through many centuries, and millions of people may enjoy telling it or listening to it. It is not the accuracy of a story which makes it live. The value of a story does not come from its accuracy but from its human interest or the way it is told.

An English novelist* wrote a new book, and a month after it was published* his publisher told him that a thousand copies had already been sold. That evening the novelist had a meal with his publisher and an American friend. They talked about the new book, and the novelist told the American that 10,000 copies had been sold. Later the publisher asked him why he had not been more accurate. "To an American," said the novelist, "a thousand is nothing. I multiplied the number by ten to give him a true idea of the success of the book." This novelist was not famous for his accuracy but for his novels; he knew how to tell stories. His best novels will probably live for a long time.

---

* a novelist = a writer of novels
 a novel = a long story. We call a story a novel if its length is more than 50,000 words or 100 pages.
* publish (verb) = get a book printed and send it to the bookshops to be sold
 a publisher = a man who publishes books

Unit I
1.5 VOCABULARY TEST

To test yourself on the vocabulary of this section, fill in the missing letters in the incomplete words.

   To make a cake, it is best to use a good b___c recipe*. If you want to make a bigger cake than the one in the recipe, you must m_____ly the qu_____s in the recipe, and if you want a smaller one you must d_____e the qu_____s.

   The qu_____s of flour, butter, and sugar must be measured ac_____y. The sugar and butter are u_____y mixed together first, and the flour and eggs a____d afterwards. But in some recipes the butter and flour are mixed first, i_____d __ the butter and sugar. N_____s many people use an electric mixer for this part of the work, which needs s_____l care.

   When you put the mixture into the cake pan, it is n_____y to a____w enough space for the cake to rise, because the mixture will e_____d when it is h_____d. St_____d s__s of cake pans can be bought which have the correct w___h and d___h for one pound, two pound, and three pound cakes.

   When you are s____ that the t_____e of the oven is right for this kind of cake, put the pan in the oven. When you take it out of the oven, you must a____w the cake to c__l before taking it out of the pan. If you follow the recipe carefully, your cake may not be p_____t but it will pr_____y be eatable.

* a recipe tells us how to prepare and cook something.

Unit II

2.1 VOCABULARY

These are the words you will practice in this unit:

VERBS		
choose		(+ noun)
chose		
chosen	(cho'sen)	
contain	(con·tain')	(+ noun)
convert	(con·vert')	(+ noun)
define	(de·fine')	(+ noun)
imagine	(im·ag'ine)	(+ noun)
imagine		(+ that)

NOUNS			
an amount	(a·mount')	an origin	(or'i·gin)
an angle	(an'gle)	the Poles	
an area	(ar'e·a)	the North Pole	
(the) atmosphere	(at'mos·phere)	the South Pole	
a barometer	(ba·rom'e·ter)	(a) pressure	(pres'sure)
(a) capacity	(ca·pac'i·ty)	a right angle	
a container	(con·tain'er)	a ruler	(ru'ler)
a definition	(def·i·ni'tion)	(a) society	(so·ci'e·ty)
a degree	(de·gree')	a solid	(sol'id)
a diagram	(di'a·gram)	a sphere	
the equator	(e·qua'tor)	a surface	(sur'face)
an instrument	(in'stru·ment)	(a) volume	
a liquid	(liq'uid)	(a) weight	
liquid volume	(vol'ume)		
a method	(meth'od)		

ADJECTIVES	
Celsius	(Cel'si·us)
cubic	(cu'bic)
derived from	(de·rived')
equivalent to	(e·quiv'a·lent)
Fahrenheit	(Fahr'en·heit)
imaginary	(im·ag'i·nar·y)
liquid	(liq'uid)
plural	(plu'ral)
singular	(sin'gu·lar)
solid	(sol'id)
Western	(West'ern)

ADVERBS	
obviously	(ob'vi·ous·ly)
originally	(o·rig'i·nal·ly)
usually	(u'su·al·ly)

17

Unit II

2.2 WORD STUDY

INSTRUCTIONS: Study the following words and the uses of them:

(a) weight   In the United States system *weight* is measured in pounds and ounces. In the metric system weight is measured in grams, centigrams, and kilograms. When you ask how heavy a thing is, you are asking a question about its w___ht.

You may notice that the word weight is used in **three ways**. Here are some examples of **one way**:

> all the weights in the box
> the two 20-gram weights
> the smallest weight in the box
> How many weights are there in the box?

In these examples, the weight is an object, a thing, a piece of metal. We can count how many weights there are in the box. There are eighteen. The word weight is called a countable noun in these examples, because the weights are things which are countable, which can be counted; we can say one weight, ten weights.

Here are some examples of the second way:

> air has weight
> the total weight
> the weight of iron
> units of weight
> the measurement of weight

In these examples the word weight does not mean a single object, a piece of metal. In these examples weight is not a thing but it is **what we measure** in different things; flour has weight, water has weight, air has weight. We can measure this, but we cannot count it. The word weight used in this way is called an uncountable noun, and since it is not countable it is not used in the plural. An uncountable noun does not have **a** or **an** before it.

Here are some examples of the third way:

> a weight of 8.250 grams
> weights of 0.040 and 0.790 grams

In these examples, we find "a weight" and "weights"; so we know that the word weight means something countable. What does the word weight mean here? It does not mean a thing, a piece of metal, but it means a **result** of weighing a thing. After weighing two apples, you may find that their weights are 5 ounces and 7 ounces. The first apple has a weight of 5 ounces and the second has a weight of 7 ounces. A nurse in a hospital may have twenty babies to look after. She weighs all the babies every day and writes their w_____ts in a book. She writes the results she gets when she weighs the babies. Results can be counted.

(a) pressure   When we push a heavy stone we put *pressure* on it. When a boy rides a bicycle, he puts pressure on
a barometer   the pedals with his feet, and this makes the wheels move around. The weight of one thing on another, or against another, puts pressure on it. (The noun pressure comes from the verb **press**, which means "put weight on something or against something.")

A pressure (countable) means "the result of measuring the pressure of something." Pressure (uncountable) is not the result of measuring the pressure of a **single thing**; it is what we measure (or feel, or notice) **every time** there is pressure on one thing by another, or one thing presses another.

Examples (uncountable): Pressure is sometimes measured in foot-pounds. Air has pressure. The pressure of the air can be measured with a *barometer*. The p_____re of the air on our bodies is 15 pounds on every square inch.

2.2 WORD STUDY

(Countable): A fish near the bottom of the sea has a pr____re of several thousand pounds on each square inch of its body. They tried using steam at different pressures.

a method

A *method* is a special way of doing something.

Examples: Our school uses modern m_____s of teaching arithmetic. He found a new m_____d of measuring the pressure of gases. Nowadays we can beat eggs quickly in an electric mixer; other m_____s of beating eggs are much slower.

a surface

The *surface* of a thing is the outside of it, the part which we can see or touch. When we say that a thing is red or blue, we mean that its s_____ce is red or blue. When we paint a wall, we paint its s_____ce.

Examples: A box has an inner s_____ and an outer s_____. The earth has only one s_____, an outer s_____. Sometimes the s_____of the sea looks green; sometimes it looks blue.

an amount

An *amount* is a **quantity**. There is not much difference in meaning between these two words, but when we talk about money we use the words "an amount."

Examples: He spends a large a____nt of money on cigarettes every week. When we measure volume we measure the a_____t of space a thing takes up. I pay $80 a week for my apartment, but my son pays only half that a_____ for his apartment. When we measure temperature we do not measure the a_____ of heat that a thing contains, but the strength (or intensity) of the heat. Summer is coming, and we will use a smaller _____ of electricity in the next few months.

(an) area

(Notice the difference between *area* and *an area*, which is like the difference between **weight** and **a weight**, or the difference between **pressure** and **a pressure**.)

Area is measured in square inches, square feet, square yards, and square miles in the United States system of measurement. In the metric system area is measured in square centimeters, square m_____s, and square k_____s. Whenever we measure a surface or part of a surface, we measure area.

Examples (uncountable): To measure a____, we multiply length by width.

(Countable): This carpet has an a____ of 60 square feet. The university buildings cover a large a____ of the land above the city. In many a____s where the storm passed, not one tree was left standing. (In this sentence area has the meaning of "a part of the earth's surface.")

(a) capacity
(a) volume
a solid
a liquid
liquid volume
solid volume

We measure a *volume* when we measure the space a thing takes up. *Liquids* like water and oil take up space and they are measured in units of *liquid volume* or *capacity*. *Capacity* is the amount of liquid which a measuring cup holds. Pints, quarts, and liters are units of liquid volume or capacity.

We measure *solid* v_____e in **cubic** inches, cubic feet, cubic yards, or in cubic centimeters or cubic meters. To find the volume of a box (or a thing with that shape) we multiply the length by the width and by the height. If the length of a box is 6 feet, its width is 5 feet and its height is 4 feet, what will its volume be (in cubic feet)? _____

Milk, water, and oil are l_____ds. Wood, iron, coal, and glass are s_____s.

What units can we use to measure the volume of a quantity of

(a) beer? _____
(b) gold? _____
(c) milk? _____
(d) stone? _____

Which of these are liquids? _____

Which are solids? _____

H = 4

W = 5

L = 6

2.2 WORD STUDY

a degree (a) *A degree* sometimes means "a unit of temperature." *Example:* Water boils at 100 d_____s Celsius.

(b) A degree sometimes means "a unit of an angle." *Example:* A right angle has 90 degrees.

(c) A degree sometimes means a certificate given to a person who studies at a university for some years and passes a university examination.

(The original meaning of "a degree" was a step on a ladder. The word degree comes from the Latin word **gradus**, which means "step." This helps us to see the likeness in the different meanings of degree. A university degree is a step upward in a student's life.)

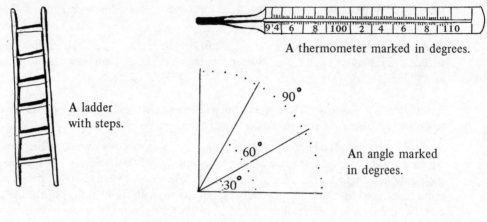

A thermometer marked in degrees.

A ladder with steps.

An angle marked in degrees.

an angle
a right angle

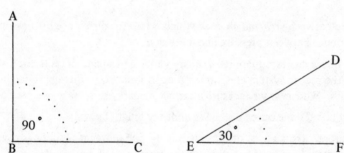

The two straight lines AB and BC meet at B and form an *angle* of 90°. The two straight lines DE and EF meet at E and form an angle of 30 degrees. An angle of 90 degrees is called a *right angle*.

a diagram This is a *diagram* of a field. A dia_____ is a drawing or a plan used to explain something. This
an area d_____m shows the length and width of the field. What is its *area*? _____

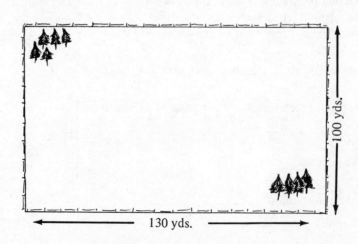

100 yds.

130 yds.

2.2 WORD STUDY

contain
a container

The larger can has sugar in it. It *contains* sugar. The smaller can has tea in it. It c_____s t___. These cans are *containers*.

The first jug c_____s water.

The second jug c_____ milk.

Both jugs c_____ liquids.

They are c_____rs.

imagine
imagine
imaginary

Imagine has two meanings.

(a)   Form a picture of something in the mind.

(b)   Think or believe that something is probable or true.

We say that something is *imaginary* when it is an idea or picture formed in the mind, not a real thing.

Examples: It is difficult to im_____e a life without electricity, movies, and airplanes. Im_____e a man as tall as a house. Poets and children are good at im_____ing things.

Don't im_____e (= think or believe) that you know everything. I can't i_____e (= think) why he came here.

The equator is an im_____ry line around the earth. To explain scientific ideas, writers sometimes use im_____y examples. The dangers he is afraid of are not i_____y; they are real.

convert

When we *convert* one thing **into** (or **to**) another, we change its form.

Examples: We can c_____t water into ice by making it colder. At school we learn how to c_____ yards into meters and meters into yards.

equivalent to

One foot is *equivalent* to 0.3333 yard. An American dollar is equ_____nt to ten dimes. One thing is equivalent to another when it is equal in quantity though different in form, or in the way we speak about it, or when it has the same results as the other thing (or action).

Examples: Two pounds are e_____t __ .454 gram. The capacity of this jug is e_____t __ the capacity of a pint bottle. Talking is not _____ __ doing.

a sphere
(the) atmosphere
the North Pole
the South Pole
the Poles
the equator

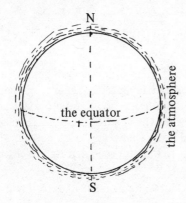

This is a diagram of the earth. The earth is a solid round thing like a ball. It is *a sphere*. (It is not a perfect sphere.) The air which covers the earth's surface is called the *atmosphere*.

This diagram shows *the North Pole* (N) and *the South Pole* (S). *The equator* is an imaginary circle around the earth, equally distant between *the Poles*. **You must always use a capital P** for the Poles, because the Poles are places which have names, like London or New York or the Cape of Good Hope.

21

2.2 WORD STUDY

an instrument
a ruler
a barometer

An instrument is something we use to measure things, or a special tool used by scientists, or something used to play music on, or a tool used for drawing. Students who take an engineering course must buy a set of drawing instr_____s. *A ruler* is an in_____ used to measure length. A violin is a musical i_____t. *A barometer* is an i_____ used to measure the pressure of the atmosphere.

These are instruments.

choose
chose
chosen

A person *chooses* a wife or husband when there are many unmarried people to choose from. A person shows his or her own wishes by choosing another as wife or as husband. People ch_____ their work when they follow their own wishes and do one kind of work though they can do something else if they wish.

When you go to a store to buy a shirt, you do not buy the first shirt you see. You look at a number of different shirts and then you ch_____ one.

A person cannot ch_____ the society (the group of people) in which he or she lives as a child. A person is born into that society. But when people grow up they can sometimes ch_____ to live in a different society. In some societies women do not _____e their own husbands. Their husbands are *chosen* for them by their parents. In some societies men do not _____e their own jobs. Their jobs are _____n for them by their parents.

Here is a story. A king who had three daughters invited a prince from another country to come and _____e one of them as his wife.

When the prince came to the palace to meet the girls, he brought a large bag with him. Two or three times he looked in the bag, then shut it again quickly.

"Why are you looking in your bag?" said the eldest daughter.

"What have you got in there?" said the second.

The youngest girl said nothing.

The prince *chose* the youngest daughter as his wife. Why did he choose her?

usually

When it is our habit or custom to do a thing, we say that we *usually* do it.

Now we will talk about the habits and customs of an imaginary family. Father u____lly gets up at about 6 o'clock. He makes coffee and brings Mother a cup of coffee. She u____lly has coffee in her bedroom and does not have breakfast till seven. The children u_____ wake up early. They play with their toys until Mother makes the breakfast. They u_____ have cornflakes and eggs for breakfast. Peter, who is ten years old, ought to start for school at eight o'clock, but he dresses and eats very slowly, so he is _____ late.

_____ Mother gets up at six-thirty, but sometimes she likes to stay in bed a little longer.

Other examples: When Mrs. Brown wants to buy a dress, she u_____ goes to three or four stores and tries on a number of dresses before she ch_____s one. In nineteenth-century England, unmarried sons and daughters _____ lived with their parents even when they were grown up. Nowadays, unmarried children _____ go to work when they are old enough and often live away from home.

22

2.2 WORD STUDY

In summer the fields are _____ dry and dusty.

Notice the position of *usually* in a sentence. It has the same position as **always, never, often,** and **sometimes.**

an origin
originally

The *origin* of a thing is its starting-point, the point (in time) or place from which it begins. Historians (people who write and study history) are interested in o_____ns. It is part of their job to find out how and where things begin. Historians of language are interested in the o_____ of words and languages. Economic historians are in_____ed __ the _____ of money and trade and economic relationships. Some physicists are in_____ed __ the _____ of the earth, the moon, the sun, and the stars. Anthropologists try to find out the _____ of customs in human societies.

What was the _____ of the earth? No one is quite sure. At one time scientists thought that *originally* (= in the beginning) the earth and the other planets formed part of the sun, then later broke away from the sun and followed their own paths. But nowadays most scientists believe that the sun, the earth, and the other planets were all formed at the same time.

O_____lly most people believed that the earth was flat. There are still a few people who imagine that it is flat. But nowadays most people know that the earth is a sphere, or that it is nearly spherical. It is not a perfect sphere, because the equator is a little longer than the circle which joins the Poles.

define
a definition

Please notice the spelling! All these words begin with **de-**

define
definition
definite
definitely

The word **design** also begins with **de-**; so you can learn this little poem:

> The man who spells **define**
> Can also spell **design.**
> He writes the letter **d**
> And then the letter **e.**

There are many words beginning with de-. Now you can spell **five** of them.

To *define* a word is to give its basic meaning in other words. *A definition* is a short, clear, complete explanation of the meaning of a word.

Here are some de_____ions:

complete and without faults. This is a de_____n of the word "p_____t."
a thousand multiplied by a thousand. This is a de_____n of the words "a million."
the length of a thing from its lowest point to its highest point. This is a d_____n of the word "_____."

Now try to write some d_____ns.

(a) Can you define the word **origin**? Please try.
     "An origin is the _____ or pl___ from which a thing b____s."
(b) Can you define the word **capacity**? Please try.
     "The c_____ty of a container is the qu_____ty it will hold."
(c) Can you define the word **method**? Please try.
     "A method is a s_____l way of d____ something."
(d) Can you define the word **multiple**? Please try.
     "A m_____le of a n_____r is that n_____r m_____d by another n_____r."
(e) Can you define the word **system**? Please try.
     "A sy_____ is a set of th____s, i___s or r___s re___ted in a sp_____l way."

In essays and scientific writing it is often necessary to give ac_____e d_____s. But in learning English it is not enough to know the definition of a word. We must also know how to use it correctly in a large number of different sentences.

23

2.2 WORD STUDY

derived from Notice the spelling. Here is another word beginning with **de-**.

We say that one thing is *derived from* another when it has its origin in the other thing.

Examples: The word **meter** is derived from the Greek word **metron**, which means "measure."
The word **degree** is de___ed f___ the Latin word **gradus**, which means "a step." Most of his
ideas are de___ed f___ Aristotle.

obviously We say that something is *obviously* true when everyone, even the most stupid person, can see that it
is true. If a road is only seven feet wide, it is obviously not wide enough for two cars to pass on it.
If a man has a temperature of 104°F., he is ob_____ly too ill to walk.

A boy who always says "No, thank you" when anyone asks him to have some chocolate
o_____ly dislikes chocolate. A man who throws himself in front of a train going at 60 miles
an hour _____ wants to kill himself.

Unit II
2.3 DICTATION EXERCISES AND DICTATION PASSAGES

A   1. The passage *The Metric System* will now be read to you. You will hear *one* of the words or phrases in each of the following pairs, in the order in which they are given here. As you listen, *cross out* the word or phrase in each pair which is incorrect (i.e., the word or phrase which you do *not* hear.) Your teacher will check the answers with you.

      (a)   a metal bar - a meter bar
      (b)   France - French
      (c)   same - the same
      (d)   unit - units
      (e)   divide - divided
      (f)   thousand - a thousand
      (g)   originally - original
      (h)   scientists - scientist
      (i)   equator - the equator
      (j)   these - the earth
      (k)   used - use

   2. When the teacher tells you to begin, underline the following words in the passage *The Metric System*. This is a race. (See instructions in Unit I.)

metal	government	divided	equator
basic	temperature	defined	unit
standard	scientists	relation	system

   3. Number the following words in the order in which you hear them. (See the instructions in Unit I.)

	relation	definition	accurately
length	distance	temperature	
	equator	system	divided

   4. Repeat the following words (as grouped) with the correct stresses.

di·vide'	re·la'tion	me'ter	ki·lom'e·ter	dis'tance	gov'ern·ment
de·fine'	def·i·ni'tion	meas'ure	cen'ti·me·ter	of'fice	tem'per·a·ture
di·vid'ed		e·qua'tor		u'nit	sci'en·tist
de·fined'				met'al	ac'cu·rate
re·lat'ed				ba'sic	ac'cu·rate·ly
				sys'tem	mul'ti·plied
				stan'dard	

   5. The passage *The Metric System* will now be given as dictation.

B   1. The passage *Accurate Measurements* will now be read to you. You will hear *one* of the words or phrases in each of the following pairs (read in the same order). Cross out the word or phrase in each pair which is incorrect.

      (a)   diagrams - diagram
      (b)   instrument - instruments
      (c)   obvious - obviously
      (d)   based on - based in
      (e)   use - used
      (f)   country - countries
      (g)   century - centuries
      (h)   divided - divide

2.3 DICTATION EXERCISES AND DICTATION PASSAGES

2. Number the following words in the order in which you hear them.

	diagrams		engineering		obviously
accurately		necessary		century	
	official		system		nowadays

3. Repeat the following words (as grouped) with the correct stresses.

a·mount'	con·tained'	nec'es·sar·y
di·vide'	de·fined'	ac'cu·rate
ex·pand'	ar·rived'	ac'cu·rate·ly
com·plete'	‾‾‾	sep'a·rate (adj.)
re·late'	ba·rom'e·ter	sep'a·rate·ly
con·vert'	ca·pac'i·ty	ob'vi·ous
‾‾‾	so·ci'e·ty	ob'vi·ous·ly
de·fine'	e·quiv'a·lent	‾‾‾
ar·rive'	‾‾‾	en·gi·neer'
con·tain'	u'su·al·ly	en·gi·neer'ing
‾‾‾	prob'a·bly	‾‾‾
di·vid'ed	quan'ti·ty	fig'ure
re·lat'ed	cen'tu·ry	pres'sure
com·plet'ed	‾‾‾	vol'ume
ex·pand'ed	or'i·gin	sur'face
con·vert'ed	di'a·gram	‾‾‾
‾‾‾	in'stru·ment	meth'od
di·vi'sion	meas'ure·ment	val'ue
con·ver'sion	sin'gu·lar	per'fect
ex·pan'sion	‾‾‾	
ad·di'tion	now'a·days	
‾‾‾	at'mos·phere	
con·tain'er	mul'ti·ple	
e·qua'tor	mul'ti·ply	
con·ven'ient		
ex·am'ple		
im·ag'ine		

4. The passage *Accurate Measurements* will now be given as dictation.

DICTATION PASSAGES

(a)   The Metric System

The standard meter was originally a metal bar, kept in an office of the French government. It was always kept at the same temperature. The meter is the basic unit of the metric system. A centimeter is a meter divided by a hundred, and a kilometer is a meter multiplied by a thousand. The length of the meter was originally fixed by French scientists, who defined it in relation to the distance from the equator to the North Pole. But they did not measure the earth accurately; so their definition is not used now.

(b)   Accurate Measurements

To make good maps and diagrams, it is necessary to use instruments which will measure accurately. For engineering, too, accurate measurements are obviously necessary. Measurements can be accurate only if they are based on official standards which do not change. Nowadays many countries use the metric system and probably most countries will use it before the end of this century. Money values in most countries will also be counted in units like the dollar, which can be divided by a hundred.

Unit II
2.4 READING PASSAGES

(a) The Earth, the Atmosphere, and the Equator

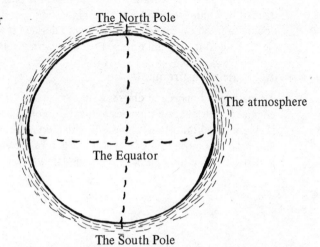

The earth on which we live is a solid sphere. Around it is the atmosphere—the air we breathe. "A sphere" means a thing with the shape of a ball. The earth is a sphere and the air around it is also a sphere; it is a sphere of air. This is the origin of the word "atmosphere." It is derived from two Greek words, *atmos*, which means air, and *sphaira*, which means a sphere.

The earth is not a perfect sphere. The distance around the earth touching the two Poles is not equal to the distance around the earth at the equator. It is a little less. The length of the equator is 40,075,594 meters. The circle which touches the Poles is 40,009,152 meters in length.

What is the distance in meters from the Equator to the North Pole?

One mile is equivalent to about 1609.35 meters. What is the difference in miles between the length of the equator and the length of the circle touching the Poles?

(b) The Meter

We know that all the units in the metric system are based on the meter. But what is the meter itself based on? It was chosen at the end of the eighteenth century (about 1790) as a new basis for the measurement of length. It was based on the distance from the North Pole to the equator, and was thought to be $\frac{1}{10,000,000}$ of that distance.

The meter is a standard unit. It is equivalent to 39.37 inches, a little more than a yard. It is the official standard of length in many countries.

(c) Equivalence and Conversion

The adjective *equivalent* means "equal in value or quantity." It does *not* mean "the same in form."

We can say that two kilometers are equivalent to 1.24 miles, because we know that one kilometer is equivalent to 0.62 mile. If we wish to *convert* English pounds *into* dollars, we must first find the value of *one* pound in dollars. (We can find this in a newspaper.) If one pound is equivalent to 2.89 dollars, then £2 will be equivalent to 5.78 dollars, and so on. In the same way, if we know that one meter is equivalent to 39.37 inches, we can convert any length in meters into inches and yards. Obviously it is much easier to convert yards into inches, which are units in the same system of measurement. We need only multiply by 36.

When we convert yards into inches we change only the form of measurement. When we convert inches or yards into meters we change not only the form but also the standard and system of measurement. How do we convert yards into meters? We know that one yard is equivalent to 36 inches and that one meter is equivalent to 39.37 inches. So we must divide the number of yards by _____ and multiply the result by _____ . How do we convert yards into inches? Here, division is not necessary. Only multiplication is necessary. Inches are equal parts or divisions of a yard, and a yard is a multiple of an inch, because both the yard and the inch are units in the same system of measurement.

(d) Volume and Capacity; Weight and Temperature

Solid volume is the space taken by a solid thing. Liquid volume, or capacity, is the amount of space a container has in it. In the metric system solid volume is measured in cubic meters, cubic centimeters, etc., and liquid volume or capacity is measured in liters. In the metric system Celsius degrees are used to measure temperature.

In the United States solids are measured in cubic inches, cubic yards, and cubic feet; liquids are measured in gallons, quarts, and pints. The volume of one gallon is equivalent to 277.4 cubic inches.

2.4 READING PASSAGES

This unit is not based on a unit of solid volume, but on the pound. The official definition of a gallon is "that which contains 10 standard pounds of distilled water at 62° Fahrenheit and at a barometric pressure of 30 inches." A barometer, you will probably remember, is an instrument for measuring the pressure of the atmosphere. In an official definition of a unit of volume the temperature and atmospheric pressure must be given, because differences in these can make a difference in volume.

(e) Family Units

When we speak of *society* in general (without using the article "a") we mean people living together, human beings in their social relations. When we speak of *a society*, we mean a large group of people living together, usually in the same country, with their own customs, language, and way of life.

In most societies the basic social unit is a family group, but the forms of such groups differ in different societies. In modern Western societies a family unit is usually small, made up of a man, his wife, and their children. In the nineteenth century the Western family unit was usually a little larger than this. Unmarried sons and daughters were part of the family even after they were grown up. Nowadays, unmarried sons and daughters do not always live with their parents after they begin going to work. They often leave home and live in their own apartments or rooms.

In other societies we find family units which are quite different. In some places, for example, a man may have more than one wife. When two or more wives live together with their husband in the same home, a child will have brothers or sisters (or both) who have the same father but a different mother. In these families the younger children sleep in their mother's room, but all the older boys may sleep together in a large room or in a separate hut and all the older girls in another.

The first wife often has a special place in this kind of family unit; she has more power than the other wives. Her husband asks her advice when he chooses his other wives, and she tells them what work they must do.

In some societies a married son and his family always live with his father. Chinese families used to be of this kind. In other societies, for example, in South India, it used to be the custom for married sons and daughters to live with their mother, not their father. In these societies men did not have much power over their own children. The uncles, the mother's brothers, had power over her children. In other words, men were masters in their *sisters'* homes, not in the homes where their wives and their own children lived. In their wives' homes they were only visitors.

In those societies where married children live with one of their parents (the father or the mother) the family unit is usually large. It is called a joint family. As more children are born, grow up, and get married, the joint family expands and gets bigger and bigger, until there may be a hundred fathers and mothers living under one roof, with their children of different ages. In Calcutta there are still one or two families as big as this. But at some point in the history of the family there must be a division. At some time a son will break away to form a new family unit. No house is big enough to contain more than a hundred married couples. In family life, where there is multiplication there must also be division at some point. This is also true of animal societies. When a group of animals becomes too large to live together, for example, when it becomes too large for the amount of food that can be found near the place where the group lives, nature finds a way of dividing it.

Unit II
2.5 VOCABULARY TEST

To test yourself on the vocabulary of this section, fill in the missing letters in the incomplete words.

During the last few years at school it is probably n_____y for pupils to c____e the subjects they want to study. They o_____y cannot study all the subjects. They must decide what interests them most.

If they c_____ science they u_____y study mathematics and chemistry, physics, or biology. In all these sciences measurement is very important. Students learn to measure temperature in degrees F_____t and d_____s C_____s. The pupils learn to c_____t ^{o}F to ^{o}C. They also learn to measure the v____e of l_____s and g___s and the w____t of s____s, l_____s, and g___s. The p_____e of gases is very important when studying the earth's a_____e.

Students of science may want to become geologists because they are interested in the s_____e of the earth and the o____n of the rocks that make up the s_____e of the earth. Geologists are interested in the a___nt of different sorts of rocks in one a__a and the a___es at which the rock s_____s lie.

All science students must be able to d____e the scientific words they use and they must learn to draw d_____s. Modern m_____s of science teaching u_____y allow the pupils to discover f___s for themselves, but sometimes this is very difficult. Only a very few of the m_____s of science students in the world will ever get the chance to travel into s___e or even to visit the N___h or the S___h P__e.

Unit III

3.1 VOCABULARY

These are the words you will practice in this unit:

VERBS			
check		(= correct, revise)	(+ noun)
compare	(com·pare')		(+ noun plural)
compare			(+ noun + with + noun)
discover	(dis·cov'er)		(+ noun)
invade	(in·vade')		(+ noun)
subtract	(sub·tract')		(+ noun + from + noun)
trade with			
travel	(trav'el)		
traveled	(trav'eled)		

NOUNS		
an American ton	(A·mer'i·can)	
a balance	(bal'ance)	(for weighing)
a basis	(ba'sis)	
a British ton	(Brit'ish)	
(a) comparison	(com·par'i·son)	
convenience	(con·ven'ience)	
a dimension	(di·men'sion)	
the East		
an Empire	(Em'pire)	
Europe	(Eu'rope)	
(a) grain		
inconvenience	(in·con·ven'ience)	
an invasion	(in·va'sion)	
a kind of		
a letter	(let'ter)	(A, B, etc.)
a metric ton	(met'ric)	
a planet	(plan'et)	
a position	(po·si'tion)	
a problem	(prob'lem)	
a row		
a season	(sea'son)	
(a) size		
subtraction	(sub·trac'tion)	
a sum		(= problem)
a total	(to'tal)	
trade		
a triangle	(tri'an·gle)	
a tribe		
the West		

ADJECTIVES			
alike	(a·like')	natural	(nat'u·ral)
Arabic	(Ar'a·bic)	Roman	(Ro'man)
convenient	(con·ven'ient)	separate	(sep'a·rate)
correct	(cor·rect')	simple	(sim'ple)
European	(Eu'ro·pe·an)	solar	(so'lar)
inconvenient	(in·con·ven'ient)	total	(to'tal)
incorrect	(in·cor·rect')		

31

3.1 VOCABULARY

ADVERBS ——————————————— separately   (sep'a·rate·ly)

PHRASES ——————————————— by air
                          by land
                          by sea

Unit III

3.2 WORD STUDY

INSTRUCTIONS: Study the following words and the uses of them:

subtract
subtraction

When we add two numbers, we write "+" for add. When we *subtract* one number from another we write "−" for subtract. When we sub____t one number from another, we take the first away from the second.

$$10 - 4 = 6$$

This means "four subtracted from ten leaves six," or "four subtracted from ten is equal to six."

What does this mean? $7 - 3 = 4$

_____

What does this mean? $25 - 7 = 18$

_____

Write the following problems in subtraction in **figures** and give the answers:

(a)   Subtract three from nine.

_____ = _____

(b)   Subtract four from forty-three.

_____ = _____

(c)   Subtract one from a hundred.

_____ = _____

(d)   Subtract thirty from two hundred.

_____ = _____

(e)   Subtract a hundred from a million.

_____ = _____

discover

A man *discovers* something or discovers a fact when **he finds** something which is there in the world or in nature, or which is true, but **which was not known before** he found it.

Examples: Columbus dis_____d America. Many new facts about nature were dis_____d by the Greeks and Arabs. Pascal d_____d that air had pressure. Travelers sometimes d_____ new kinds of plants and animals.

the total
total

When we add two or more numbers, the result is *the total*. When we do a problem in arithmetic, the result is the t_____. We can also speak of the t_____ number of chairs in a room, the t_____ amount or quantity of water in a lake, a man's t_____ income or wages, and so on. The total means the amount reached and recorded after everything has been added up or all the necessary arithmetic has been done.

Exercise: Do the following problems.

1. Add 4, 10, and 5, subtract 3 and give the total. _____

2. John went shopping and bought 2 pounds of potatoes, 3 pounds of tomatoes, and 3 pounds of flour. Find the total weight of the things he bought.

_____

3. During the summer (June, July, August, September) 300 guests a month visited a hotel. 100 guests a month visited the hotel during the rest of the year. What was the total number of guests during the year?

_____

33

3.2 WORD STUDY

When Mary goes to work the bus takes her to the center of the town. The bus ride takes half an hour, and after that it takes her 10 minutes to walk to her office. Find the total time it takes her to get to work.

---

a season

In the United States there are four *seasons*: spring, summer, autumn, and winter. In India there are three s_____ns; the rainy season, winter, and summer. In Cambodia there are only two seasons; a cold dry s_____n and a hot wet s_____n.

convenient
convenience
  (uncountable)
inconvenient
inconvenience

We say that something is *convenient* when it is easy to use, to do, or to reach; when it gives us no difficulty or trouble. It is *inconvenient* when it gives us trouble or difficulty.

Examples: This table will be very con____ient for my work. We must find a more conven____t place for the meeting. Will it be con_____t for you to start work tomorrow? The great con_____ce of your house is its position. I hope the change of time will not cause you inconvenience. When I put these things here I was thinking only of your con_____ce. The con_____ce of the yard as a unit of length is that it is about as long as a man's arm.

Mr. X. (the house agent)   Mr. Green (the poet)

Mr. X.   Well, here's the house. When will it be convenient for you to see it?
Mr. Green   I see it now.
Mr. X.   I mean, when will it be convenient for you to go and look at it?
Mr. Green   I'm looking at it now.
Mr. X.   Well, what do you think about it?
Mr. Green   I don't think about it. I'm a poet. I don't think, I only imagine things.
Mr. X.   Well, what do you imagine?
Mr. Green   I imagine there's no telephone. I imagine there's no electricity. And I imagine my wife won't like it.
Mr. X.   Oh, you have a wife? That's inconvenient.

natural

(a)   If something is the work of nature, not of human beings, it is *natural*.

(b)   We sometimes say a thing is natural when it is ordinary, like what usually happens, or when it is the usual result of other happenings.

Examples:

(a)   Wind, rain, thunder, and lightning are natural forces. Gas which is not made from coal but comes from the land or the sea is called n_____l gas. It is n_____ for birds to fly. It is n_____ for children to love their parents.

(b)   Don't copy other people but speak in your n_____ voice. He died a n_____ death. His interest in your success is quite n_____. The n_____ result of the new highway will be greater pressure on road space in the center of the city. It will be n_____ if they choose a man who can drive a car.

3.2 WORD STUDY

simple

A thing is *simple* if it (a) is unmixed, or (b) is not divided into parts or has very few parts, or (c) does not have many parts of different kinds, or (d) is very easy to learn or to do.

Examples: You must try to write s_____ sentences. A can opener is a s_____ machine; it has only two or three parts. He has a simple mind. He can do s_____ arithmetic. In our first biology class we will study only s_____ forms of life.

solar
a system
a planet

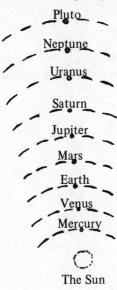

Pluto
Neptune
Uranus
Saturn
Jupiter
Mars
Earth
Venus
Mercury

The Sun

This is a diagram of the *solar system*. Solar means "of the sun," and the s__ar s_____m is the s_____m which has the sun as its center. There are a number of *planets* which go around the sun. You can count them in the diagram. How many are there? The sun and the pl____s together f__m the s_____ s_____. What is the name of the pl ___t nearest the sun? M_____y. This is also the name of a liquid metal. (It is not necessary to remember the names of all the planets.)

a triangle

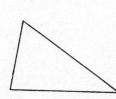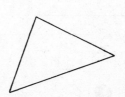

These shapes are called *triangles*. (Tri- means **three**.) How many sides does a t_____le have? How many angles does a t_____le have? Can you define a triangle? It is a _____
_____

When you add the three angles of a triangle together, the total is always 180º (180 degrees). (Do you know how to prove this?)

(a) size

The *size* of a thing is its largeness or smallness or its measurement.

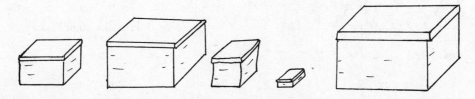

These boxes have different s___s. Their s___s are different. Some of them are larger; some are smaller. They do not have the same s__e.

3.2 WORD STUDY

What is the size of this box?

It is _____ x _____ x _____ ft.

These two baskets are about equal in s____, but one is wider and the other is taller.

a row   Pronounced like **go** or **show** or **no**.

This is a *row* of trees.

2   3   4   5   8

This is a r__ of figures. The third f____re in the r__ is _____.

There are two r___s of students in this class. John is the second boy from the right in the front r__.

Here is a ____ of cans and bottles on a shelf.

These children are standing in a ____.

36

3.2 WORD STUDY

a position

In this picture, what is the *position* of the man? He is in front of the horse.

What is the _____ of the woman? She is b_____d the horse.

John looks at the notice board to see his position in the list of examination results. John is pleased, because he is at the top of the list. He has the top position.

Mr. X. has a very high p_____ in the Government. He is Secretary of State. How can you go to sleep in that p_____n?

a balance

We use *a balance* to measure weight. A b_____e is an instrument for measuring the weight of something.

a problem
a sum
check
compare
correct
incorrect

Checking Answers and Checking Numbers.

All arithmetic books contain *problems*. Some arithmetic books give the answers to the problems, and usually the answers are given in the last pages.

Students who do problem 12 in section B on page 16 can look in the "Answers" for "P. 16, B 12." Then they can *compare* their answer with the answer given in the book. They can find out whether their answer is *correct* or not.

The easiest way of *checking* whether work is correct or not is to compare it with work which is correct.

Often we do not have correct work or correct answers, and so we cannot check our work in this way.

There are other ways of checking whether work is correct or not. One easy way of checking work in arithmetic is to do it again. You can compare the first answer with the second answer. If they are the same, perhaps the answer is correct. If they are not the same, at least one answer must be *incorrect* and you must do the work again.

3.2 WORD STUDY

The Boss: I hope you checked your arithmetic carefully.

Girl: Yes, Sir. I checked it three times—

The Boss: Good!

Girl: —and here are the three answers.

In schools and colleges there are many tests and examinations. The person who marks a student's work c _____ s the student's work with work which is c_____ t. If the student's work is correct, the marker puts a check (✓) by it; if the student's work is _____correct, the marker puts a cross (x) by it.

In a test some students answer the questions, but do not ch _____ whether the work is c_____t or in_____ . One way of _____ ing work in arithmetic is to _____ _____ again. Then the student can _____ the first answer _____ the second answer. If the answers are not _____ _____ at least one answer must be incorrect. The new office girl gave three different answers to her boss. We know that _____ _____ two _____s must be _____! It is possible that all three _____ are _____!

In a test there is usually not enough time to do all the work two times in order to compare the answers.

French children learn a short way of checking their answers in arithmetic.

A French schoolboy does a subtraction problem and wants to check whether the answer is correct or incorrect.

Here is the problem: $\begin{array}{r} 7685 \\ - 5398 \\ \hline \end{array}$

Here is his answer: 2287

The boy adds the figures in the first row: 7 + 6 + 8 + 5. The total is 26. He adds the two figures: 2 + 6. The total is 8.

He adds the figures in the second row: 5 + 3 + 9 + 8. The total is 25. He adds the two figures: 2 + 5. The total is 7.

He subtracts 7 from 8. The answer is 1.

Now he adds the figures in the third row (his answer): 2 + 2 + 8 + 7. The total is 19. He adds the two figures: 1 + 9. The total is 10. He adds the two figures 1 + 0. The answer is 1.

He compares the two answers. They are the same: 1. The boy knows that his work is correct. If the answers are not the same, there is a mistake.

The schoolboy does an addition *sum* and wants _____ whether the answer is _____ or _____ .

Here is the sum: $\begin{array}{r} 992 \\ 1068 \\ 5437 \\ + 106 \\ \hline \end{array}$

Here is his answer: 7603

To check the answers, the boy adds the figures in each row. When the result of an addition contains two (or more) figures, he adds these until he has a total with one figure:

3.2 WORD STUDY

9 + 9 + 2 = 20	2 + 0 =	2
1 + 0 + 6 + 8 = 15	1 + 5 =	6
5 + 4 + 3 + 7 = 19	1 + 9 = 10 1 + 0 =	1
1 + 0 + 6 =		7

He adds the figures: 2 + 6 + 1 + 7. The total is 16. He adds the two figures of the total: 1 + 6. The answer is 7.

He adds the figures in the last row (his answer): 7 + 7 + 0 + 3. The total is 17. He adds the two figures of the total: 1 + 7. The answer is 8.

He compares the two answers. The two answers (7 and 8) are not the same, so the boy knows that his work is incorrect.

The boy does a multiplication problem and wants _____ _____ whether the answer is _____ or _____ .

Here is the problem:

$$\begin{array}{r} 8934 \\ \times\ 5862 \\ \hline 44670000 \\ 7147200 \\ 536040 \\ 17868 \\ \hline \end{array}$$

Here is his answer: 52371108

To _____ his answer, the boy _____ the figures in each number in the problem, and then _____ the figures in each total:

8 + 9 + 3 + 4 = 24	2 + 4 = 6
5 + 8 + 6 + 2 = 21	2 + 1 = 3

Since the problem is a m_____ problem, he multiplies the two totals: 6 x 3 = 18.

He adds the two figures: 1 + 8. The answer is 9.

Now the schoolboy _____ the figures in his answer: 5 + 2 + 3 + 7 + 1 + 1 + 0 + 8. The total is 27. He _____ the two figures: 2 + 7. The answer is 9. He compares the two answers. The two answers are _____ _____ ; so the boy knows that his work is _____ .

The way of checking a division problem is slightly different. Here is a division problem: 92872 ÷ 76. The boy's answer is 1222.

The boy adds the figures in the number he divides by: 7 + 6. The total is 13. He _____ the two figures: 1 + 3. The t_____ is 4.

He adds the _____ in his answer: 1 + 2 + 2 + 2. The total is 7.

Now he **multiplies** the figures of the two totals: 4 x 7 = 28. He _____ the two _____ : 2 + 8. The _____ is 10. He _____ these two _____ . The answer is 1.

Now he adds the figures of the number he divides into: 9 + 2 + 8 + 7 + 2. The _____ is 28. He _____ the two _____ : 2 + 8. The _____ is 10. He _____ these two _____ : 1 + 0. The answer is 1.

He compares the two answers. The two _____ are _____ _____ ; so the boy _____ _____ _____ _____ is _____ .

compare
compare
a comparison
a basis
alike
a dimension

Comparison and Measurement.

When Mrs. Smith wants to buy some cloth for a dress, she goes to a store. She sees two pieces of blue cloth and says, "This is darker than that." She *compares* the colors of the two pieces. When she buys apples of two different kinds, she eats one of each kind and then says, "This apple is sweeter." She c_____s the apples by tasting them.

But it is not always convenient to make *a comparison* of this kind. When Mrs. Smith wants a bedcover for her bed, she does not want to take her bed to the store and c_____e the bed with the bedcover.

3.2 WORD STUDY

She wants to know if the bedcover is long enough for her bed. But the clerk may not allow her to take the bedcover home and _____ it with her bed.

When Mrs. Smith wants to make sleeves for a dress, she does not take two pieces of cloth and compare them. She does not _____ the piece of cloth _____ her own arm. She takes a tape measure and _____s the marks on the tape with the length of her arm. She compares the length of her arm with the number of units marked on the tape measure. She writes the number on a piece of paper. In other words she measures the length of her arm. Then she measures the cloth; she compares the tape measure with the cloth. After this she can cut the cloth.

When a grocer gives you two pounds of apples and two pounds of tomatoes, he does not compare the apples with the tomatoes. He does not hold the apples in one hand and the tomatoes in the other hand and compare them like this. (You would be very angry if he did!) No, he compares them separately with the weights on his scales (or balance). First he compares the apples with the weights on his scales and then he _____ the tomatoes with the _____ on his _____. So measurement is a kind of comparison. It is an accurate way of making comparisons. It is also very convenient when we want to compare things which cannot be brought together, or when we want to compare a large number of things.

All measurement is based on comparison. Measurement is the comparison of *dimensions*. A dimension is something which can be measured, like length or area. We do not always compare dimensions; sometimes we compare things which cannot be measured, like shape or taste or usefulness. But when we compare, we must have some *basis* for comparison in our minds. What is comparison based on? It is based on the fact that things are *alike* in some ways but different in other ways. We cannot compare the area of a triangle with the area of a line because a line has no _____. We cannot compare the weight of a triangle with the weight of a tomato because a _____ has no weight. We cannot compare the price of air with the price of oil _____ air _____ _____ price. We cannot _____ the shape of the wind _____ the shape of a tree because _____ _____ has no _____. Weight, length, shape, color, each of these can be the basis of a comparison. But a comparison must have a basis. It must be based on something which is the same in things. Please remember this when you are asked to make a comparison between two things.

**separate
separately**

Here is a log of wood.

A woodman comes with his ax.

He cuts the log.
Now it is in three *separate* parts.

3.2 WORD STUDY

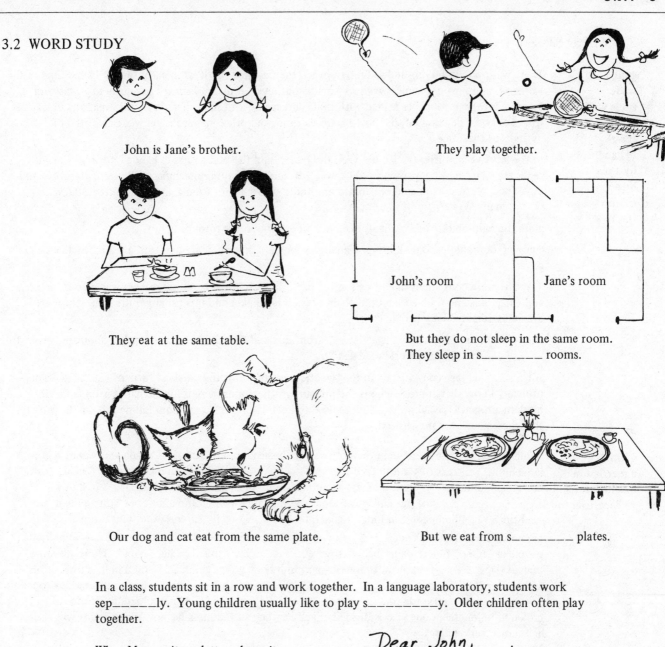

John is Jane's brother.

They play together.

They eat at the same table.

John's room   Jane's room

But they do not sleep in the same room.
They sleep in s_____ rooms.

Our dog and cat eat from the same plate.

But we eat from s_____ plates.

In a class, students sit in a row and work together. In a language laboratory, students work sep_____ly. Young children usually like to play s_____y. Older children often play together.

When Mary writes a letter, she writes each letter of the word separately.

Dear John,
I hope you had
a good vacation and

When John writes a letter, he joins the letters together.

Dear Mary,
The vacation will
soon be over, and

What are the two meanings of "a letter"?

3.2 WORD STUDY

grain
trade
trade with
travel
travel
by land
by sea
by air
the East
the West

There was *trade* (= buying and selling) between *the East* and *the West* in early times. In the time of the Roman Empire many people *traveled* (= made journeys) from one country to another *by land* and *by sea*. European countries traded with India and even with China. They sold oil, weapons, ships, and works of art. They bought silk, cotton, spices, gold, and other metals. Steel was one of the metals sold by India at that time.

In the last five centuries tr____ between the E____ and the W____ has expanded greatly. Canada sends *grain* to China. Japan sells radios, watches, and many other machines to Western countries and buys food, wool, cotton, and oil from them. India tr____s with Russia, and the United States t_____s w____ many Western and Eastern countries.

grain (uncountable) = corn, wheat, rice, and other food in the form of grains.

a grain (countable) = something very small, e.g., a grain of sand, a grain of salt, a grain of wheat, a grain of rice.

Travel is more convenient than it was in the past. In early times t_____ by sea was incon_____t and dangerous and took a long time. Nowadays it is quicker and it is usually quite safe. Ships are driven by steam. Many people t_____ *by air*.

It now takes only eight hours to t_____ from England to India by ____. It takes about six weeks to _____ from England to New Zealand by ____.

Air t____l is very convenient. In the twentieth century it is the quickest form of t_____. You probably know that at great heights the pressure of the atmosphere is lower than it is on land. In modern airplanes special m_____ds are used to keep the p_____re from falling too much. We say that these planes are pressurized.

grain
a metric ton
a British ton
an American ton

Some countries grow more grain than others. With the help of machines, Canada and America grow large qu_____s of grain to feed their own people and people in other countries. Canada grows about 20 million metric tons of wheat a year and more than 12 million tons of oats and barley. Large qu_____s of rice and other kinds of grain are grown in India, but not quite enough to feed the 600 million people in India. Large qu_____s of r____ and other kinds of gr____ are grown in China, but not en_____ to feed the Chinese people. There are more than 800 million people in China.* Indonesia probably grows en_____ gr____ to f____ her people. There are more than 100 m_____ people in Indonesia, and Indonesia grows about 23 million metric tons of rice a year. One British ton is eq_____t to 2,240 pounds. An American ton is eq_____t to 2,000 pounds. A metric ton is e_____t to 2,204.6 pounds or 1,000 kilograms. If the rice grown in Indonesia in one year is divided equally among all Indonesians, how many *grams* will each Indonesian get per *day*?

You can do this problem in the space below.

*This figure was given by Chou-en-lai in January 1975. Other figures given in this paragraph are the latest available in June 1979.

Unit III
3.3 DICTATION EXERCISES AND DICTATION PASSAGES

A 1. The passage *The Metric System (2)* will now be read to you. As you listen, you will hear *one* of the words or phrases in the following pairs (in the same order). Cross out the word or phrase which is incorrect.

    (a) official - the official   (f) standard - standards
    (b) other - others   (g) ordinary - originally
    (c) country - countries   (h) end of - enter
    (d) without - with a   (i) a nation - and Asian
    (e) part of - party   (j) unit - units

2. Number the following words in the order in which you hear them:

comparisons   European   Asian
           necessary   familiar with   definitions
trade   duty   metric

3. Practice the stresses of the following words, as grouped.

pos'si·ble	de·fine'	fa·mil'iar	Eu'ro·pe·an
im·pos'si·ble	be·come'	com·par'i·son	def·i·ni'tion
ac'cu·rate	with·out'	of·fi'cial	cal·cu·la'tion
in·ac'cu·rate	be·tween'	o·rig'i·nal·ly	
nec'es·sar·y		sub·trac'tion	
un·nec'es·sar·y			

4. The passage *The Metric System (2)* will now be given as dictation.

B 1. A Note on Meanings of Words

A barbarian (noun), *barbarian* (adjective). The Romans gave this name to people who were not Romans, especially those outside their Empire.

An Empire. A group of countries under one ruler or government.

A tribe. A group of people having the same language and customs; an early form of society which can still be found in some countries.

Invade (verb). Go (without permission) into a place or country which is not your own.

An invader. Someone who invades (a country, etc.).

An invasion. The action of someone who invades (a country, etc.).

2. The passage *The Barbarian Invasions* will now be read to you. As you listen, cross out the word or phrase in each of the following pairs which is incorrect.

    (a) century - centuries   (g) draw - drawn
    (b) the Empire - their Empire   (h) Easter - eastern
    (c) tribe - tribes   (i) invasions - invasion
    (d) number of - a number of   (j) fifth - fit
    (e) invade - invaded   (k) ready - readily
    (f) travel - traveled   (l) among the - among them

3.3 DICTATION EXERCISES AND DICTATION PASSAGES

3. Number the following words in the order in which you hear them:

tribes   Societies   armies
      size   origin   imaginary
triangle   invasions   Europe

4. Practice the following words, as grouped, with their correct stresses.

con·tain'   Eu'rope   sep'a·rate (adjective)
ex·act'   A'sia   nat'u·ral
in·vade'   Em'pire   u'su·al·ly
in·vad'er   Ro'man   sep'a·rate·ly
in·va'sion   Ger'man
di·vide'   Ger'ma·ny
di·vi'sion   Af'ri·ca
di·men'sion

5. The passage *The Barbarian Invasions* will now be given as dictation.

C   Dictation Passage

Work in pairs. The passage *Air Travel* will be read to you two or three times at intervals of 3 minutes.
Fill in the blank spaces, using the vocabulary given below. (No other words may be used.)

Air _____ ___ _____ convenient. In the _____ _____ it is _____

_____ _____ _____ travel. You _____ _____ that at _____ _____

_____ _____ of the _____ _____ _____ than it ____ ____ _____.

In _____ _____ special _____ ____ _____ _____ to _____ _____

_____ _____ falling.

atmosphere	is	probably	of	great
century	is	very	on	lower
form	is	the	from	modern
land	used	the		quickest
pressure	keep	the		twentieth
airplanes	are			
heights	know			
methods				
travel				
pressure				

3.3 DICTATION PASSAGES

(a)   The Metric System (2)

The meter is the official standard of length in France, and it is also used in many other countries as a standard. Trade between countries is impossible without accurate comparisons of measurement. But these comparisons cannot be made without standard units, and nowadays it is part of the duty of a government to fix or define standards. The meter was originally chosen as a standard by the French government at the end of the eighteenth century. It is necessary for European and Asian students to become familiar with the definitions of units in the metric system.

(b)   The Barbarian Invasions

Between the third and the fifth centuries the Romans lost much of their Empire. Under the pressure of the Huns and other invading tribes, Europe broke up into a number of separate societies under separate rulers. The exact origin of the Huns is not known. They invaded Europe from the northeast and their armies traveled quickly. An imaginary triangle drawn to contain Italy, Germany, France, eastern Spain, and a small part of North Africa will give some idea of the size of the invasions and the area covered by them. In the fifth century the invaders lost some ground. They fought one another as readily as they fought the Romans, and the divisions among them made it possible for Roman armies to drive them back.

(c)   Air Travel

Air travel is very convenient. In the twentieth century it is the quickest form of travel. You probably know that at great heights the pressure of the atmosphere is lower than it is on land. In modern airplanes special methods are used to keep the pressure from falling.

Unit III
3.4 READING PASSAGES

(a)   The Origin of Measurement

The history of mankind is, in part, a history of measurement. The origin of measurement was comparison. By looking at two groups of animals and comparing them, people could tell that one group was larger than the other. When numbers were discovered, people could compare groups more accurately by counting them.

But counting and calculation (which means working with numbers) were useful only for the comparison of groups of *separate* things. People who wished to compare sizes and distances could not do it just by counting. They had to find a way to divide the size or the distance into equal parts which could be counted. And so a new science was born—the science of measurement.

The first units of measurement were very simple. People already knew how to use their fingers to count with. (The word *finger* itself is probably derived from a word which means "five.") Now they began to use their feet, hands, thumbs, or steps to measure length. They found this set of units very convenient. Since they were parts of their own bodies, they could use them anywhere and at any time. To measure weight, they used stones or grains. They used the sun or the moon to tell the time or the season.

But these units of measurement were not always alike. Some feet were larger than others, some stones were heavier than others, and some days were longer than others. So, when people began to build houses, travel in ships, trade and divide the land, these natural ways of measuring were not good enough. Now they needed standard units of measurement. They needed measures that would be the same for everybody.

(b)   Arabic Figures and Arab Science

Who discovered mathematics? No one can say. The person who first discovered that fingers could be used to count with was the first mathematician. We do not know who he or she was. But we know that mathematics began and grew in Babylonia, Egypt, and Greece. Later it was also studied in India and Arabia, and from there it reached the West.

We still use Arabic figures (1, 2, 3, 4, 5, 6, 7, 8, 9) when we do arithmetic. The Romans used figures which were different. The Roman numbers are I, II, III, IV, V, VI, VII, VIII, IX, X, XI, and so on. L stands for 50 and C stands for 100 (*centum* in Latin). What is the Roman figure for *five*? _____

What is the Roman figure for *ten*? _____

How is *eleven* written in Roman figures? _____

How do we write *eight* in Roman figures? _____

How do we write *twenty-eight*? _____

(c)   Meters and Degrees

At the end of the eighteenth century there was a revolution* in France. Many of the new leaders were interested in science, and the new French government formed a committee to work out a completely new system of measurement.

This committee believed that the basic unit of length should be based on some natural measurement, some fact of nature. The most obvious fact of nature was surely the earth itself; so the committee began by trying to measure the earth. They hoped to do this by measuring the distance from the equator to the North Pole, on a line running through Paris. This distance is a quarter (¼) of the distance around the earth, and it is called a *quadrant*. The word *quadrant* is derived from a Latin word meaning "a quarter."

To make sure of this distance, the committee told their workers to measure distances between places in France and Spain from which the length of this quadrant could be accurately determined (= fixed). They finished their work and gave the result to the committee. The next problem was what to choose as the basic unit. A ten-millionth of the quadrant seemed to be a convenient length for everyday use; so this was taken as the basic unit. This ten-millionth ($\frac{1}{10,000,000}$) of a quadrant was called a *meter*; the word is derived from the Latin *metrum* and

3.4 READING PASSAGES

Greek *metra,* which both mean simply "measure."

The system based on the meter, as you know, is called the metric system. Everyone in France began to use it. Unfortunately (= unluckily) it was found many years later that the measurements which had been made by the committee's workers were not quite accurate and that the real length of the quadrant was just a little bit more than its originators thought it was. If the meter was exactly a ten-millionth of a quadrant, the distance from the equator to the North Pole would obviously be equivalent to 10,000,000 meters, no more and no less. But in fact the distance is 10,002,288.3 meters.

The mistake was discovered, but by this time it was too difficult to change the length of the meter. It was used by shopkeepers, traders, and the whole of French society and all kinds of measurements were based on it. If the French government had tried to change it there might have been another revolution—a revolution of shopkeepers and traders! So the government had to forget about using nature as a basis of measurement. They had to go on using the meter just as it was—a standard made by people, based on their planning, their work, and also on their mistakes. (You can calculate the difference between a "natural" meter and a "real" meter. It is not very large.)

Now we will think about another kind of unit. The line around a circle is called its circumference. The circumference of any circle can be divided into 360 *degrees.* This division originated with the Babylonians, who discovered that the sun took 365 days to go around the sky. However, 365 is an inconvenient number; so the Babylonians chose to divide the circle into 360 parts instead. This was more convenient, because 360 is a multiple of 22 different numbers, while 365 is a multiple of only two numbers. (You can find out what they are by doing a few simple division problems.)

Each degree was divided into 60 minutes and each minute was divided into 60 seconds (just like the divisions of an hour). This system was called *angular* measure because it could be used to measure angles as well as circumferences, and it is still used in this way. You can see the relation between a degree as a measure of length (of part of a circumference) and a degree as a measure of an angle if you draw a circle like this.

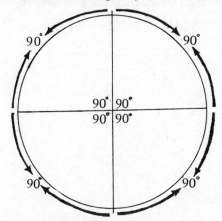

It is obvious that degrees (measuring distance along a circumference) are not very useful if we wish to compare the length of one circumference with another, because every circumference has exactly the same number of degrees. They are useful only when we want to compare one part of the *same* circumference with another part of the *same* circumference, and that is the way we use them—to make maps of the earth and compare distances on its surface.

To measure distances on the earth's surface is not simple. Special methods and special instruments are needed. The Greeks used Polaris (the star above the North Pole) to help them determine the position of places on land and ships at sea. The earliest maps were based on their calculations (= the sums they worked out). About 200 B. C. a Greek scientist called Eratosthenes calculated the size of the earth. Although his methods and instruments were not very good by our standards, his result was nearly correct. The French scientists who determined the length of the meter had better instruments and used better methods, and came still closer to the truth. The methods and instruments used nowadays can give still more accurate results, but even now we cannot be quite sure that our measurements are correct. A measurement is never perfect.

---

* a revolution = a complete change in a society, in its system of government, and in the basis of power in that society.

Unit III

3.5 VOCABULARY TEST

To test yourself on the vocabulary of this section, fill in the missing letters in the incomplete words.

When people have more money than they need for ordinary things, they sometimes use their extra money to t_____l and see other parts of the world. E_____n people go to t__ ___t and people from the E___t go to t__ ___t. Long before people t_____d for pleasure ships went from one country to another to t____e with each other. The men who sailed in these old ships used to use the stars and the p_____s to help them find the way. When they saw an island they c_____d their maps to see if the island was marked on their map. If it was not marked there, they knew that they had d_____d an island. If we c_____e the maps of today with those used by the early sailors we will notice many differences.

N_____s the quickest and most c_____t way to travel is b_ ___r. Some people who do not like cold weather fly to a warmer place when the cold s_____n comes. Their only p_____m is that if they move every year to avoid the cold or rainy s_____n they need two s_____te houses, one for each half of the year. Some people prefer to t_____ __ ___a because it gives them a chance to make new friends. The most n_____l way to t_____l is by l__d. No two places are a____e and if we t_____l slowly we have time to c_____e one place with another. We can make a better c_____n between two countries if we know both languages. This may mean learning not only new sounds, new words, and new ideas but also learning new and different letters. R_____ _____s are used by Indonesian, English, and Vietnamese, A_____ l_____s are used by Urdu, Javi, and Arabic, I____ _____s are used by Tamil, Hindi, Thai, and Burmese. The Chinese languages have quite a different writing s_____m from any of these. The signs do not mean g____ps of l_____s. They are pictures of ideas.

Unit IV
4.1 VOCABULARY

These are the words you will practice in this unit:

VERBS			
belong to	(be·long')	(+ noun)	
calculate	(cal'cu·late)	(+ noun)	
determine	(de·ter'mine)	(+ noun)	
displace	(dis·place')	(+ noun)	
dissolve	(dis·solve')		
flow			
happen	(hap'pen)		
notice	(no'tice)	(+ noun)	
obtain	(ob·tain')	(+ noun)	
record	(re·cord')	(+ noun)	
refer to	(re·fer')	(+ noun)	
repeat	(re·peat')	(+ noun)	
represent	(rep·re·sent')	(+ noun)	

NOUNS			
(an) action	(ac'tion)	an interval	(in'ter·val)
(a) calculation	(cal·cu·la'tion)	an object (= thing)	(ob'ject)
the center	(cen'ter)	a pattern	(pat'tern)
a circle	(cir'cle)	a radius	(ra'di·us)
the circumference	(cir·cum'fer·ence)	a rectangle	(rec'tan·gle)
a class		(a) repetition	(rep·e·ti'tion)
a cube		a route	
a diameter	(di·am'e·ter)	a scale	
an edge		a statement	(state'ment)
a fluid	(flu'id)	a symbol	(sym'bol)
a formula	(for'mu·la)		

ADJECTIVES			
alike	(a·like')	impossible	(im·pos'si·ble)
certain (= particular)	(cer'tain)	indirect	(in·di·rect')
chemical	(chem'i·cal)	irregular	(ir·reg'u·lar)
direct	(di·rect')	possible	(pos'si·ble)
fluid	(flu'id)	rectangular	(rec·tan'gu·lar)
important	(im·por'tant)	regular	(reg'u·lar)

ADVERBS	
conveniently	(con·ven'ient·ly)
directly	(di·rect'ly)
fortunately	(for'tu·nate·ly)
generally (= usually)	(gen'er·al·ly)
indirectly	(in·di·rect'ly)

PREPOSITION	
without	(with·out')

PHRASE	
at sea	

Unit IV
4.2 WORD STUDY

INSTRUCTIONS: Study the following words and the uses of them:

(an) action

(a)   *An action* is something which is done by a person. We know what a man is like from his a_____ns.

(b)   An army, or a football team, or a fire engine is in *action* (uncountable noun) when it is doing its own kind of work. Action (uncountable noun) can be used about machines and substances, not only about people or groups.

Examples:

(a)   As a result of his action, the town was saved. People do not always know what the results of their a_____s will be. His next a_____n was to telephone the hospital.

(b)   Children like to watch a fire engine in a_____. Today we will study the a_____ of oxygen on iron and on other metals. Napoleon was a man of a_____. The government must take action (i.e., do something) to help the farmers.

calculate
a calculation
calculation
  (uncountable)

When we *calculate* we do sums or work with numbers, or find out something by working with numbers. This work is called *calculation* (uncountable). A calculation is a sum, or a piece of work done by calculation.

Examples: Can you c_____te the cost of the journey? He has a c_____ting machine. These c_____ns will take a long time. You can find the answer to this problem without much c_____tion.

an object

An object is a thing that can be seen or touched, usually a solid separate thing.

How many o_____s do you see here?
I can count _____ ob____s.

What is that ob____t in the distance, in the middle of the road?

a formula
pl. formulas

A formula is a rule, fact, or relation written in a short form, usually in numbers, letters, or other symbols. H_2O is the formula for water, used in chemistry.

Examples: L x W x H is a f_____a for a rectangular solid.

4.2 WORD STUDY

Physicists will know the f_____a for Boyle's law, a famous law relating the volume of a fixed amount of gas to its pressure and temperature. The formula is:

$$P \propto \frac{1}{v} \text{ or } P = k, \frac{1}{v}; \text{ } PV = \text{const. or } P_1V_1 = P_2V_2$$

It is not necessary to learn this now! It is given here as an example of a f_____a in physics. Students of physics and chemistry must learn many f_____s.

a symbol A cross (✝) is a *symbol* of the Christian religion. A crown 👑 is a sym____ of a king. Black is a s_____ of death. Red is often a s_____ of danger. These are mathematical s_____s.

A symbol is a written mark or a thing which stands for another thing. The meaning of a s____l is given to it by people, by human beings. Red things, for example, are not naturally dangerous. But the color red is often used by people as a s____l of danger. The meaning of a s____l is not in the object or mark or color which is used as a s____l but in the minds of the people who use it in this way.

displace One thing *displaces* another when it pushes it out of the way and takes its place. When we put a solid object into a glass of water so that the water covers it, some of the water is dis____ed.

dissolve A solid *dissolves* when it mixes with a liquid and itself becomes liquid. Salt d_____s in water. Sugar also d_____s in water. A piece of iron will not d_____ in water.

determine One meaning of *determine* is "find, fix, or measure" (a dimension or set of dimensions) exactly.

Examples: Early sailors did not know how to d_____e their position. They had to find a way of d_____ning their position. A. A. Michelson, a German scientist, spent many years trying to d_____e the speed of light. He succeeded and was given a Nobel Prize in 1907.

Another meaning is "to be the fact, or the kind of fact, or to be the unit or formula by which a **feature** or **a dimension** is fixed or measured."

Examples: The size of your feet d_____es the size of your shoes. Colors are d_____ed by the length of light waves. Actions d_____e character. The volume of a rectangular solid is d_____d by the formula L x W x H.

Note: Things, objects, and dimensions can be **measured**. Only dimensions or special features of things can be **determined**. We can speak of measuring or determining the position of a ship. We can speak of measuring a ship. But we cannot speak of determining a ship.

repeat
(a) repetition We *repeat* something when we do it again or say it again. A machine can repeat a movement. An action, a movement, or part of a pattern is r_____ed when it is followed by something which is the same, or which is a copy of it. *A repetition* of a movement or an action is that movement or action done a second time. There may be many r_____ions of the same movement. *Repetition* (uncountable) means "repeating." We learn words by r_____n. This means that we learn words by repeating them.

Examples: Please r_____ what you said, because I couldn't hear it. Our teacher usually r_____s a new word two or three times. In this song you can hear the same musical phrase r_____ed five times. There are five r_____ns of the phrase. Most people cannot remember a word or a name after a single r_____n. In learning, r_____ and understanding must go together.

refer to
referred
referring When I say "I have two hundred dollars in the bank," I am using the word dollar to *refer to* a unit of money. When I say "I have three pounds of sugar in the cupboard," I am using the word p___d to r___r to a u___ of weight. Instead of using the word dollar to r____ to a unit of money, a writer can use the symbol $. When John says "I will see you tomorrow," he r____rs __ the future. Not one word only, but his whole sentence r____rs to the future. We use sentences of this kind to r____r __ the future. A speaker may refer to something without naming it. For example, I may say "In the place where I work there are no large classrooms." If the person I am speaking to knows where I work, he

4.2 WORD STUDY

knows that I am r____rring to the English Language Institute, though I have not named it. If I walk into my son's apartment and say "Where is he?" his friends will probably know that I am r___rring to my son, though I have not named him.

Words, symbols, and sentences can be used in different ways to r_____ __ different things (or persons, places, times, actions, etc.). The words in a dictionary do not r_____ to anything. The "meaning" of a word which we find in a dictionary is a definition or explanation which shows what this word **usually** refers to. But a word does not refer to anything until someone uses it to refer to that thing. A word or a sentence only r_____s __ something when it is **used** by a speaker or a writer to refer to that thing, i.e., to turn our thoughts toward that thing.

More Examples of refer to, referred to, referring to:

The word **degree** may r_____ __ a unit of temperature, or to a unit of the earth's circumference, or to an angular unit, or to a certificate of examination successes given by a university.

When I spoke of my brother, I was r____rring __ John, not Peter.

In his speech he r____rred once or twice to the price of rice.

We will forget this quarrel; please don't r_____ __ it again.

regular
irregular

Regular, when it refers to something in space, means "having parts which are the same, which are repeated in the same way."

This is a regular shape, because the right side is the same as the left side.

This is an *irregular* shape, because one part of it does not repeat any other part.

Regular, when it refers to something in time, means "done at the same time" or "repeated in the same way." A man who is regular in his habits does things at the same time every day and in the same way. Regular can also mean "following a rule."

Examples: R_____r solids can be measured easily, but it is not easy to measure irr_____ar solids. To find the volume of an irr_____ solid we must use special methods.

His attendance in class is irr_____. He is not a r_____r student; he only attends a few courses. The movements of a clock are r_____, and that is why we can use it to measure time. It is a r_____ custom in our home to invite friends on Christmas day. I will allow you to take the examination without paying your fees, though this is irr_____r (i.e., against the rule).

an interval

An interval is a space or time **between** two points in space or between two times or happenings.

In this row of trees the in_____l between two trees is ten yards.

4.2 WORD STUDY

To measure length, we use a piece of wood called a ruler, marked **at regular intervals**. Most rulers are marked at intervals of one inch.

In this school the bell rings at i_____ls of one hour. At 12 o'clock there is an i_____l for lunch.

flow
a fluid

A fluid is something which can *flow*, as gases and liquids do. A f____d is either a gas or a liquid. All gases and liquids are f____ds, because they can all flow. Air is a _____. Milk is a _____. Iron is not a _____. A solid thing is not a _____ because it does not f__w. It stays in the same place and does not change its shape. Gases and liquids move and change their shape if they are not kept in solid containers. They flow. They are f_____s.

a pattern

These are *patterns*. We can call them geometrical p_____rns, because the forms in them are triangles, squares, and other regular geometrical forms. Not all p_____ns are geometrical, but in every p_____n there are forms which are repeated regularly. We find p_____ns in carpets, on wallpaper, and on many things made by men. We often find them in nature. A leaf has a pattern.

We can also hear p_____ns in music. A piece of music is a p_____n of sounds. In music sounds are grouped and repeated in a regular way. Some of the p_____ns of music are determined by the intervals between sounds.

We can speak of p_____rns of society, p_____ns of family life, or the p_____n of an essay. A p_____n of society is a form of society which we find regularly repeated. A p_____n of family life is a f__m of family life which we find re_____ly rep___ed. The p_____n of an essay is a f___ which can be re_____ed. Two essays can have the same p_____n though the ideas in the essays may be quite different.

represent

When one thing is a **picture**, a **diagram**, a **map**, a **symbol**, or an **example** of another thing, it *represents* the other thing.

What does this drawing represent?

It r_____nts a house between two rows of trees.

4.2 WORD STUDY

What does this diagram represent? It
r_____s the e___th.

What do N. and S. represent? They
r_____t the North P____ and
the South P____.

What does the line AB represent? It
r_____ts the equ_____.

What does this map represent? It r°_____
S__th A_____a.

+   —   x   ÷   **What do these symbols represent?**

They r_____ _____, _____, _____ , and _____ .

When students are asked to write an essay on "American Cities," they cannot describe **all** American cities;
there are too many of them. So they choose three or four cities **as examples,** to r_____nt American
cities in general. Students will try to choose **representative** cities, cities which have features found in
many other American cities. They may choose Chicago (or Detroit, or St. Louis) to r_____t the
industrial cities of the north. Chicago r_____s these cities.

It is impossible for all the people in the United States to become members of Congress and make laws.
There are too many of them. So the people in a certain district choose a person to represent them and
speak for them in Congress. That person becomes their representative in Congress. So to represent can
also mean "to be a person who stands for or speaks for people."

important   We say that something is *important* when we ought to take notice of it or pay attention to it.   A
teacher who says "This rule is very important," means that we must pay attention to it and not forget it.
Boyle's law is an im_____t law in physics; it is a law which most students of physics need to know.
When we learn English we find that some words are more i_____ than others. The i_____
words are the words which we use or read most often.

a scale   The word *scale* has many meanings. The most important one for you to learn now is "a set of marks at
fluid   regular intervals for the purpose of measuring or regulating." The marks on a scale represent units or
regular multiples of units. What kinds of units are represented on the following scales?

The scale on a speedometer represents units of _____

The scale on a thermometer represents units of _____

4.2 WORD STUDY

The scale on a barometer represents units of _____

The scale on a measuring glass represents units of _____

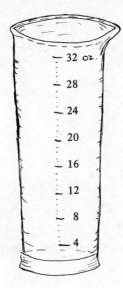

A measuring beaker with a scale showing *fluid* ounces, which are units of volume. Every fluid ounce is marked on the scale and every multiple of 4 fluid ounces is numbered on the scale, up to 32.

without

Today Mr. Smith went for a walk with his dog.

Yesterday he went for a walk *without* his dog.

4.2 WORD STUDY

without   (before nouns and pronouns) = not having, not with.
without   (before -ing noun) = not doing (something).

Examples: I came to the office w_____t my raincoat.

She did all the work w_____ help.

She went for a holiday _____ her husband.

He went out w_____ shutting the door.

He can't write anything _____ making mistakes.

She sat there half an hour _____ speaking.

happen
happened
happening
fortunately
  (= luckily)

Mr. A.   You are very late for work. What *happened*?

Mr. B.   The house burned down.

Mr. A.   Oh dear! Are you hurt?

Mr. B.   No, *fortunately* I was in the garden when it happened.

Mr. A.   Is it your own house?

Mr. B.   No, fortunately it is not my house. I only rent it. (= I pay some money every week or every month for it.)

Mr. A.   What happened to your wife?

Mr. B.   Nothing happened to her. She was not there.

Mr. A.   Where was she?

Mr. B.   Fortunately she was out. She had taken the children to school.

possible
impossible

(a)   A   B   C

E   W

Puzzles

A, B, and C are houses.
E is an electric power station.
W is a waterworks.

Is it *possible* or *impossible* to connect E with A, B, and C separately, and W with A, B, and C separately, without any of the pipes or wires crossing each other? (Try to do this by drawing lines from the wires and water pipes.)

(b)   A   B   C

E   G   W

A, B, and C are houses.
E is an electric power station.   G is a gas station.   W is a waterworks.

4.2 WORD STUDY

Is it possible or impossible to connect E with A, B, and C separately, G with A, B, and C separately, and W with A, B, and C separately, without any of the pipes or wires crossing each other? (Try to do this by drawing lines for the electric wires, gas pipes, and water pipes.)

a circle
the center
  (of a circle)
the circumference
  (of a circle)
a (the) radius
  (of a circle)
(the) radii
  (of a circle)
a (the) diameter
  (of a circle)

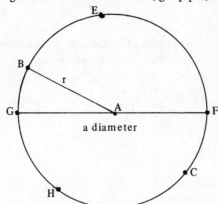

This is a *circle*. The point A is the *center* of the circle. The line AB is a *radius* of the circle. AG is another radius. All the *radii* (plural) of a circle are equal in length. In a formula the r_____s is often represented by r. The *circumference* of the circle is the line equidistant (=at equal distance) at all points from the center. The circumference is defined by the length of the radius. All the points B, E, F, C, H, G are on the c_____ of this circle.

The line GF which goes across the circle and through the center is called a *diameter*. The length of a d_____r is equal to two r____i. Every line which joins the center with the c_____ is a r_____s. The size of a circle is d_____ned by the length of its radius.

The formula for the length of the circumference of a circle is 2Πr. The symbol represents 3.14159.

a cube
an edge

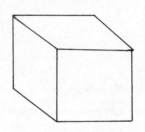

This is a diagram of a *cube*. A c____ has six sides and twelve *edges*. It is a three-dimensional object. It has length and width and height. Every side (or face) of the c____ is a perfect square. The length of this c____ is two feet. Its height is two feet. Its w__th is two feet. What is the **volume** of this cube?

An edge of a thing is a line which joins two surfaces. A ruler has a straight e____.

How many edges does this have?

Answer _____

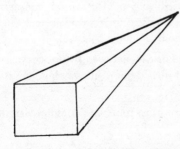

How many edges does this have, if it is a regular solid? How many sides?

Answer (a) _____ (b) _____

a rectangle
rectangular

A shape with four sides meeting to form four right angles is a *rectangle*.

57

4.2 WORD STUDY

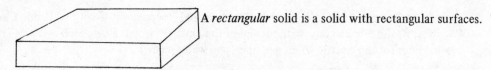

A *rectangular* solid is a solid with rectangular surfaces.

a statement

A *statement* is a sentence which says something or **tells us something**, not a sentence which asks a question (this is called a question) and not a sentence which tells someone to do something (this is called an order, or a command, or a request).

A st_____nt begins with a capital letter and ends with a period. All sentences begin with capital letters, but not all sentences end with a period. A period is a symbol (representing the end of a statement). What symbol does a question end with?

Here are some st_____nts.

(a) Paris is the largest city in France.

(b) The value of this house is $40,000.

(c) A barometer is used to measure pr_____re.

(d) A metric ton is equ_____nt to 1000 kilograms.

(e) A triangle has two sides.

A statement may be true or false (= untrue). Are any of these s_____ts false? Which do you think are false? _____

Here are three statements. One of them is a definition. Which one?

(a) This container holds water.

(b) Volume is the space taken by a thing or a substance.

(c) There are nine planets in the solar system.

direct
directly
indirect
indirectly
a route

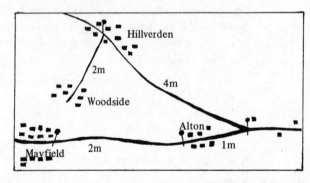

Look at this map. There is a *direct* road from Mayfield to Alton. There is no d_____t road from Mayfield to Woodside. If you want to drive from Mayfield to Woodside, you must go through Alton, take the first turning on the left, and turn left again at Hillverden. The *route* is *indirect*. You can only reach Woodside ind_____ly. It is only 2 miles from Mayfield to Woodside across the fields and through the wood, but because of the in_____t route it is 9 miles by road.

A connection or relation between two things, or a road or way between two places (called a route) is direct if there is nothing between them, and if it is not turned out of its way but goes by the shortest possible way.

A man goes to a place *directly* if he goes there by the shortest route and does not visit other places on the way.

When we measure a line with a ruler we make a direct measurement; we d_____ly compare the length of the line with the intervals between the marks on the ruler. We can see the results as soon as we do this; it is not necessary to do any work **between** making the measurement and finding the result of the measurement.

58

4.2 WORD STUDY

But we usually measure an area *indirectly*. We do not d_____y compare the size of one surface with the size of another s_____ce. We measure the length and width of the s_____ce and then multiply the two figures. Between making the measurements and getting the answer we must do some cal_____n. The answer is reached in_____ly.

Many actions have indirect results in addition to d_____t results. The direct results are those which people **try** to obtain (= get) or those which they think will happen. The in_____ results are another set of results which happen later, or which are not thought of at first. For example, a man may work hard from morning till night, and forget about his family and friends. Perhaps he wants to get a lot of money by working day and night, and the d_____ result of his work is that he becomes a rich man. This is pleasant. But the in_____t results may be unpleasant. Perhaps he loses his health and his peace of mind, or he now lives in such a grand house that his friends are afraid to come and see him, so he loses them too. He never thought of these indirect results.

When something happens, we may hear about it d_____ly from someone who saw it (or who did it himself) or we may hear about it in_____ly from someone who only heard about it or read about it. When their son is going to be married, parents are usually happy if they hear about it d_____ from him and not i_____ from another person.

We can refer to something d_____ly, by naming it, or we can refer to it ind_____tly in some other way. For example, the Greek word "barbaros," which means "those who speak in a way which we do not understand" was an indirect way of r____rring to anybody who was not a Greek.

alike
a class   = the set of all the things or people which are alike in a certain way.
belong to
directly

Counting and Measuring

To use the passage:

1. Fold or cut a strip of paper to cover the words in the column on the right.

2. Read the first sentence (line 1).

3. Read the second sentence and write the missing word in the underlined space. (The information in the previous sentence tells you what to write.)

4. Move your strip of paper downward to uncover the first word in the column. It is the word you should have written.

5. If you wrote the right word, go on. If you wrote the wrong word, read the previous sentences again.

6. Go on in the same way. Each time you fill the blank space(s) in a line, move your strip of paper down to the line below and check your word(s).

Work carefully. The ideas and words of the passage are repeated so that you learn them thoroughly. Don't hurry!

1. **Unus, duo, tres**: these are the Latin words for **one**, **two**, and **three**. From **unus**, meaning _____, we get the word **unit**. **Units** are **ones**. In order to count (one, two, three . . .), we must be able to see **ones**.

one

2. We can count apples, spiders, and girls because each apple grows separate and complete, each spider grows _____ and complete, and each girl grows separate and _____ .
We can count bottles, typewriters, and hats because each bottle is made separate and complete, each typewriter is made _____ and complete, and each hat is made separate and _____ .

separate
complete

separate
complete

3. This ⬛ is a bottle and this ⬛ is a bottle. The bottles are not *alike* in height. They are not alike in width. They are not alike in size. They are not alike in shape. They are

4.2 WORD STUDY

alike in being bottles. Each bottle is one of the things which we call **bottles**. All the bottles in the world form the *class* of things we call bottles. Mary is a girl and Joan is a girl. These two friends are not alike in _____ . They are not _____ in width. They are _____ alike in size. They are not alike in _____ . They are alike in being _____ . Each _____ is one of the things which we call _____ . All the girls in the world form the _____ of things which we call _____ .

height	alike
not	
shape	girls	girl
girls	
class	girls

4. When we count bottles, we do not think of the differences between one bottle and another; we think of them as separate complete things which we call bottles. In the same way, when we count girls, we do not think of the _____ between one _____ and another; we think of them as _____ complete things which we call _____ . We think of the bottles as units of the class of things which we call bottles. We think of the girls as _____ of the _____ of things which we call _____ .

differences	
girl	separate
girls	
units	class
girls	

5. We cannot count together units which do not *belong to* the same class of things. Two girls and one boy are not three units of the class of things which we call **girls**. Two bottles and one cup are not three units of the class of things which we call **bottles**. Two dogs and one cat are not three _____ of the _____ of things which we call **dogs**.

units	class

6. Two boys and one girl do not belong to the class of girls, but they belong to the class of **persons**. Each boy and each girl is one unit of the class of persons. Two bottles and one cup do not _____ to the _____ of cups, but they belong to the class of **containers**. Each bottle and each cup is one _____ of the _____ of _____ . Two dogs and one cat do not _____ to the _____ of dogs, but they _____ to the _____ of animals. Each dog and each cat is one _____ of the _____ of animals.

belong	class
unit	
class	containers
belong	class
belong	class
unit	class

7. When we count units of the class of **persons**, we do not think of the differences between a girl and a boy. When we count units of the _____ of containers, we do not think of the _____ between a bottle and a cup. When we say a **boy** is a **person**, and that a **girl** is a **person**, we think of the ways in which a boy is like a girl. All units of a class are alike in some ways; these are the ways which make us say they belong to that class.

class
differences

8. It is easy to count things which grow separate and complete, like spiders, or which are made separate and complete, like bottles. It is difficult to think of counting the water in the river, or the heaviness of a parcel, or time. We cannot count these things *directly* because water, heaviness, and time are not separate and complete.

9. Water is not separate and complete. If we want to count water, we must divide it into parts which are separate and complete. We can count separate amounts of water by using a container of a known size. Heaviness is not separate and complete.

4.2 WORD STUDY

If we want to count heaviness, we must _____ it into
parts which are _____ and _____ . We
can count separate amounts of heaviness by using an object with
a known weight. Time is not _____ and _____ .

divide

separate   complete

If we want to _____ time, we must _____it into
_____ which are _____ of time by using an
object which moves at a known speed.

separate   complete
count   divide
parts   divisions

10. Water is not separate and complete and so we cannot count water directly. When we divide it into
separate, complete parts, we can count the parts. Counting parts of something we cannot count directly
is called *measuring*.

11. Spiders grow separate and complete. Each spider is a unit of
the class of spiders. Bottles are made _____ and
_____ . Each bottle is a _____ of the _____
of bottles. We can count bottles and spiders directly. Water is
not separate and _____ ; so we cannot _____
water directly. We must _____ it into separate,
_____ parts. To do this we need a container. The
container is our instrument of measurement. An instrument of
measurement is needed for measuring all things which are not
separate and complete. A balance is an instrument for measuring
weight. A clock is an _____ for measuring time. A
ruler is an _____ for _____ length.

separate
complete   unit   class

complete   count
divide
complete

instrument
instrument measuring

12. A measuring instrument is used to divide uncountable things
into parts. Each part is a unit of measurement.

certain   (used with countable nouns) = known but not named.
notice   = see or hear something which catches your attention.
record   = put something in writing, on a tape, etc., or keep it for later use by writing it, putting it on a tape, etc.
a record   = something recorded, i.e., written or put into a form in which it can be read or heard again.
obtain   = get (something).

When you look around the university library, you will probably *notice certain* rooms which students are
not allowed to use. Some of these rooms are offices used by the librarians, but others are rooms where
special books are kept. These books can only be read when special permission is ob_____ed from the
head librarian. They are often old books which can no longer be ob_____d in bookstores.

In the reference room you will n____ce many large dictionaries and encyclopedias. Students are not
all____d to take them out of the library, but are a_____ to read them in the reference room.

Before you take any books out of the library you must o_____ a library card. You will probably
n_____ that the librarian uses a special machine to *record* your name on the card and in her register.

The library catalogue is *a record* of all the books in the university library. On the cards in the catalogue
the librarians have recorded the name of each book, the name of the writer, the name of the publisher,
and the year in which the book was published.

In a ce_____n part of the library, historical r_____ds are kept, which give interesting and important
facts about the history of the country. Some of these r_____s are not books, but letters and
government papers.

If you want r_____ds for your record player, you will not find these in the university library. You can
ob___n them from a store, or from the public library in the town. You can use the r_____s in the
public library by paying 25 cents a week for each r_____d that you take out.

Unit IV

4.3 DICTATION EXERCISES AND DICTATION PASSAGES

A 1. The passage *Movies and Photographs* will be read to you. Give the correct forms of the following verbs in the order in which you hear them.

(a) travel _____   (f) obtain _____

(b) happen _____   (g) look at _____

(c) watch _____   (h) choose _____

(d) imagine _____   (i) notice _____

(e) record _____   (j) represent _____

2. Number the following words in the order in which you hear them.

certain	accurate	important	ordinary
	distant	completely	necessary
impossible	sure	historical	

3. **A recognition race.** Underline the following words in the passage *Movies and Photographs*.

happenings	happens	record	imagine	ordinary
photographs	represents	notice	travel	instrument
discoveries	chooses	discover	obtained	method

4. Practice the following words, as grouped, with their correct stresses.

cam'er·a	gen'er·al·ly	im·pos'si·ble
pho'to·graph	nat'u·ral·ly	his·tor'i·cal
in'stru·ment	sep'a·rate·ly	con·ven'ient
rep're·sent	or'di·nar·y	dis·cov'er·y
con'fer·ence	nec'es·sar·y	

5. The passage will be read again. As you listen, write the articles (if any) which come before the following adjectives, and the nouns which follow them. Give the noun endings correctly (singular or plural).

(a) _____ other _____

(b) _____ easier _____

(c) _____ important historical _____

(d) _____ ordinary _____

(e) _____ living _____

(f) _____ distant _____

(g) _____ certain _____

(h) _____ this _____

(i) _____ scientific _____

(j) _____ many historical _____

6. Work in pairs. A paragraph will be read to you two or three times at intervals of about five minutes. After the readings (not during the readings) try to fill in the blank spaces in the framework given on the next page. **All** the missing words are given below the framework.

4.3 DICTATION EXERCISES AND DICTATION PASSAGES

Camera _____ _____ _____ _____ _____than _____ _____

_____ _____ and _____ . When a _____ _____ _____ _____ _____ , he

_____ what _____ _____ to see. He often _____ _____ _____

_____ not to _____ _____ things. But a _____

_____ _____ _____ _____ _____ and _____ .

Without _____ _____ _____ , many _____ _____ _____

_____ impossible, and we _____ _____ _____ _____ _____ _____ _____ facts.

discoveries	every	of	accurate	completely	are	
eyes	many	of	convenient	less	chooses	
eyes	this	it	historical	more	finds	
instrument	the	he	scientific	more	looks at	
man	the		sure	only	notice	
men			certain	truthfully	represents	
object				generally	sees	
women					would be	
world					would be	
camera						

7. The passage *Movies and Photographs* will be given as dictation.

B   1. The passage *A Train Robbery* will be read to you. Give the correct forms of the following verbs in the order in which you hear them. (If the verb has two parts, give both.)

(a) travel _____   (c) notice _____

(b) happen _____   (d) contain _____

(e) steal _____   (g) say _____

(f) refer to _____   (h) arrive _____

2. Number the following words in the order in which you hear them.

traveling   happened   unusual

referred to   conference   robbery

fortunately   official   thefts

3. Practice the following words, as grouped, with their correct stresses.

in·di·rect'ly   po·lice'
sci·en·tif'ic   re·cord' (verb)
cal·cu·la'tion   a·sleep'
def·i·ni'tion   with·out'

4. The passage will be read to you again. As you listen, cross out the word or phrase in each of the following pairs which is incorrect.

(a)   a robbery - robbery   (f)   a suitcase - the suitcase
(b)   Paris - palace   (g)   official - officials
(c)   happen - happened   (h)   speak - speech
(d)   asleep - sleep   (i)   directly - indirectly
(e)   notice - noticed   (j)   shirts - shirt

5. The passage *A Train Robbery* will now be given as dictation.

4.3 DICTATION PASSAGES

(a)   Movies and Photographs

If we want to learn about other societies, it is not always necessary to travel. We can discover what happens in other parts of the world by watching movies. It is difficult to imagine an easier method of learning about other countries. Nowadays movies not only tell stories or record important historical happenings. They also record for us the actions and habits of ordinary people. Much of our present knowledge of living forms and of objects in distant space, too, is obtained from movies and photographs.

Camera eyes are generally more accurate than the eyes of men and women. When a man looks at the world, he sees only what he chooses to see. He often finds it more convenient not to notice certain things. But a camera represents every object completely and truthfully. Without this instrument, many scientific discoveries would be impossible and we would be less sure of many historical facts.

(b)   A Train Robbery

Last night there was a robbery on the special train in which a government official was traveling to speak at the Paris conference on European trade. It happened while everyone was asleep, and even the police did not notice anything unusual until eight o'clock next morning. Fortunately the suitcase containing the official papers was not stolen. In his speech on the radio this afternoon the official referred to the thefts indirectly when he said that he arrived in Paris with only two shirts.

Unit IV

4.4 READING PASSAGES

(a) Measuring a Rectangular Solid

Probably the easiest kind of volume to measure is liquid volume, which we can measure directly in a container marked with a scale, like the measuring breaker on page 55. A liquid is easy to measure because it is a fluid; in other words it can flow. It can take the shape of any container which is not too small.

To measure regular solids with straight edges we use a cube with edges of a certain length as a unit of volume. If the length is one inch, it is called a cubic inch. For larger spaces we use cubic feet, cubic yards, or cubic meters and for smaller spaces we use cubic centimeters, cubic millimeters, or parts of a cubic inch. But perhaps one of these statements is incorrect. It is not perfectly true to say "we use a cube" to measure solid volume. We do not use the cube itself; we take its size as a unit and after measuring the length, width, and height of the solid we do a little calculation.

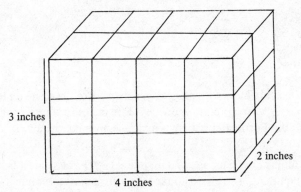

a rectangular block

3 inches

2 inches

4 inches

This diagram represents a block with sides of 4, 3, and 2 inches.

Perhaps you wish to determine its volume. If you count the one-inch cubes contained in the block, you will find there are 24. But obviously there is no need to count them. You calculate 4 x 3 x 2 and that gives you the answer. When we measure in this way we do not measure volume directly. We use another kind of measurement (the measurement of length) to help us find the result. This is an example of indirect measurement.

If you know a little geometry you can use it to calculate the volumes of other regular solids. How do we generally measure area? Directly or indirectly? To calculate volume or area, do we add, divide, or multiply?

(b)   Formulas (Plural of Formula)

We represent the solid volume of a rectangular box or rectangular solid by the simple formula L x W x H. What does L represent in this formula? What does W represent? What does H represent? To calculate area we use the formula L x W.

A formula is a short statement of a rule or general fact. Very often *symbols* are used in formulas. In the formula L x W x H, L is a symbol for length. H_2O is the chemical formula for water. H is the symbol for hydrogen. Do you know what O is the symbol for?

The symbol Π represents the number 3.14159, which is the circumference of a circle divided by its diameter.

The formula for finding the area of a circle is Πr^2. The symbol r represents the length of the radius of a circle. By using this formula you can determine the area of any circle if you know the length of the radius.

Is this an example of direct or indirect measurement?

4.4 READING PASSAGES

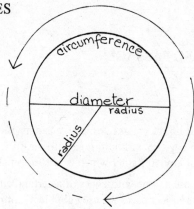

(c)   Measuring the Volume of an Irregular Solid

a stone

Perhaps you want to measure the volume of a solid object with an irregular shape, like the stone represented above. How can you do it? You will find it impossible, or very difficult, to divide it into cubes (or regular solids of any kind) and measure their length, height, and width. Fortunately, there is a more convenient way to measure its volume.

First obtain a measuring glass with a scale of units of volume marked on one side. The glass must be big enough to hold the stone conveniently. Next put some liquid into this glass and record (write down) its volume. Now drop the stone into the glass. You will notice that the surface of the liquid gets higher. This happens because the stone takes the place of some of the liquid, pushing it higher up the glass. Now you can measure the new height of the liquid, and subtract the original height from this. This calculation will determine the volume of the stone. Its volume is, of course, equal to the volume of the water displaced. This method of measurement can only be used for solids which do not dissolve in the liquid in which they are placed.

(d)   Ships, Stars, and Clocks (1)

Nowadays ships are often used for scientific purposes. There are special ships used by oceanographers (scientists who study the sea and its depths) and by scientists who travel to the Poles. The earliest ships were not built by men who traveled to discover nature's secrets. They were built by men who wished to trade with people across the water, or to find routes which were quicker and more convenient, or to find good land to feed their families, or to invade their enemies' countries.

But some of the most important discoveries about the earth, the stars, and time were probably made by early sailors—men who sailed on ships. They were among the first who learned that the earth was a sphere. Sleeping and living under the open sky, they came to know the stars well and discovered important facts about them.

Before ships were made, men were interested in the stars. Shepherds who spent the night in the fields noticed that the movements of the stars followed a pattern, repeated over and over again. There were sailors who were familiar with this pattern in their own countries, just as they were familiar with the pattern of houses and fields in their own towns or villages. When their voyages (= journeys by sea) took them to new places, these sailors noticed that the familiar stars seemed to have fallen a little lower toward the edge of the sea or to have risen a little higher above their heads.

A Greek scientist called Anixamander noticed that the big group of stars which we call the Great Bear was so close to the Pole star that it was always above the horizon*. Then he visited Egypt. He saw the Great Bear again, but its position had changed. In the Egyptian sky it seemed to hide below the horizon for a short time every night.

4.4 READING PASSAGES

Anixamander believed that this meant the world was not flat, but a sphere. If the world was flat, the Great Bear would always stay in the same place in the sky. It might look farther away if you traveled away from it, but if the world was flat it would not go down behind the horizon. Anixamander could only explain what he saw by saying that the earth was a sphere.

Scientific facts are often discovered not because they are interesting but because they are *needed*. People often get into difficulties because they do not know enough. Men on ships had a problem in those early times which men on land did not have. What was this problem? When they were far out at sea and could not see the land, they did not know *where they were*. They did not know their *position*. What do we mean by a position? The position of a thing is its relation to other things or points in space. In the game of baseball, for example, the position of the batter is his relation to the catcher and to the other people on the baseball field.

On land, we can tell our position from the trees, houses, roads, and hills and other things that we can see. Men at sea on a ship could not see anything except water around them. Their problem was to determine the position of the ship and keep it on the route which would take them where they wanted to go.

Sailors on a ship sailing north or south could tell how far it had gone by looking at the Pole Star. When the ship went north, the Pole Star seemed to rise in the sky. When it went south, the Pole Star seemed to fall toward the horizon.

But when a ship sailed east or west the Pole Star could not help the sailors. If a ship sailed along the line of the equator, for example, the Pole Star did not change its position in relation to the horizon.

In an earlier passage in this book we read that people found a way of dividing the surface of the earth into small areas. They divided the circumference of the earth from North to South into a number of parts called degrees. (The length of each degree was about 69 miles.) For each degree they drew an imaginary line (north or south of the equator) running east and west. The Romans referred to these lines as lines of *latitude* and we still refer to them in this way.

The earth, showing lines of latitude and longitude

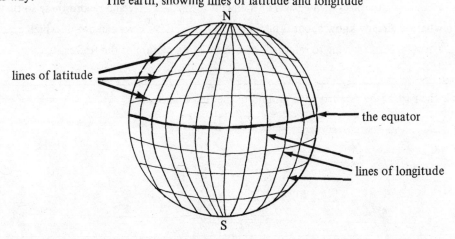

They also drew imaginary lines of *longitude* running north and south. A ship sailing north or south crossed imaginary lines of latitude which marked its position. A ship sailing east or west crossed imaginary lines of longitude which marked its position.

But how could the sailors on a ship *find* their position in relation to these imaginary lines? The problem was still there. They could determine their latitude by the position of the Pole Star or by the sun's angle with the horizon at midday, but they needed another method to determine their longitude.

(In the next unit we will read about methods which were used to solve (= find the answer to) this problem.)

---

* horizon = the line at which the earth and the sky or the sea and the sky seem to meet: the edge of the sea or land as we see it.

Unit IV
4.5 VOCABULARY TEST

To test yourself on the vocabulary of this section, fill in the missing letters in the incomplete words.

The sha____ of n_____al ob____ts are not u_____y p_____t c____s, s_____, or re_____ar s____ds. They do not often have st_____t ed___. Although the shapes of n_____ o_____ are either very i_____ar or slightly i_____r, we can find in nature many pa_____ that are r_____ted. Scientists use these r_____ to help them to classify things into different groups. U_____ all the leaves on a plant have almost the same p_____ and the leaves occur at r_____ i_____ in relation to the growing point. Flowers also have regular shapes and the parts of a flower are grouped in ci_____ around a c_____.

It is possible to d_____ the age of a tree by counting the rings which occur across the d_____er of the tree trunk.* The dark rings are autumn growth and the pale rings are spring growth. A dark and a pale ring together r_____t one year's growth. By c_____ing the widths of the rings we can d_____ which years had a good growing season. We can also c_____e the amount of wood in a tree than can be used for building, by multiplying the height of the tree trunk by the c_____.

If we find a plant and we do not know which c____s it belongs to we can look at it c_____ to d_____ those features which help us to classify plants. We must r_____d where we found it growing and how it was growing. We must d_____ the sizes of the parts of the plant se_____y and record these so that we can c_____ them with what we already know about other plants. G_____ we can decide which c_____. the flower b_____ t_ w_____ having to refer to a description or a picture of the flower.

---

* The trunk of a tree is the part of the tree from the ground to the first branch.

Unit V

5.1 VOCABULARY

These are the words you will practice in this unit:

VERBS

classify	(clas'si·fy)	(+ noun)
classify		(+ noun + as + noun)
depend on	(de·pend')	
enter	(en'ter)	(+ noun)
exist	(ex·ist')	
fall	(in level, prices, etc.)	
limit	(lim'it)	(+ noun)
practice	(prac'tice)	(+ noun or + -ing)
produce	(pro·duce')	(+ noun)
prove		(+ noun)
require	(re·quire')	(+ noun)
rise	(in level, prices, etc.)	
solve	(a problem)	
stretch		
stretch		(+ noun)
suppose	(sup·pose')	(used at the beginning of a sentence)

NOUNS

an abbreviation	(ab·bre·vi·a'tion)	a limit	(lim'it)
a block		mercury	(mer'cu·ry)
a cone		a politician	(pol·i·ti'cian)
economics	(e·co·nom'ics)	a price	
an edge		a purpose	(pur'pose)
an effect	(ef·fect')	a relation	(re·la'tion)
an example	(ex·am'ple)	a relationship	(re·la'tion·ship)
existence	(ex·ist'ence)	a right angle	(an'gle)
a feature	(fea'ture)	a sentence	(sen'tence)
a harbor	(har'bor)	a situation	(sit·u·a'tion)
intensity	(in·ten'si·ty)	the standard	(stan'dard)
knowledge	(knowl'edge)	a thermometer	(ther·mom'e·ter)
a level	(lev'el)	a tube	

ADJECTIVES

actual	(ac'tu·al)	numerous	(nu'mer·ous)
common	(com'mon)	political (situation, etc.)	(po·lit'i·cal)
economic (relations, etc.)	(e·co·nom'ic)	related (to)	(re·lat'ed)
intense	(in·tense')	right-angled	(an'gled)
limited (to)	(lim'it·ed)	sealed	
narrow	(nar'row)	various	(var'i·ous)

ADVERBS

actually	(ac'tu·al·ly)
directly	(di·rect'ly)
generally	(gen'er·al·ly)
indirectly	(in·di·rect'ly)
regularly	(reg'u·lar·ly)
slightly	(slight'ly)

Unit V

5.2 WORD STUDY

INSTRUCTIONS: Study the following words and the uses of them:

solve　　　We *solve* a problem when we find the answer to it.

Examples: The problem of determining the speed of light was not s___ed until the twentieth century. There are some mathematical problems which have never been s_____d. To s___e this problem, special measuring instruments will be needed. His teacher gave him ten problems to do, and he s_____d all of them in twenty minutes.

limit
a limit
limited (by, to)　　A headmaster *limits* the number of children in a class when he does not allow the number to go beyond a certain number which he has fixed. We limit the length of a speech when we do not allow it to go beyond a certain fixed time. The warden of a prison l_____s the movements of the prisoners when he does not allow them to go beyond the walls or the boundaries (= lines which enclose something) of the prison.

This school only admits a l_____ed number of children. Speeches are l_____ed to five minutes each. The amount of food in the house is l_____d; it will be enough for only two weeks.

The limits of the scale on this beaker are zero (0) and 32 fluid ounces.

There should be some l___t to the amount of food you eat; the amount of food you eat should not go beyond a certain l___t. School and university examinations always have a time limit; so do football matches. There is no l___t to his kindness. Within the city l___ts there are speed l___ts fixed by the police.

a right angle
right-angled

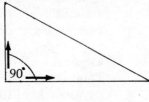

A right angle is 90 degrees. This is a *right-angled* triangle.

The angles of a square are r___t a_____s.

enter　　= go in or come in

We did not hear her when she *entered* the room.

When an empty glass is pushed into water with its mouth downward, no water can enter it. Why not?

5.2 WORD STUDY

stretch

This is a small rubber band.

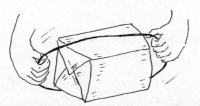

It can be *stretched* so that it will go around a parcel.

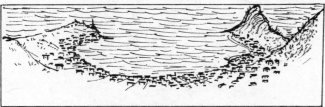

The town stretches from the foot of the hills to the sea.

The elephant stretches its trunk toward his hand.

a tube

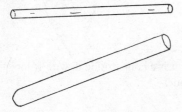

A tube is a long circular container, usually made of glass, rubber, or metal. If it is open at both ends, fluids (gases and liquids) can flow through it. The tube inside a bicycle wheel is made of rubber and contains air at high pressure.

A test tube, used in a chemistry laboratory, is closed at one end and open at the other.

narrow

We use this adjective about objects whose length is much greater than their width. It is usually used to describe the width of **surfaces**.

A *narrow* belt.

A narrow road

A narrow stream

sealed

A container is *sealed* when it is closed in such a way that something must be broken to open it.

This bottle is sealed.

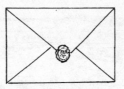

This letter is sealed.

5.2 WORD STUDY

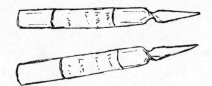

Some liquids are often sold in small sealed glass tubes. To get the liquid out, the top of the glass must be broken off.

These are sealed glass tubes.

an edge The *edges* of a surface are the lines which limit it. A rectangular block has 12 edges.

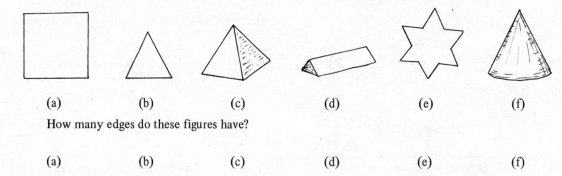

(a)   (b)   (c)   (d)   (e)   (f)

How many edges do these figures have?

(a)   (b)   (c)   (d)   (e)   (f)

a cone A *cone* is a three-dimensional object which has only two surfaces. How many edges does a cone have?

    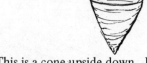

This is a cone.

This is a cone upside down. It looks like an ice cream cone.

a block Children like playing with *blocks* of wood.

This is a block of stone.

This is a block of ice. Water is running from it.

a harbor

A *harbor* is a place where ships can come safely near to land. Often the land which forms the harbor is high and does not allow the winds to blow strongly. San Francisco has a natural h____r. Not all

72

5.2 WORD STUDY

h_____s are natural. Some h_____rs are built by people.

practice When we *practice* something, we make a habit of it; we do it regularly or habitually.

Examples:

(a)   When we practice English sentences, we repeat them often because we want to learn them well.
When we practice something (in this sense of the word) we do it again and again; we repeat the action,
usually at regular intervals, because we want to learn to do it well.

(b)   If he p_____ces these habits he will find it difficult to make friends. When you stay in another
country, you will be more popular if you p_____ce the local customs. If you p_____ce getting up
early and going to bed early, your health will be better.

Make sentences from this table.

I	II	III	IV	V
You	must	practice	singing	everyday.
He	should		typing	regularly.
She	will		playing the piano	
I			swimming	

an abbreviation *An abbreviation* is a short form of a word or phrase. When we write an abb_____tion we usually use
the first letter or the first few letters of each word. An abb_____n is used to save time or space
in writing or printing, and sometimes in speaking.

Here are some abbreviations. Give their full forms.

(a)   U.N.   _____

(b)   lab.   _____

(c)   St.   _____

(d)   pl.   _____

(e)   n.   _____

(f)   v.   _____

(g)   adv.   _____

(h)   U.S.A.   _____

(i)   sci.   _____

(j)   Univ.   _____

(k)   Y.M.C.A.   _____

(l)   A.D.   _____

an example *An example* is a single thing, fact, sentence, problem, etc., which represents a class of things or a general
statement or a general rule.

1. Give an example of a chemical formula.

_____

5.2 WORD STUDY

2. Draw an example of a right-angled triangle.

3. Give an example of a problem in subtraction.

_____

4. Give an example of the general fact that gases expand when they are heated.

_____

_____

knowledge
(uncountable)

Our *knowledge* of a thing or a subject is what we know about it.

Examples: An engineer must have some kn_____e of mathematics.

A historian should have some k_____e of economics.

By watching films we can add to our k_____e of other societies and other countries.

A good k_____ of English is useful for scientists.

Note: Knowledge has **no** plural form, but is sometimes used after "a," as in the last example.

**intense
intensity**

Energy, or heat, or a feeling is *intense* when it is strong and powerful. The *intensity* of heat is called temperature and can be measured with a thermometer. The int_____y of a feeling (for example, love or anger) or of a man's interest in something cannot be measured, but is shown by its effect on his speech and actions, by the way in which it changes his speech and actions.

mercury
(uncountable)

Mercury is a liquid metal, much heavier than water, which is often used in thermometers because it expands in a regular way when it is heated.

numerous
(= many)

Do not use this word. Use the word **many** instead. It is better to use short, simple words when you can. But you should know what *numerous* means, so that you understand it when you hear it.

Aircraft designers use numerous (many) types of different metals.

There are numerous (many) different ways of solving this problem.

a level

Levels are surfaces which may be above or below each other, but are at an equal distance above or below. A level is the height of a surface in comparison with a limit or with another surface. Sea level is the level of the sea.

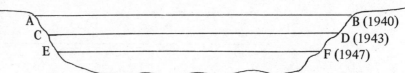

In this diagram, the lines represent various levels of a lake. In 1940, the level of the water was AB. In 1943 it fell to CD. In 1947 the level was EF.

prove

To *prove* something means to show by reasoning or by facts that something is true.

How will you prove that $(a + b)(a - b)$ is equal to $a^2 - b^2$?

How will you p__ve that the angles of a triangle, when added, give a total of 180 degrees?

How can you p_____ that most metals expand when they are heated?

How can you p_____ that it is hotter today than it was yesterday?

5.2 WORD STUDY

rise
fall
the level
the price
the standard

In each blank space in the following sentences, use **one** of the words given, where the meaning requires it.

1. When it is a good year for apples, the price of apples _____s.

2. When a thermometer gets warmer, the _____ of the mercury _____s.

3. When the weather is dry, the _____ of the water in the lake _____s.

4. When it is a bad year for potatoes, the _____ of potatoes _____s.

5. When everyone works hard and there are more things in the stores, the cost of living _____s.

6. When everyone works hard, the _____ of living _____s.

7. In summer if the weather is dry the _____ of raincoats _____s.

8. When water begins to boil, its _____ _____s.

9. When the stores are full of things and people do not have much money, the _____ of _____s _____s.

10. When the farmers grow more grain, the _____ of living _____s.

a purpose
various

A purpose is an idea. It is an idea of what we want or of what we want to do. When we want to obtain something or when we want to do something we have a purpose. A purpose is an idea which gives meaning to our actions. It is also an idea of what we want to do with a thing (for example, a tool or a machine), which gives meaning to that thing.

When Mrs. Brown has *various* things in her bag, she has a number of different things in her bag. When she spends the morning visiting v_____s friends, she visits a number of different friends.

Mr. Brown uses his car to do a number of things; he uses it for various purposes. Sometimes he uses it to drive himself to work; sometimes he uses it to take his wife shopping; sometimes he uses it to take his children to school. A man with a family uses his car for many p_____s.

Last week he drove his car to the station. He went there for a special p_____e, but he did not tell Mrs. Brown what it was. Women do not always know the p_____s behind their husbands' actions. They do not always know why their husbands do what they do.

But when Mr. Brown came home, Mrs. Brown discovered his p_____e in going to the station. In the back of the car there was a big new refrigerator!

Mrs. Brown uses her refrigerator for v_____s p_____s. She uses it to keep vegetables fresh and to keep meat and eggs from going bad. She also uses it to make ice cream and to freeze the little cubes of ice that she puts into cold drinks. Her husband and children come home at various times, after work or after school, and want something cold to drink. So she finds her refrigerator very useful.

In a modern house you will see v_____ machines. Do you know their names, and the p_____s for which they are used? There is a refrigerator, which is used to keep things cold. There is a washing machine, which is used to wash clothes and sheets. There is a vacuum cleaner, which ____ _____ _____ clean carpets and to do v_____s other cleaning jobs. There is sometimes an electric mixer, which can change solids into liquids, beat up eggs, mix butter and sugar, and do v_____s other things.

Note: Various means "a number of **different unnamed** things, people, etc." It means "an **uncounted** number of different things, etc." We use this word when we do not think it is necessary to name the different things we are talking about or to say how many there are.

purpose
political
various
a politician

In many countries, most people believe that people should be free to say what they think about the way the country is governed, in other words about politics, which is the science or art of government. *Political* groups (sometimes called parties) are groups which believe that they have ideas about government.

Television is sometimes used for pol_____l pu_____s. Speakers from v_____s po_____l groups are allowed to make speeches on television, and sometimes important speeches are made by the President and other p_____ans. Most people feel that there is no harm in this.

5.2 WORD STUDY

But it is probably dangerous for a country if only one p_____ group or party is allowed to speak on television. The use of television should not be limited to a single p_____ group. V_____s groups should be allowed to say what they like about the p_____ situation.

exist
(= be; be there)
existence

Tigers still ex____ in India and Africa, but they no longer ex____ in certain parts of these countries because many of them have been killed. In early times people believed that gods ex____ed in the trees, the sun, in rivers, and in other places. Some people still believe this. Most scientists think that water cannot ex__t on the surface of the moon. Societies still _____ in which men can have three wives or more. The standards of measurement which _____ed in early times made it difficult to compare distances and quantities accurately.

The ex_____ce of minds separate from bodies is very difficult to prove. This is the oldest steel bridge in ex_____ce.

a relation
related (to)

A relation exists **between** things, or people, or actions, or ideas, or words. Things can be *related* in various ways. There is a relation between a cause and its effect (= the change which the cause makes). For example, there may be a r_____n between bad weather and the high price of grain. Two things can be r_____d by having the same origin, for example, the words **meter** and **measure**, which are both derived from the same Latin word. Another kind of r_____ is the r_____ between a thing and a certain part of that thing, for example, the r_____n of the earth to the solar system. There are also r_____s between the various parts of a thing; for example, the human brain is r_____d in certain ways to other parts of the body. An idea is r_____d to another idea which forms part of its meaning; for example, the idea of work is r_____ed to the idea of energy. There are r_____s in time. "Before" and "after" are words for relations in time.

depend on

We *depend on* plants for our food. We either get food from them directly, or we get food from them indirectly by eating animals which grow by eating plants. We d_____d on the farmers who grow plants and vegetables. Children d_____ __ their parents for food and clothes. We _____ __ the government (or the local government) for the water we use in our homes, for the safety of the roads, and for v_____s other things. We depend on people or things when we have a certain r_____n to them. The r_____n is this; we need them in order to exist (= to be or to live) or to succeed in our pur_____s.

Writers d_____ on their power to write well. Workers may _____ __ buses or taxis to take them to work.

One thing d_____s on another when it often needs that thing in order to ex___ or be successful. Good health d_____s on good food, sleep, and physical exercise, for example, walking. The amount of money a man gets for himself or for his family does not always d_____d __ the amount of work he does. Sometimes it d_____ds __ his position in society, or the money that people are ready to pay him for the kind of work he does.

A man's happiness d_____s __ v_____s things; on his pur__se in life, on the kind of work he does, on his success in his work, on his relations with his family, and on many other things. But perhaps it mainly d_____s __ his peace of mind.

a situation

A situation is not a thing. It is a set of relations at a certain time. It is the way a person or thing is related to other people or things at a certain time; or it may be the relation which exists between a group of people at a certain time. A woman with a family who goes out to work is in a certain s_____n. She is in a different s_____n from a woman with a family who stays at home, because her relations with people (for example, the work she does for them) are different. The **political** s_____n in a country at a given time is the relations between the Congress, the ministers, and other powerful people (for example, the head of the army, the king, or the President), groups in Congress or Parliament and groups outside Congress or Parliament such as the army, the traders, various groups of workers, the farmers, and religious groups. The **economic** s_____n in a country depends on the quantity of food and other things which exist in the country at a certain time and on the relations between people who make, grow, sell, or buy these things. Relations can change; so can situations.

5.2 WORD STUDY

economic
political
economics
(uncountable)

These are various relations between human beings. One kind of relation is an *economic* relation. The r_____n b_____n a farmer and the people who buy grain or milk is an e_____c relation. The r_____n between workers and the people they work for or the people who pay them is an ec_____c r_____n. E_____c r_____s ex___ be____n people because of the work they do for each other or the things they grow or make for each other or because of the money or things they give for other people's work.

Another kind of relation is *political*. People enter into p_____l r_____s when they form p_____l groups or parties or allow certain people to govern them. P_____l r_____ns ex___ b_____n people and those who have power over them, or those who use power for them. My r_____n with the person who repr____ts me in Congress is a p_____al r_____n.

Note: Economics is used with singular verb forms.

In a university a student may study economics or political science. Economics is the study of e_____c r_____s; political science is the study of p_____l r_____s and of v_____s systems of government.

The p_____al sit_____n in a country depends on the p_____al r_____s between the government and various groups of people. The ec____ic s_____n de___ds on the people's needs in relation to what is produced and on relations between producers and buyers.

a relationship

When a relation has a natural basis, or a basis in the meanings of words themselves, or when it cannot be changed or does not change for a long time, we call it *a relationship*. A relationship is a basic, unchanging relation.

A father may have good or bad relations with his sons, or he may have various economic relations with them, but he cannot change his basic relationship with his sons. He is a father; they are his sons. Teachers may have various relations with their students, but the relationship of a teacher to a student cannot be changed because it is fixed by the meanings of the words "teacher" and "student." One teaches and the other learns with the teacher's help.

When we speak of family relationships, we mean the **basic** relations which exist between father and son, nephew and uncle, wife and husband, and so on.

The relationship between the **words** "career" and "current" is a relationship based on their derivation. It is a historical relationship. There is very little relationship between their meanings.

slightly
(= a little)

Make sensible sentences from the following tables:

I	II	III	IV	V	VI
My	shoes	are slightly	older bigger	than yours	.
His	trousers		smaller cleaner	than hers	.
Those	gardening tools		better stronger	than these	.
			thicker longer	than the others	.

5.2 WORD STUDY

I	II	III	IV	V
This	list	is slightly different from	the other one	.
	problem			
Her	example		the first one	.
	statement			
His	formula		the others	.
	diagram			
The new	total		the one in the book	.
	system			
	calculation			
	scale		the earlier ones	.
	definition			

I	II	III	IV	V	VI	VII
If you compare	the	(two) shirts	you will	see		.
If you look at	these	carpets		notice	that they are	.
If you examine	those	lists		find	slightly	.
		cars		discover	different	.
		colors				
		problems				
		lengths				
		diameters				
		routes				
		totals				
		definitions				
		situations				
		thermometers				
		tubes				
		maps				
		diagrams				
		copies				

produce Farms *produce* grain and vegetables, milk and eggs, butter and cheese. Some farmers only produce grain. Canada pr____es large quantities of grain. The earth p_____s many different kinds of plants. Factories p____ce various things; some factories p_____ machines, others p_____ automobiles, others p_____ soap, others p_____ shoes. Poets p_____ poems.

The cows on Mr. Green's farm p____ce 200 gallons of milk a day; his hens produce 400 eggs a day. The new factory produces 30,000 bicycles a year.

Nowadays furniture is mainly p_____ed by machinery; fifty years ago it was mainly p_____ed by hand.

When a farm, or a field, or a country, or a factory, or a cow, or a man produces something, it (or he) brings that thing into existence or causes it to exist—either by making it or growing it.

We use the verb produce when we think of the thing **resulting** from our work or actions, or even from natural causes. An earthquake is produced by natural forces. Better methods will produce better results. Kuwait produces oil. Success is produced by hard work. Great thinkers produce new ideas.

actual = real, not imagined or guessed
actually = in fact, really

Examples: The newspapers say that 5000 people were killed in the war last year, but the *actual* number is probably much higher. The a____l number is probably closer to 10,000. Some people say that the government will fall, but no one ac____lly knows what will happen.

78

5.2 WORD STUDY

A man has a watch which keeps correct time. He leaves New York at 12 o'clock (by his watch) and takes exactly two hours to fly to Chicago. When he reaches Chicago the time is 2 o'clock by his watch, but a_____lly it is 12 o'clock in Chicago. The a_____l time at any place on the earth's surface depends on the position of the earth in relation to the sun.

Mary Jones and Helen Jones look alike and dress alike. They often walk to school together. Many people think that they are sisters, but a_____lly there is no relationship between them. They are only friends.

Why do you think people are your enemies and want to hurt you? You are frightened of situations of which you a_____y have no kn_____ge.

require   = need for a special purpose

Tomorrow Mrs. Smith will begin teaching English to a small class in her house. She will *require* a blackboard and some chalk. She will r_____ enough chairs for six people. Her students will _____ exercise books and pens.

To start a factory, a large amount of money is r_____ed. Engineers, office workers, and factory workers are also r_____; a factory cannot start without them.

Note: When you speak or write English, it is generally better to use the verb "need" than the verb "require." Always use a simple word when you can.

a feature
classify
common

John has a large room in an apartment. The room is narrow and the walls are high. It is a sunny room with two large windows. There are two cupboards built into the walls. The size of the room, its height, its narrowness, and its warmth are *features* of the room. The narrowness of the room is a f_____e of the room. The two large windows are f_____s of the room. The cupboards are built into the walls and belong to the room; they do not exist separately. Not all rooms have cupboards like these. They are special f_____s of the room. When we describe the room we describe these f_____s. To describe something is to say what its most important f_____s are.

How would you describe Wellington, the capital of New Zealand? Wellington is a hilly, windy city with a beautiful harbor. The natural harbor, the hills on which the city is built, and the winds which blow over it are f_____s of Wellington.

When two things have f_____s which are alike we can compare them. Wellington and San Francisco have f_____s which are alike. Both cities are near the sea. Both have beautiful har___s. Both are built on hills. But there are important differences too. San Francisco has two famous bridges which stretch from one side of the harbor to the other. Wellington harbor has no bridges.

When things have the same f_____s, we can *classify* them by these f_____s. When we cl_____y things, we do not think of the special f_____s which make them different from each other, but the f_____s which they all have. We cl_____ certain living things as birds not because they have long legs or short legs, but because they all have feathers. Parts of the earth are mountains. They all have the same f_____re. What is it? Some men are called postmen. What feature of their work makes it possible to classify them in this way? Some sentences are class__ied as statements. The f_____e of a statement is that it gives a fact or has the same form as a sentence which gives a fact.

Different things have different features. But each thing has a number of features. It has v_____s f_____s. So we can cl_____fy things in v_____s ways. Flour can be cl_____ied as a food, because we eat things which are made of flour. But flour can also be cl_____fied as a powder, because it has the form of a powder. Students of chemistry may cl_____fy it in another way, by the carbohydrate it contains.

One important feature of the earth is its spherical shape. So we can cl_____y it as a sph___ (though it is not a perfect sph___). Another feature of the earth is its r_____ship with the sun. It goes around the sun. What do we call the spheres which move around the sun? We call them pl_____s. We classify them as pl_____s. A word like sph___ or pl___t is a classification. It classifies the things which it names.

How do we classify substances which flow? We classify them as f_____s.

5.2 WORD STUDY

How do we classify the fixed quantities we use to measure things? We classify them as u____s.

How do we classify instruments used to measure temperature? We classify them as th_____ters.

We can compare and classify situations. For example, a woman with a family who goes out to work is in a certain kind of situation. She is in a different situation from a woman with a family who stays at home. But both these situations are **often found** in families; they are *common* situations. Situations exist in time and can change, but history repeats itself and so do situations. For example, the members of a government may be divided among themselves and form groups which do not have the same purposes. This is a common situation in the world of politics. The situation of a working man with a large family who does not have enough money to feed them all is unfortunately very c_____n. People who study sociology, history, economics, and political science have to classify situations. They can then make comparisons between different kinds of situations.

an effect
directly
indirectly
generally
a thermometer
a tube

It is often said that science is the study of causes and *effects*. An effect is a change made in one thing by another. We often speak of the effect of one thing **on** another.

We cannot measure temperature di____ly, because we cannot d_____y compare a lower temperature with a higher temperature and obtain an accurate measurement. We can make some kind of comparison of temperatures by putting our hands into cold water, then into warm water, then into boiling water, and so on. But no one wants to do this, and obviously our hands cannot give ac_____te measurements of temperature.

But our eyes can compare lengths accurately. They are a_____e instru_____s for this pu___se. With their help, we can compare a length marked on a ruler with the length of a table quite a_____ly. But the feeling of heat through human skin does not help us to make accurate comparisons of temperatures.

If you put your right hand into very hot water and your left hand into very cold water and then put both hands into warm water, what will happen? Your right hand will find the water cold and your left hand will find the same water hot. This shows that our hands cannot safely be used to measure temperature, though people sometimes try to use them in this way. A mother sometimes puts her hand on her child's head to find out if he has a high temperature.

Doctors do not use their hands to measure temperature. They *generally* (= usually, most often) use a *thermometer*, which is a special instrument. A th_____ter is a *tube* closed at both ends which contains a liquid. This liquid expands in a **regular** way when it is heated; in other words an equal amount of heat produces (= causes) an equal expansion, so that there is a regular relation between the rise in temperature and the expansion of the liquid. Mercury and alcohol are the two liquids g_____y chosen for this purpose, because their expansion is noticeable and regular.

Heat has an effect on liquids; it changes their volume. This eff___ makes it possible for us to measure t_____e. We cannot d_____ly co_____e a lower temperature with a higher one. But we can measure temperature in_____ly, because we can compare the e____ct of a lower temperature on a liquid in a thermometer with the e____ct of a higher t_____re on that liquid.

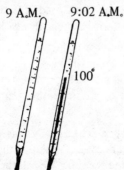

9 A.M.   9:02 A.M.

100°

Here are two diagrams of the same thermometer, shown at 9 a.m. and 9:02 a.m. At 9 a.m. all the mercury is below the lower limit of the scale. It has not risen. Then the thermometer is put into a boy's mouth. It is taken out two minutes later, at 9:02 a.m. The mercury now stands at 100°. It has expanded, and traveled a short **distance** up the tube. What do we look at? What do we compare? We look at the **length** of the narrow line of mercury in the tube and compare it with the original length. We do **not** look at the heat of the mercury; no one can look at heat! So what we **actually** measure is not one temperature compared with another but one length compared with another, and from this we read the temperature.

How is this possible? It is only p___ible because the rise in temperature has a regular e_____t on the volume of mercury. We measure temperature by the e_____ it produces on another thing. We cannot measure the e_____ of temperature on our bodies; so we measure its e_____ on the volume of a liquid. This is an example of in_____ measurement.

Unit V

5.3 DICTATION EXERCISES AND DICTATION PASSAGES

A 1. The passage *The Measurement of Temperature* will be read to you. Write the articles (if any) which come before the following adjectives, which you will hear in the same order, and the nouns which come after them.

(a) _____ accurate _____

(b) _____ total _____

(c) _____ certain _____

(d) _____ large _____

(e) _____ boiling _____

(f) _____ smaller _____

(g) _____ both _____

(h) _____ good _____

(i) _____ Fahrenheit _____

(j) _____ other _____

(k) _____ boiling _____

(l) _____ two _____

2. Number the following words in the order in which you hear them.

	definition	amount	instruments
total	thermometers	Celsius	degrees
	obviously	scale	convenient

3. When the teacher tells you to begin, underline the following words in the passage *The Measurement of Temperature*. This is a race.

accurate	quantity	scientists	certain
both	intensity	temperatures	contains
boiling	amount	Fahrenheit	accurately

4. Practice the following words, as grouped, with their correct stresses.

ther·mom'e·ter	im·pos'si·ble	tem'per·a·ture	e·co·nom'ic
di·am'e·ter	po·lit'i·cal	Fahr'en·heit	cal·cu·la'tion
ir·reg'u·lar	e·quiv'a·lent	Cel'si·us	sit·u·a'tion
rec·tan'gu·lar	a·rith'me·tic	clas'si·fy	Eu·ro·pe'an
in·ten'si·ty	re·la'tion·ship	in'stru·ment	def·i·ni'tion

5. The passage *The Measurement of Temperature* will be read again. As you listen, cross out the word or phrase in each of the following pairs which is incorrect.

(a) try - tries	(f) small - smaller	(k) doctors - doctor
(b) a total - the total	(g) have - has	(l) scientists - scientist
(c) its heat - the heat	(h) instrument - instruments	(m) selling - Celsius
(d) quantity - quantities	(i) depend - depends	(n) boil - boils
(e) contains - contain	(j) use - used	

6. The passage *The Measurement of Temperature* will now be given as dictation.

5.3 DICTATION EXERCISES AND DICTATION PASSAGES

B   1. Number the following words in the order in which you hear them.

               traveled   practice   regularly

  separating   effect   existence   purpose

          situation   expand   political

2. Number the following words in the order in which you hear them.

          pattern   necessary   knowledge

  position   voyages   relations

          friendly   intervals   depended

3. Write the past tense of the following verbs.

    (a)   travel   _____   (e)   compel   _____

    (b)   model   _____   (f)   label   _____

    (c)   expel   _____   (g)   rebel   _____

    (d)   quarrel   _____

4. Read the two following sentences:

    (a)   Changes in the political situation have an effect on patterns of trade.

    (b)   He wanted to discover the effect of changes in the political situation on patterns of trade.

Now finish the *second* sentence in each of the pairs given here, making the same kind of change in the words and their order.

    (a)   Changes in temperature have an effect on liquids.

    (b)   He studied the _____.

    (a)   Experiments in learning have an effect on teaching.

    (b)   He was interested in the effect _____.

    (a)   The ideas of great men have an effect on the way we think.

    (b)   He explained the effect _____.

    (a)   The customs of society have an effect on our lives and actions.

    (b)   Anthropologists study the effect _____.

5. The passage *Mr. Ali's Visits to Europe* will now be read to you. *After* the reading is finished, write as many past tense verbs, with the regular -ed ending, as you can remember from the passage.

6. Shut your workbook and write the missing prepositions in the blank spaces in the passage, as given here.

Mr. Ali visited Europe regularly, _____ intervals of about three years. The purpose _____ his visits was to discover the effect _____ changes _____ the political situation _____ patterns of trade _____ Europe and the Far East. He believed that good trade _____ nations depended _____ the existence of friendly relations _____ them.

Mr. Ali did not believe _____ separating business _____ pleasure. When he visited Europe he usually traveled _____ sea. He enjoyed the long voyages, which gave him the chance to make new friends who helped him to expand his business. He practiced tennis and practiced speaking English. A good knowledge _____ English was necessary _____ a man _____ his position.

7. The passage *Mr. Ali's Visits to Europe* will now be given as a dictation.

5.3 DICTATION EXERCISES AND DICTATION PASSAGES

C   1. Number the following words in the order in which you hear them.

representing   determined   multiplying

           two-dimensional   figure   triangle

calculate   area   surface

2. Number the following words in the order in which you hear them.

edges   rectangular   sphere

        symbol   circumference   spherical

width   height   formulas

3. Complete the following sentences:

    (a)   A triangle has _____ dimensions.

    (b)   A sphere has _____ dimensions.

    (c)   A line has _____ dimension.

    (d)   A cube has _____ d_____ s.

    (e)   A circle (i.e., the space inside a circle) has _____ d_____ s.

    (f)   A cube has _____ edges.

    (g)   A sphere has _____ e_____.

    (h)   All points on the c_____ e of a circle are at equal distances from its center.

    (i)   All points on the surface of a _____ are at equal distances from its center.

    (j)   The size of a circle is determined by the length of its _____.

    (k)   The _____ representing the volume of a rectangular solid is L x H x W.

    (l)   The area of a circle is _____ than four times the square of the radius.

4. Without looking at the passage, fill in the missing words or letters in the passage as given below:

A f_____e sometimes means a w_____n or printed symbol r_____ing a number, but it may also _____ a two- or three-dimensional shape, such as a t_____e, a c_____e, or a s_____e. A circle is a r_____r, two-dimensional _____ . Its size is determined by the l_____h of the radius, which is the _____ from the center to a point on the c_____ce. A sphere, which has no _____ and only one s_____e, is a _____ -dimensional f_____e. Its s____ is determined by the _____ from the center to a p_____ on the s_____. The _____ of each face of a rectangular s____d can be c_____ed by multiplying the h_____ by the w_____. Other f_____s are required to c_____ the area of a circle or of a sp_____al surface.

When you have finished, you can check your answers.

5. The passage *Circles and Spheres* will now be dictated to you.

5.3 DICTATION PASSAGES

(a) The Measurement of Temperature

It is difficult to give an accurate definition of "temperature," but we can try. Temperature is not the total amount of heat in a thing but the intensity of its heat at a certain time. When we measure temperature we do not measure the quantity of heat but its intensity. A large pan of boiling water obviously contains more heat than a smaller pan of boiling water, but their temperatures are the same. The water in both pans has a temperature of 100 degrees Celsius.

To measure temperature accurately we need good instruments. The accuracy of a measurement depends partly on the instrument which is used. Most instruments used to measure temperature are called thermometers. In thermometers two scales are used, the Fahrenheit scale and the Celsius scale. American doctors find the Fahrenheit scale convenient for measuring the temperature of the body, but other doctors and scientists often use the Celsius scale. The boiling points of water are different on the two scales. On the Celsius scale, water boils at 100 degrees. On the Fahrenheit scale it boils at 212 degrees.

(b) Mr. Ali's Visits to Europe

Mr. Ali visited Europe regularly, at intervals of about three years. The purpose of his visits was to discover the effect of changes in the political situation on patterns of trade between Europe and the Far East. He believed that good trade between nations depended on the existence of friendly relations between them.

Mr. Ali did not believe in separating business from pleasure. When he visited Europe he usually traveled by sea. He enjoyed the long voyages, which gave him the chance to make new friends who helped him to expand his business. He practiced tennis and practiced speaking English. A good knowledge of English was necessary for a man in his position.

(c) Circles and Spheres

A figure sometimes means a written or printed symbol representing a number, but it may also mean a two- or three-dimensional shape, such as a triangle, a circle, or a sphere. A circle is a regular, two-dimensional figure. Its size is determined by the length of its radius, which is the distance from the center to a point on the circumference. A sphere, which has no edges and only one surface, is a three-dimensional figure. Its size is determined by the distance from the center to a point on the surface. The area of each face of a rectangular solid can be calculated by multiplying the height by the width. Other formulas are required to calculate the area of a circle or of a spherical surface.

Unit V
5.4 READING PASSAGES

(a) Direct and Indirect Measurement

We know that a measurement is often made by comparing the units marked on a measuring instrument with an object to be measured. This is the way we measure length with a ruler, liquid volume with a measuring cup, or weight with a balance on which standard weights are placed. Measurements obtained in this way, by direct comparison with standard units, are called direct measurements.

But there are some kinds of measurement which cannot be obtained by direct comparison. Temperature, for example, can only be measured indirectly. The measurement of temperature is indirect not because it requires mathematical calculations, but because it depends on our knowledge of the effect of heat on liquids. When a fluid is heated, it expands. If we put some mercury or alcohol into a sealed glass tube, the amount it expands can tell us how much the temperature has risen. Thus the unit of temperature recorded by a thermometer is based on the amount of heat required to expand the liquid until it reaches a certain level. Many modern instruments of measurement are based, like the thermometer, on our knowledge of causes and effects.

(b) The Learning Situation in the Modern University

Students who enter a university in the second half of the twentieth century are in a new situation. They are not like the young students of the early nineteenth century who came to sit at the feet of the masters and left as a master. That situation no longer exists, because now it is not only students who change. They may grow fast, but science grows still faster.

The young German philosopher Hegel, writing at the beginning of the nineteenth century, believed that one man's mind could contain all the knowledge of his times. At that time it was perfectly possible for a man to hold such a belief and to base his life on it. Hegel's friend Goethe wrote a famous poem about a young man who hoped to translate this purpose into reality. The young man in the poem was called Faust. But Hegel's situation was slightly different from Faust's, because Faust, the hero of the poem, had the devil to help him, while Hegel had only his professors.

Today a very different situation exists, a situation in which the professors and the devil have lost most of their power. Today students cannot master knowledge; they can only be its servant. They know that they can become familiar only with a small corner of knowledge, and that their learning will always be imperfect and incomplete. But they can still hope to add something to the sum of knowledge, and so make the situation slightly more difficult for those who come after them.

(c) Causes and Effects

How is a photograph produced? It is produced by the effect of light on certain chemicals. Certain chemical substances change when light reaches them. Where the light is intense they get very dark. Where weaker light reaches them they get less dark. For this reason the "negative" picture taken by a camera represents light objects as dark shapes, and dark objects as lighter shapes. It was possible to take photographs only when scientists had discovered something about the effects of light.

Scientific discoveries have important effects on society. The discoveries about light made by scientists had far-reaching effects. Life would not be the same without the camera, the motion picture, and the television set.

When Sir Alexander Fleming discovered penicillin, he was not in a position to know the effect on society which his new drug would produce. The effect of penicillin on a human body is to kill some of the dangerous germs* which enter the body. Penicillin kills these germs quickly, before they have time to produce very harmful effects on the sick person. Before penicillin was discovered, millions of people died every year of the diseases caused by these germs. The number of deaths was greatly reduced by penicillin. So the effect of penicillin on human societies was to make them much larger, by adding millions of people to the numbers which existed before.

---

* germs = very small living things which cause diseases.

5.4 READING PASSAGES

(d) Family Systems in South India

Not very long ago, a special family system existed in certain parts of South India. In this system, the actual head of a family unit was the mother's eldest brother, though the mother also had an important position in the family. In families of this kind, a husband was actually no more than a visitor. He did not live with his wife, but with his own mother, brothers, and sisters in another house. He saw his sons and daughters sometimes, but the man who actually fed and cared for them and acted as their father was their uncle—their mother's brother.

But this system, in which brothers and sisters take the place of the father, no longer exists in South India except in a few villages. Economic changes have had a far-reaching effect on family life. Family life began to change when men went out to work in factories and offices instead of working with their mothers, brothers, and sisters on the land. When a man went out to work he had money of his own and could buy his own land and build his own house. He wanted to be the head of his own family, instead of depending on his mother and his brothers. He wanted to be *independent*. This is an example of the way in which economic relations can have an effect on family relationships.

(e) Ships, Stars, and Clocks (2)

At the end of a reading passage in Unit IV of this book you were asked to think about a problem. It was this. How did sailors on ships discover how to determine their longitude? You will probably remember that lines of longitude are imaginary lines running north and south.

Between the fifteenth and eighteenth centuries many new trade routes were discovered; trade between Europe and America and between the East and the West expanded greatly and there were thousands of sea voyages, so that the problem of determining longitude became more and more important. In England the Royal Observatory was started to produce charts* of the stars, and in 1714 a Board of Longitude was formed. This Board was a group of men who tried to solve the problem of longitude, and get other people interested in solving it. One of the members of the Board was a well-known astronomer*, Mr. Maskelyne.

The Board promised to give a large amount of money as a prize to the man who found a method of determining longitude accurately. Mr. Maskelyne thought that this could be done by using special charts showing the changing position of the moon in relation to certain stars. He thought that the pattern of the night sky, if accurately mapped, would help the captain of a ship to fix his own position.

A watchmaker, Mr. Harrison, had noticed the obvious difficulties in Mr. Maskelyne's method, and thought of a simpler idea. His idea depended on one thing only; the accurate measurement of time. He reasoned as follows. Any place on the earth, except the two Poles, goes around the earth's axis* once in 24 hours. That is, it moves 360° in 24 hours, 15° in one hour, $\frac{1}{4}^o$ in one minute, and so on. The difference in longitude between two places A and B can therefore be measured by a ship's captain if he knows the difference in time between the time at A and the time at B.

Now if a ship's captain has a very accurate clock there is no difficulty in knowing the exact time at the place where his voyage began; he can just read the time on that clock.

If the ship's captain can find out the local time, i.e., the time at the spot where his ship is, he can calculate the difference in time and change this into difference of longitude. If his accurate clock keeps London time and the local time is later than London time, his position is east of London, and if the local time is earlier than London time, his position is west of London.

How does the ship's captain find out the local time?

Anywhere on the earth's surface the sun reaches its highest point in the sky at midday. Ships' officers start measuring the angle between the horizon* and the sun a short time before midday. At the moment the angle stops getting larger, local time is 12:00. London time is known from the captain's clock, the difference in time between 12:00 and London time is converted into degrees, and the ship's longitude is known.

In Harrison's time, no clock was accurate enough to give the exact time over a period of months and years, and voyages often lasted for months and years. Therefore, Harrison tried to make a very accurate clock or chronometer, which was called Harrison's No. 4 because it was the fourth clock he had tried to make. It looked like a big watch and had a diameter of three inches. In 1763 a ship had to sail to Barbados, and its voyage was used to test Maskelyne's method and Harrison's method (and his chronometer). Prize money was promised to Harrison if he won the test. On the voyage it was found that the error (the mistake) in the results obtained by using Maskelyne's method was four times greater than the error obtained by using Harrison's method. Harrison was the obvious winner.

5.4 READING PASSAGES

Unfortunately for Harrison, Maskelyne was one of those people who dislike changing their ideas even when the facts prove them wrong. He would not allow the Board to give Harrison the total prize money. Harrison received only half of it, and the other half was not paid until three years before he died.

---

* a chart = a special map used by sailors, showing features of the land, sea, or sky.

* an astronomer = a scientist who studies the stars.

* an axis = a straight line going through the middle of a body or a system.

* the horizon = the line which seems to join the earth (or the sea) and the sky, the circle limiting the distance a person is able to see over the sea or flat land.

Unit V

5.5 VOCABULARY TEST

To test yourself on the vocabulary of this section, fill in the missing letters in the incomplete words.

Most people think that they have not got enough money. We r_____y hear our friends saying that they r_____e more money but a_____y they probably have enough for food and clothes and they only want the extra money for u_____ry things. In a country like New Zealand it is difficult to believe in t__ e_____e of m_____s of people whose daily a_____t of food is below the l____l needed to keep a person healthy. Some countries do not p_____e enough food for their people, and other countries produce more than they need. This is a world p_____m and for many years governments have been trying to s___e this p_____m. The s_____n is difficult because often the countries without enough food do not have enough money to pay h__h p____s for the food they need.

There is no s_____e a_____r to the p_____m. Sometimes p_____ r__e and sometimes p_____ ___l. Students of e_____s study the e_____s of changing prices on the economic situation of the country; but every s_____n is slightly different from every other s_____n. There is a l____t to how much m___y a country can pay for food and this limit is often related to how much money that country can earn by selling v_____us other things or substances. S_____se country A has g___n to sell and country B needs g___n but has no money. Then country C may lend money to country B to buy t__ _____n from country A. Instead of paying back country C with money, country B gives country C some other substance, for example, rubber.

The economic r_____s among these three countries are not s_____e. They d_____ _n one another and they o_____y also depend on a peaceful p_____l s_____n so that e_____ p_____s can be s_____d w_____t worrying about war or i_____n.

Unit VI

6.1 VOCABULARY

These are the words you will practice in this unit:

VERBS		
accept	(ac·cept')	(+ noun)
agree	(a·gree')	(+ to + stem)
agree		(+ with + noun)
belong to	(be·long')	(+ noun)
disagree	(dis·a·gree')	(+ with)
distinguish	(dis·tin'guish)	(+ between)
expect	(ex·pect')	(+ noun)
expect		(+ to)
expect		(+ noun + to)
expect		(+ that, optional)
guess		(+ noun)
precede	(pre·cede')	(+ noun)
remove	(re·move')	(+ noun)
state		(+ noun)

NOUNS			
(an) agreement	(a·gree'ment)	minus	(mi'nus)
alcohol	(al'co·hol)	an operation	(op·er·a'tion)
brightness	(bright'ness)	a paragraph	(par'a·graph)
a chapter	(chap'ter)	plus	
(a) convention	(con·ven'tion)	a prefix	(pre'fix)
(a) custom	(cus'tom)	a quarter	(quar'ter)
a decimal	(dec'i·mal)	a rod	
disagreement	(dis·a·gree'ment)	a speedometer	(speed·om'e·ter)
a distinction	(dis·tinc'tion)	a subject	(sub'ject)
a fraction	(frac'tion)	a substance	(sub'stance)
a guess		a tenth	
a hundredth	(hun'dredth)	a thousandth	(thou'sandth)
a member (of)	(mem'ber)	traffic	(traf'fic)

ADJECTIVES			
approximate	(ap·prox'i·mate)	given	(giv'en) (length,etc.)
common	(com'mon)	intense	(in·tense')
conventional	(con·ven'tion·al)	ordinary	(or'di·nar·y)
countable	(count'a·ble)	social	(so'cial)
decimal	(dec'i·mal)	traffic	(traf'fic)
distinct	(dis·tinct')	unconventional	(un·con·ven'tion·al)
exact	(ex·act')	uncountable	(un·count'a·ble)
general	(gen'er·al)	willing (to)	(will'ing)

ADVERBS			
almost	(al'most)	exactly	(ex·act'ly)
approximately	(ap·prox'i·mate·ly)	generally	(gen'er·al·ly)
distinctly	(dis·tinct'ly)	quite	(= completely)

PHRASE	
to the nearest (inch, gram, etc.)	

Unit VI

6.2 WORD STUDY

INSTRUCTIONS: Study the following words and the uses of them:

precede **a prefix**	pre- is *a prefix*. A prefix is a part of a word which comes at the beginning of the word and which has the same meaning when it comes at the beginning of other words. What is the meaning of **pre-**? What is the meaning of the prefix **un-** in **unhappy, unnatural, uncountable**? One thing *precedes* another when it comes before it. *Examples:* A statement about trade in early times was made in the preceding paragraph. A singular countable noun is usually preceded by an article. In a language course listening should pre_____ speaking, and speaking should pre___e writing.
state	When a man *states* something, he makes a statement; he says something in an official way or gives an important fact. *Examples:* Last night the President st___ed that the value of the dollar had fallen during the last three months. In his book he st____s that economic relations always precede political relations; but this cannot be proved. Please do not take more than the st____d amount (i.e., the amount stated on the bottle of medicine).
willing **willingly**	If a man is *willing* to do something (for example, to help his friend), this means that he is ready to do it, he will do it when he is asked, it will not be against his wishes to do this. If he helps his friend *willingly*, this means that he helps his friend because he wishes to do so. *Examples:* John says he is w____ing to reduce the price. He is not w____ing to travel without his wife. He supplied the information w____ingly. I will w____ingly allow you to go.
accept	= be willing to take (something) When someone wants you to take a gift or some money, or asks you to take it, and when you do not say "No" but are willing to take it, you *accept* the gift or the money. You accept a statement or the truth of a statement when you do not question its truth but are willing to believe that it is true, without further questions. You acc____ a custom when you are willing to follow it, to practice it as one of your own customs. If a principal says "I cannot acc____ this boy as a student," he means that he is not willing to take the boy as a student in his school. *Examples:* I invited him to the party, but he did not acc____ my invitation. He wanted Jack to take half the money, but Jack did not acc____ it. I said I was sorry, and they acc____ed my apology. Will you acc____ this small gift? We must either acc____ the college rules or try to get them changed. Teachers will not acc____ exercises which are given to them after the stated date.
remove	To *remove* a thing is to take it off, or take it away from its usual place or take it to another place. We often speak of removing a thing when we have some good reason for wanting to take it off or take it away from its present place. *Examples:* You must remove all these dirty marks from your shirt before you wear it. Please r___ve your hat. The boy was so ill that he had to be r____ed from school. The last paragraph of your essay should be r____ed.
alcohol (uncountable)	*Alcohol* is a colorless liquid which is present in beer, whiskey, and other strong drinks. It is used in some thermometers. *Examples:* Too much a_____l is not good for anyone. The a_____l in this test tube is pure.

6.2 WORD STUDY

traffic
(uncountable)
traffic

The cars, buses, bicycles, and moving machines on the roads are *traffic*.

Examples: It is difficult to cross the road because there is so much tr_____. The t_____c problem in our city is becoming worse every day.

an operation
plus
minus

An operation is a piece of work done on something, or a piece of work of a special kind.

Examples: In mathematics the symbols + and − represent *plus* and *minus*, which are the mathematical o_____ns of addition and subtraction. Yesterday the doctors in the hospital did a big o_____n. They removed a man's heart and put another heart in its place. Engineers must study the o_____s of various machines. A changeover from pounds, shillings, and pence to a decimal currency is a big o_____n.

a member (of)

A member of a society, a club, a group, a class, etc., is one of the people in that society, club, group, class, etc. We sometimes speak of a thing as a member of a class of things, e.g., "A bottle is a member of the class of bottles and also a member of the class of containers."

Examples: Are you a m_____r of the club? Every m_____r of my family has been to a university. The University Debating Society has 54 m_____s. In English, when a class of things has only one m_____r (e.g., the earth, the equator, the North Pole), the noun is often preceded by "the."

given

= certain or stated

Examples: A *given* quantity of mercury will expand by a certain number of cubic centimeters if there is a stated rise in temperature. The difference between the pressure of the atmosphere at sea level and the pressure of the atmosphere at a g____n height is always the same.

intense

This adjective is used about pressure, heat, brightness, energy, and certain feelings. It means strong or high in degree.

Examples: The *intense* heat sent everyone indoors. He read the book with in____se interest. Under this i_____e pressure some of the rocks even became liquid. The brightness of the sun is so _____ that it can cause blindness.

ordinary

= usual, not different from most things or people of the same kind

Examples: Today was not an o_____ry day, because I had two unexpected visits from old friends. Most o_____ry children like playing better than working. This dress is too good for o_____y use. Our house is o_____y, but its situation is unusual. No o_____ person can remember everything that happens on a given day.

belong to

(a) A thing (e.g., a book) *belongs to* me if it is mine.
(b) A book belongs to the public library if it is one of the public library books.
(c) A man belongs to a certain club if he is a member of that club.

Exercise: In the following sentences, which are **incomplete**, **put in** the words "belongs to" or "belong to" at some point to give each sentence a meaning. Rewrite each sentence below, after completing it.

1. This thermometer the doctor.

_____ .

2. In some South Indian families the land and money used to the mother.

_____

_____ .

3. Who does this object?

_____ ?

6.2 WORD STUDY

4.   In some societies a husband and his wife do not the same family unit.

   _____

   _____ .

5.   This barometer the physics laboratory.

   _____ .

6.   The earth and the other planets the solar system.

   _____ .

7.   These two houses my uncle.

   _____ .

8.   This set of instruments me.

   _____ .

9.   Five acres of this land the university.

   _____ .

10.   He does not the University Football Club.

   _____ .

expect to   We *expect* to do something when we think that we will probably do it.

Make ten **sensible** sentences from the following table:

I	II	III	IV
I expect to	see him	on Tuesday	.
We expect to	hold the meeting	in 1975	.
Do you expect to	visit Europe	in a few minutes	?
Most people expect to	get a phone call	some time today	.
She expects to	find the index	on the first page of the book	.
Professor Parker expects to	find the writer's name	at the end of the book	.

expect (that)   We *expect* (that) something will happen when we think (that) it will happen.

Make ten **sensible** sentences from the following table:

I	II	III	IV	V
Do you expect	(that)	he will have time	tomorrow	.
I don't expect		it will rain	to meet him	.
Some people expect		he will come here	next year	.
Farmers expect		prices will rise	for a meal with us	?
Everyone expects		there will be an election	at the wedding	.
No one expects		there will be anyone	before the end of the month	.

expect   Two meanings of the word:

1. expect someone to do something
2. expect something to happen

We *expect* someone to do something when we think he will do it.

We expect something to happen when we think it will happen.

6.2 WORD STUDY

Make ten **sensible** sentences from the following table:

I	II	III	IV	V
Do you expect	him	to rise	before the examination	.
I expect	the President	to come	every day	
We all expect	them	to make a speech	soon	?
The students expect	us	to leave	in the summer	.
I don't expect	anyone	to check their work	at night	.
He doesn't expect	prices	to arrive	at 10 o'clock	.
He expects	the professors	to fall	next month	.
Who expects	the cost of living	to work	at once	.

quite   = completely (usually used with "not")

In the following sentences, **put in** the word "quite" (meaning "completely") before a suitable verb, adjective, or -ed form. Rewrite each sentence.

1.   The work is not finished.

   _____.

2.   Please wait a few minutes; I am not ready.

   _____.

3.   I couldn't believe what he said.

   _____.

4.   I can't understand why you want to leave.

   _____.

5.   These apples are not ripe.

   _____.

6.   Your answer is not accurate.

   _____.

7.   This line isn't straight.

   _____.

8.   He didn't succeed in proving it.

   _____.

9.   This box isn't large enough to hold all the books.

   _____.

10.   He isn't old enough to go to school.

   _____.

11.   Even when both ends are stretched, they don't meet.

   _____.

12.   It is impossible to obtain long grained rice here.

   _____.

6.2 WORD STUDY

a speedometer
a rod

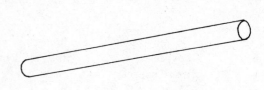

A speedometer is an instrument which shows how fast a car (or any machine which moves) is traveling.

A rod is a thin, long piece of metal (or wood or glass or some other solid substance). A rod is thicker than a wire but narrower than a bar, and it cannot be pulled into different shapes like a wire.

In most typewriters there is a metal r__d to keep the paper in its place.

a fraction
a quarter
a tenth
a hundredth
a thousandth
a decimal
decimal

1, 2, 3, 4, 5 are whole numbers.

1/2, 1/3, 2/45, 3/4, 9/10 are *fractions*.

We use fractions to count parts of units.

This is one inch.

When one inch is divided into 4, one of these divisions is *a quarter* of an inch. We write this "1/4 inch."

Three of these divisions are **three-quarters** of an inch. We write this "3/4 inch."

Here is a square. What fr_____n of it is black? What f_____n is white? Give the answer in figures.

Black _____   White _____

When we divide one unit into ten, we can write the fractions like this: 1/10, 2/10, 3/10, 4/10, 5/10, and so on.

But there is another way of writing them, which was probably first thought of in India, and was later used by Arab and European mathematicians.

Instead of writing 1/10, 2/10, 3/10, etc., we can write .1, .2, .3, .4, and so on. The point (.) which precedes each figure is called *a decimal* point and the figures after the point are called decimal fractions or decimals. .1, .2, .3, .4 are called d_____al fr_____ns, because these figures represent fractions and are written in decimals.

Note: In many countries a comma (,) is used instead of a point.

When we use d_____ls, instead of writing 25/100, we write .25, and instead of writing 253/1000 we write .253. For every zero (0) of the dividing figure **we move one place away (to the right) from the decimal point.** Now write the following fractions **in decimals**.

1. $\frac{2}{100}$ (This is written .02)

2. $\frac{3}{100}$ _____

3. $\frac{32}{100}$ _____

4. $\frac{9}{1000}$ _____

94

6.2 WORD STUDY

5. $\dfrac{92}{1000}$ _____

6. $\dfrac{928}{1000}$ _____

7. $\dfrac{9296}{10,000}$ _____

8. $\dfrac{9274}{100,000}$ _____

9. $\dfrac{1}{1,000,000}$ _____

10. $\dfrac{999,999}{1,000,000}$ _____

approximately
approximate
guess
a guess
a fraction
exact
exactly
almost

Look at this line. It is not quite straight, is it? Don't measure this line.

Guess its length. What do you think it is? Different people will gu__ss differently, because when we gu____ an answer we do not reach it by counting, measuring, or using a standard. We only say what we think, and this may be wrong.

What do you guess? 4½ inches? Now measure the line. Your gu____ was not a very good one. The line is *almost* (= nearly) five inches long.

We can also say that the line is *approximately* five inches long. This means that it is either a little less than five inches or a little more than five inches. It is not *exactly* five inches.

Five inches is the *approximate* length of this line. If the line is 4.999 inches long, we can say that its length is approximately 5.00 inches.

When we say that a measurement is accurate, we do not mean that we cannot make it better. You will remember that accuracy depends on being careful and using a certain standard to check your measurements or statements. Perhaps the inch on your ruler is divided into tenths. If this ruler is your standard, then it will be accurate enough, if you give your measurement in inches and tenths of an inch.

When we say a measurement is accurate, we mean that it is carefully made with an instrument which shows units (and fractions of units) which are small enough **for the purpose of our work**. For example, a scale of weights (tons, hundredweights, pounds) which will give us accurate results when we use it to weigh coal will not give accurate results when we use it to weigh gold or drugs.

Our standards of measurement depend on our purposes. In weighing coal, a difference of one ounce or one gram is not important, but in weighing drugs (= medicine) it may make the difference between life and death.

This difference in standards of measurement can be represented in decimals. When we count, 2.0, 2.00, and 2.000 are the same number. When we measure, 2.0, 2.00, and 2.000 are very different.

When we see 2.0, we know that something has been measured, and that the result of the measurement is app_____ly two units. We know that the approximation is to the nearest tenth of a unit. A measurement above 1.95 units, by this standard, would be written as 2.0, and a measurement above 2.05 would be written as 2.1. 2.0 means between 1.95 and 2.05.

When we see 2.00 we know that _____ _____ _____ _____ , and that the r_____t of the measurement is app_____y two units. We know that the app_____n is to the nearest hundredth of a unit. By this standard a measurement above 1.995 would be written as 2.00 and a measurement above 2.005 would be written as 2.01. 2.00 means between _____ and 2.005.

When we see 2.000 we know that something _____ _____ _____ , and that the r_____t of the m_____nt is app_____ two units. We know that the measurement is to the nearest th_____th of a unit. A measurement above 1.9995, by this standard, will be written

95

6.2 WORD STUDY

as 2.000, and a _____ above 2.0005 will be wr_____n as 2.001. 2.000 means between
_____ and _____ .

It costs more money to make a thing to the nearest thousandth of a unit than to make a thing to the nearest tenth of a unit. The standards of measurement used will be different and the measuring instruments will also be different. You cannot use a wooden ruler to measure thousandths of an inch. You must use an instrument which costs more money.

a substance
common

Water, oil, gold, lead, milk, leather, and wood are *substances*; a glass of water, a drop of oil, a piece of gold, a bar of lead, all these are things or objects.

Water, ice, and snow are not different substances; they are the same s_____ce in different forms. Salt is a *common* s_____ce; it is found in large quantities in many places. Sugar is another very c_____n s_____ce. You will find some in every house. Gold is not a c_____n s_____ce; so it costs a lot of money. There is not much of it in the world and it is difficult to obtain.

S_____ces which can flow are called fluids. S_____ces which cannot flow and have a fixed form are called solids. But a solid s_____ce can often be converted into a liquid one by heating it.

Houses made of wood are very c_____n in my hometown. Stone houses are not so c_____n. One of the most c_____ cars on the road is the Ford. The most c_____ letter in the alphabet is E. The most c_____ word in the English language is "the"; so don't forget to use it where it is required.

The word "substance" is **countable**; the plural is "substances," because there are obviously many different s_____ces—gold, milk, wood, and so on. The words "a solid" and "a liquid" are also **countable**, because there are many different solids and liquids. The words for **special** substances are **uncountable**; we say that a box is made of gold, a glass is full of water, that water is a liquid.

expect

When we *expect* something, we think that it will happen or we think that it will probably h_____n. For example, if I say "I expect rain today" or "I ex_____ that it will rain today," I mean that I think it will pr_____ly rain today. This does **not** mean that I want it to rain or that I hope that it will rain! What we ex_____ is not always what we want or hope for.

Social life (= life in society, life among other people) would be very difficult if we did not ex_____ things. Imagine a man going to work. When he reaches the bus stop, he e_____s to find a bus there at a certain time, and when he gets on the bus he e_____s it to take him to a certain place. He e_____s the driver to drive the bus. He does not e_____ the driver to sit on top of the bus, or get off and play cards by the roadside, or start fighting a policeman. When this man reaches his office, he probably e_____s to find the door open and his office clean. Perhaps he works for another man, Mr. Y. He e_____s Mr. Y. to say "Good morning" and he e_____s Mr. Y. to give him some work to do. He does not e_____ Mr. Y. to start singing in a loud voice and throwing the typewriters out of the window.

Unexpected happenings are sometimes pleasant, sometimes unpleasant, sometimes interesting. It is very pleasant to have an un_____ed visit from an old friend. It is sometimes interesting when something un_____ed happens. If one of your teachers arrived at the university on the back of an elephant, this is the last thing you would _____ and you would find it interesting. But things which we do not _____ can also be unpleasant. If you arrived home and found that your house had been burned down in your absence this would be un_____ed and obviously very unpleasant for you.

Knowing a language means having a certain set of expectations. For example, when we are talking about this animal, I expect you to use the word "elephant," if we are speaking English, though I do not ex_____ this if we are speaking Malay.

When you use the verb "depend," I expect to hear the preposition "on" because "depend" is nearly always followed by "on."

6.2 WORD STUDY

agree (to)
agree (with)
disagree (with)
(an) agreement
disagreement

Two friends *agree to* meet at the public library at 10 o'clock. What does this mean? It means that they both say they will meet there and that they ex_____ to find each other at the library at 10 o'clock. When two women agree to call each other by their first names, this means that they say or promise that they will do this and that each of them ex_____s the other one to use her first name in the future. If one of them forgets to do this, perhaps the other one will say "Don't you remember our *agreement*"?

Mr. Smith lives in Florida and Mr. Brown lives in Quebec. They agr__ to exchange houses every year for the summer holidays. If Mr. Brown talks about going to Mexico one year, Mrs. Brown may say "Have you forgotten your ag_____nt **with** Mr. Smith"? Mr. Brown has made an agr_____nt with Mr. Smith. He may keep to it; he may break it. Perhaps he will ask Mr. Smith to change it. A written agreement, for example, an agreement about the use of land, a house, or a sum of money, cannot be broken and cannot be easily changed. Such ag_____s are often called contracts.

Suppose Mrs. Brown says to Mr. Brown "Young people nowadays are more sensible than they were thirty years ago," and Mr. Brown says "Of course you are right, dear." If he says this, Mr. Brown *agrees with* Mrs. Brown. But if he says "No modern young person, in my opinion, has any sense at all," then he obviously *disagrees with* her. (This is a short way of saying that he disagrees with her statement.) A man a_____s _____ someone when he thinks that person is right about something. He _____ _____ a statement when he believes that it is true. He dis_____s _____ a person when he thinks that person is wrong or mistaken about something, and he dis_____s _____ a statement when he thinks that it is not true. When he says "Yes" he expresses a_____nt, and when he says "No" he ex_____s dis_____t.

a custom
a convention
conventional
unconventional
social

Here is a symbol (?). This symbol is *a convention* used in writing. Everyone who writes English uses it at the end of a question. It is a written con_____ion.

In this country it is *a custom* for the bride to wear a long white dress. Not all brides wear this kind of dress, but many do. It is one of the c_____ions of a wedding in this country.

It is a c_____n of driving in England that drivers keep to the left side of the road. In Europe and America the convention is that drivers keep to the right.

The last example is interesting. These driving conventions have the force of law, but they are obviously not laws of nature. And the man who breaks a c_____n of the road is in a different position from a man who steals or kills someone. English people do not think that Americans are strange because they drive (in their own country) on the right side of the road.

From these examples we can discover the important features of a c_____tion.

First, it is clear that a c_____tion is a way of doing something in a certain situation that is practiced by the members of a certain *social* group; or something generally used in a certain situation by the members of a s_____l group, a group of people in society. The group which practices or uses a c_____ion may be small or large, but there must be at least two people in it. A husband and wife, for example, may have a c_____ion which no one else has. For example, they may always knock on the door in a special way.

Secondly, a c_____ion is known to the members of the group (which may be as small as a family unit or as big as a nation) and is **accepted** by them. They show that they accept it by practicing it or using it at the right time.

Some c_____s, like certain conventions used in games or the rules of the road, are agr__d to by the members of a group; others are acc____ed and used because they already exist in the social group to which a person belongs. Most of the c_____ions of a language are of this kind. We acc__t them and use them because they are already part of the language. So a c_____ion may exist already or may be the result of an ag____ment; but it must be acc____ed by a group of people.

Thirdly, a convention is a way of doing something or something used by members of a group, in a certain kind of situation. For this reason a convention often has the force of a rule among the members of the group which practice it or use it. This is true not only of useful or necessary conventions like the conventions of grammar or driving conventions; it is often true of conventions which do not seem useful, like the clothes we are expected to wear at a party. Here is a true story. Some students invited two

6.2 WORD STUDY

friends, Bob and Dick, to an evening party to meet their parents. They told Bob and Dick that they must wear white shirts and dark ties. These things—a white shirt and dark tie— were a convention for evening parties in the social group to which the parents belonged. The students who gave the party gave this convention the force of a rule. So Bob and Dick did not acc___t their invitation.

A fourth feature of a convention is that it is not really necessary, or even if it seems to be necessary (like the convention of driving on the right side of the road, or using "s" to show the plural form of a noun) it can be replaced by a different convention in a different social group. Some conventions, like wearing a special kind of dress for a wedding, are not necessary at all. Other conventions (like driving on the right or left side of the road) are based on the fact that in certain situations it may be difficult or dangerous, or it may be impossible for people to understand each other, if everyone does **not** do the same thing. A policeman stands in the middle of the road and moves his hands in a certain way when he allows people to cross the road. These movements are *conventional*, and could be different (in another country they are different), but the important thing is that all policemen and everyone who uses the roads should know them and accept them.

Some conventions are necessary for a s_____l group living in a certain way; others depend on customs or fashions. We say that a man is conventional if he accepts and practices the customs of his social group, or *unconventional* if he does not. If he does not accept the necessary conventions of language or of the road we do not say he is unconventional but that he is mad. When we say that a man is unconventional in his language, we probably mean that he uses a few expressions of his own, or does not try to copy the speech of a limited social group. But he must accept the basic conventions of language; otherwise no one will understand him.

a chapter
a paragraph
a distinction
distinguish
distinct
distinctly

When it is a fine day, objects in the distance can be seen clearly and separately; they are *distinct*, they can be seen *distinctly*. When the day is cloudy ob_____s in the dis____ce cannot always be seen dis_____ly; they are not always d_____t. If a man speaks with his mouth full, his words are not d_____t. We cannot hear each word clearly and separately; in other words we cannot hear the words d_____ly.

The shapes of things seen at a d_____ce are not a____ys d_____t; they are not always clear and s_____te. We cannot count things unless they are s_____ and d_____. To count them we must be able to see the difference between them clearly; if we cannot make any *distinction* between them we cannot count them.

Here is a map showing some roads joined at various places. How many roads are there on the map? It is very difficult to count them, isn't it? You cannot see where one road begins and another ends. There is no basis for d_____tion; so we cannot *distinguish between* one road and another. We cannot make a d_____n between them.

When scientists classify things, or put them into classes, they d_____sh between different kinds of things; they show the ways in which they differ. Some people, for example, think that bats and birds are alike because they fly, but a scientist knows that there are important dis_____ns between them and that they do not belong to the same family of living things. In nature it is not always easy to d_____sh between things which are alike in some of their features, and in language it is not always easy to dis_____ between words which look or sound alike or which have nearly the same meaning.

Can you distinguish between (make a distinction between):

(a)   a ship and a sheep?
(b)   a book and a newspaper?
(c)   a pen and a pencil?
(d)   expecting that something will happen and hoping that something will happen?
(e)   a pyramid and a cone?
(f)   a cause and an effect?

6.2 WORD STUDY

Writers often want to show the d_____ion between different parts of a subject. They do this in in various ways. They can divide a book into *chapters*, but they may want to make smaller divisions within each chapter. They can do this by dividing each chapter into *paragraphs*. They make a new p_____h by beginning a sentence a short distance to the right of the beginning of a line, instead of at the beginning of a line. Here is a long p_____h. Can you divide it into two shorter p_____s?

Liquid volume or capacity can be measured by using a special kind of container. This container is made of glass or another substance which we can see through, and has a scale on one side marked in units of liquid volume, for example, liquid ounces. When a quantity of liquid is poured into the container it reaches a certain point on the scale. This point shows the level of the liquid and represents its volume. Solid volume cannot be measured in the same way because solid things do not flow. They are not fluid and cannot take the shape of a container. We know this very well when we try to pack a box with books or other solid objects. It is impossible to make them fit exactly into the space in the box. To measure the volume of a solid object we must use a different method.

Look at the reading passages in this unit, page 103. How many paragraphs are there in the first reading passage? How many paragraphs are there in the second? How does a division into paragraphs help us to d_____sh between the different steps or divisions in a writer's thinking?

Unit VI

6.3 DICTATION EXERCISES AND DICTATION PASSAGES

A 1. The passage *Symbols* will now be read to you. When you hear the following adjectives, write the articles (if any) which precede them and the nouns which follow them.

    (a) _____ two important   _____

    (b) _____ conventional   _____

    (c) _____ busy   _____

    (d) _____ traffic   _____

    (e) _____ narrower   _____

    (f) _____ very short conventional   _____

    (g) _____ capital   _____

    (h) _____ special   _____

    (i) _____ logical   _____

    (j) _____ mathematical   _____

    (k) _____ separate   _____

2. Number the following words in the order in which you hear them.

          operations   symbols   chemistry
    traffic   chemical   capital
          notice   sign   symbolic

3. When the teacher tells you to begin, underline the following words in the passage *Symbols*. This is a recognition race.

    substances   busy   subtraction   actually
    formulas   separate   circumference   conventional
    operations   special   logic   calculate

4. The passage *Symbols* will be read again. Write the correct form of the following verbs, in the order in which you hear them.

    mean   walk   have   mean   call   use   represent   call

5. The passage *Symbols* will now be given as dictation.

B 1. The passage *Describing a Harbor* will now be read to you. *Listen* to the *prepositions* used after the following words in the passage: classify (+ object); distinguish (+ object); belong; alike. Now write the missing prepositions in the following sentences:

    (a)   We can classify most sentences _____ statements, questions, and commands or requests.

    (b)   Wars may not be alike _____ their causes, but they are usually alike _____ their effects.

    (c)   This book does not belong _____ the college library.

    (d)   It is usually possible to distinguish a definition of a word _____ a description of a thing.

    (e)   It is sometimes difficult to distinguish artificial silk _____ real silk.

    (f)   Psychology is not always classified _____ a science.

    (g)   I do not belong _____ any political group.

6.3 DICTATION EXERCISES AND DICTATION PASSAGES

2. Number the following words in the order in which you hear them.

features   natural   artificial
          harbor   safely   certain
members   class   classify

3. Number the following words in the order in which you hear them.

distinguish   alike   features
          definition   description   formed
special   suppose   belongs

4. The passage *Describing a Harbor* will be read again. It is given below, with fifteen words (not counting articles) left out. *After* listening to it, write the missing words in the blank spaces. They are given here, but not in the correct order.

Verbs	Nouns	Adjectives and Adverbs
classify	a description	certain
formed	the definition	safely
suppose	the sea	artificial
distinguish	mouths	alike
	harbor	special
	members	
	features	

_____ you want to describe Portsmouth harbor. You will not say that it is a place where ships can lie _____ near the land, because this is part of _____ _____ of a harbor, not _____ _____ of Portsmouth _____. To describe something you must do more than _____ it as a thing of a _____ kind; you must point out its _____ features; in other words you must _____ it from other _____ of the class to which it belongs. Harbors are not _____ in all their _____. Some are natural; some are _____. Some are formed by the _____ of rivers; others are _____ by the shape of the land where it meets _____ _____ .

5. The passage *Describing a Harbor* will now be given as dictation.

6.3 DICTATION PASSAGES

(a) Symbols

The word "symbol" has two important meanings. It may mean anything used as a conventional sign for something else. In this sense all words are actually symbols. Next time you walk in a busy street, try to notice the traffic symbols and count them. What color is the symbol for danger?

In mathematics, science, and logic the word "symbol" has a narrower meaning. It means a very short conventional sign, like the symbols for plus and minus in mathematics or the capital letters used in chemical formulas. One branch of logic, the science of reasoning or thinking, is called symbolic logic, because it uses special symbols to represent logical operations.

Multiplication, division, and subtraction are called mathematical operations. Each of them can be represented by a separate symbol. There are other mathematical symbols, for example, the symbol used to calculate the circumference of a circle. In chemistry the names of substances are also generally represented by symbols.

(b) Describing a Harbor

Suppose you want to describe Portsmouth harbor. You will not say that it is a place where ships can lie safely near the land, because this is part of the definition of a harbor, not a description of Portsmouth harbor. To describe something you must do more than classify it as a thing of a certain kind; you must point out its special features; in other words you must distinguish it from other members of the class to which it belongs. Harbors are not alike in all their features. Some are natural; some are artificial. Some are formed by the mouths of rivers; others are formed by the shape of the land where it meets the sea.

Unit VI
6.4 READING PASSAGES

(a) Units of Measurement

You can make an exact count of a number of horses, a number of apples, and even a number of hairs (if you have time), but no one can measure exactly the time it takes for a horse to run a race, the weight of an apple, or the diameter of a hair. The reason for this is that things or objects are separate and distinct, and so they are themselves ones or units. But the quantities we measure are not separate and distinct. They are not *things* but the *length* of a thing, the *temperature* of a thing, and so on. We do not find these quantities naturally separated into units. They are not units in themselves and they do not have units of their own.

If we wish to count quantities we must fix our own units, conventional units, to count them with. These conventional units are units of measurement. Though they may be derived from things we are familiar with, the inch and the gram are not found in nature. They are fixed and agreed to by people. Space and time, as we find them, are not already divided into parts. They have no parts in nature. We can only count them by comparing them with the conventional units fixed by human agreement; in other words, we can only count them by measuring them.

(b) Societies

People live in groups, which we call societies. Societies and social relations are the subjects studied in the social sciences.

People depend on other people and on the world around them. The sun brings them warmth and light, day and night, summer and winter. Plants grow where there is air and sunshine, earth and water; animals depend on plants; people depend on water, air, sunshine, and the plants and animals around them.

Wherever people live and whatever they look like, many of their requirements are the same. They need food and places to live in, warmth and sleep. They need a social existence; they need friendships and relationships which will lead to marriage and family life. The members of a society depend on one another.

In different societies we find different ways of finding food and different methods of preparing it. Societies have various habits and customs. They teach their children, care for sick people, look after old people in various ways. They have different beliefs about life, death, and the world into which they are born.

Most people want to live in peace. The members of every social group accept certain rules and customs and expect other members to know them. Children are taught to follow these rules, and what they do in later life depends partly on the habits they learned when they were young.

When human beings enter the world they do not and cannot form their own habits, customs, and purposes independently. They find them ready-made in the society into which they are born. Some people never travel more than three or four miles from their parents' village, and naturally the habits of these people do not change much. Others who for various reasons are able to travel from one country to another may have a chance to choose between different societies and different customs. But they cannot change their way of life, their way of thinking completely. Even when a man believes that he is totally different from the other members of his original social group, we can still see in him some family likeness. A society prints its own features on the human beings who belong to it.

Social scientists study societies and can show how people develop customs and conventions, how these are passed on by older people and changed by younger people. They show the effect of these customs on people's health and happiness. They show how societies produce things and use them, how they divide food and other necessary things among themselves. They show how different groups living side by side or mixing together are changed, how their disagreements lead to quarrels or to wars, how they end their disagreements and how people succeed in living together peacefully.

Social scientists classify societies. The basis of their classification is often the family unit. As we have seen, family units can be of very different kinds. A good classification helps a student of society to make interesting comparisons and useful distinctions, and to understand human purposes and actions.

6.4 READING PASSAGES

(c) Customs and Conventions

When you begin to play a card game with a friend, someone has to play the first card. Who will play it? Probably you make some rule about this, or agree to follow a rule made in other games. You may agree that the two players will take one card each from the pack (= the set of cards) before the game starts, and that the player who picks the card with the highest value will play first.

This rule, reached by an agreement, is a convention. The most important feature of a convention is that it is accepted by everyone and that everyone uses it or practices it—everyone belonging to the same group. It will not make very much difference to your game if you choose a different convention for starting it. You may, for example, agree to let one of the players guess which side of a penny or a cent thrown into the air will face upward when it reaches the ground.

In England, there is a convention that all cars must keep to the left side of the road. In Europe and America cars must keep to the right. This is not a law of nature, and it is not a question of right and wrong. The Americans do not think that English people are strange because they always drive on the left. It is a convention which has become a law in every country, because it would be impossible to drive safely if drivers were allowed to choose between the left and the right.

Language is conventional; its patterns and vocabulary are accepted by a social group. When we speak a language we use words which have a certain form and sentences which have a certain form. If we did not do this we would not easily understand each other. Here again it is the acceptance of these forms which is important, because it would not really matter if English people called a horse by another name.

Some conventions (like the driving conventions, and certain conventions of language) are necessary, because social life would be impossible without them. Other conventions are not necessary, but very convenient; they save time by letting us know what to expect. For example, on the first or second page of a book you will usually find the title (= the name) of the book, followed by the author's name, with the publisher's name at the bottom of the page. On the back of the same page you will often find the year of publication. It is accepted as a convention by publishers and writers that this information shall be given in the same place in their books, and readers also have a hand in this convention because they look in the same place for the information. There is no law about this. A publisher will not be sent to prison if the writer's name is given at the end of the book instead of at the beginning, but readers find the convention very convenient, when it is followed, because they find the information where they expect to find it.

But we should not imagine that every convention is good or useful and that no convention ought to be changed. Before we choose to follow a certain convention we should look closely at its purpose. Many conventions have a bad or stupid purpose, the purpose of keeping some people in a group and others out and making those who are "in" feel proud of themselves. A short time ago I read that there was a grand hotel very close to some beautiful mountains where visitors were expected to wear ties with their shirts. A man without a tie was not allowed to enter this hotel. This was not a sensible convention, because most people who love climbing mountains or walking among them also like to feel free when they are on vacation. Some people accepted this convention because the hotel was good in other ways. Probably the real purpose behind the convention was to make the people using the hotel (the tie wearers) feel different from the untidy people outside, who possibly did not have ties.

All units of measurement are conventions. Some of them are inconvenient and should be changed, because their use requires a lot of difficult and unnecessary calculation. You can think of examples for yourself. The conventions of English spelling are often very inconvenient, not only for English-speaking children who have to learn to spell at school. But it is easy to see why governments are not in a hurry to change these conventions. To change conventions like these means changing the habits and regular actions of millions of people, a major operation which may prove more inconvenient than the conventions themselves.

Unit VI
6.5 VOCABULARY TEST

To test yourself on the vocabulary of this section, fill in the missing letters in the incomplete words.

Almost every society uses a_____l for some purpose. In our s_____ certain c_____ are followed when drinking. Drinking a_____ is part of a social situation. G_____ly people are willing to a_____ the c_____ and they behave in an ac_____ way. Unf_____ly, however, there are always a few people who, i_____ o_ drinking a small amount of alcohol, drink it in large qu_____. They probably e_____ t_ get an i_____ly pleasant feeling from this experience, but often all they get is a pain in the head.

As free members of a s_____ we think we are free to choose whether to a_____ c_____ or not. In fact we are not q_____ free because some c_____ have become so important to s_____ that those who break them are not allowed to be part of society. Sometimes people who are w_____ t_ b_____ in an o_____ c_____al way are happier than those people who disagree with the c_____ of the s_____. Sometimes members of a society de_____ not to take any n_____ of the c_____ of that society and to b_____ e_____y as they want to. However, sometimes this person still e_____ other people to behave in a c_____ way. Sometimes a whole group __ ___ple a_____ not to follow the c_____ of the s_____ and they try to live in some other way. Almost always this group begins to a_____ some rules for b_____r and these become the c_____ for those who b_____ t_ the group. The group then e_____ its m_____s to follow the new c_____. Perhaps the most sensible c_____ are based on co_____ce and not on ideas about how people ought to live.

Unit VII

7.1 VOCABULARY

These are the words you will practice in this unit:

VERBS

continue (to)	(con·tin'ue)	
develop	(de·vel'op)	
devise	(de·vise')	
discuss	(dis·cuss')	
drop		
estimate	(es'ti·mate)	
expect	(ex·pect')	
express	(ex·press')	(+ noun)
express		(+ noun + in + noun)
guess		
imitate	(im'i·tate)	
lead to		
lift		
matter	(mat'ter)	("it does not matter")
reduce	(re·duce')	
rely on	(re·ly')	
repeat	(re·peat')	
suppose	(sup·pose')	

NOUNS

(an) ability	(a·bil'i·ty)	(an) imitation	(im·i·ta'tion)
(an) activity	(ac·tiv'i·ty)	(an) industry	(in'dus·try)
a datum	(da'tum)	(a) possibility	(pos·si·bil'i·ty)
(a) development	(de·vel'op·ment)	(a) practice	(prac'tice)
an estimate	(es'ti·mate)	precision	(pre·ci'sion)
an error	(er'ror)	a quarter	(quar'ter)
(an) experience	(ex·pe'ri·ence)	(a) repetition	(rep·e·ti'tion)

ADJECTIVES

artificial	(ar·ti·fi'cial)	precise	(pre·cise')
continuous	(con·tin'u·ous)	safe	
dangerous	(dan'ger·ous)	several	(sev'er·al)
experienced	(ex·pe'ri·enced)	suitable	(suit'a·ble)
final	(fi'nal)	unlikely	(un·like'ly)
inexperienced	(in·ex·pe'ri·enced)	unsuitable	(un·suit'a·ble)
practical	(prac'ti·cal)		

ADVERBS

about	(a·bout')	(= approximately)
continuously	(con·tin'u·ous·ly)	
finally	(fi'nal·ly)	
over	(o'ver)	(= more than)
precisely	(pre·cise'ly)	
under	(un'der)	(= less than)

Unit VII

7.2 WORD STUDY

INSTRUCTIONS: Study the following words and the uses of them:

it does not matter When we say that something *does not matter*, or *"It doesn't matter,"* we mean that it is not important,
it doesn't matter or that it makes no difference, or that there is no need to worry about it.

> *Examples:* When coal is weighed, an error (= a mistake) of half an ounce doesn't matter, but when we weigh drugs it may make the difference between life and death.

> It d__s n__ m_____ what you say, I still can't believe that he did it. It d___n't m_____ to me whether you have your class in the morning or in the afternoon. We reached the lecture room 20 minutes late, but it didn't m_____, because the speaker had not arrived.

a datum (This word is generally used in its plural form.)
pl. data

> *Data* are facts. We often speak of the data (the facts) which we have in front of us when we have a problem to solve. The laws which scientists discover must be based on the data, the facts which are "given," which they already know. (In Latin the word "datum" means something which is given.)

> *Examples:* We do not yet have enough data to solve this problem. He is collecting d____ on people's smoking habits.

a possibility If a thing or a situation or an action or a result is *a possibility*, this means that it may be or may not be a fact. When we speak of the possibility of something happening, we are speaking of the chance that it will happen.

> *Examples:* A trade agreement between Canada and Japan is a p_____ty, and the two countries have agreed to work toward it. Have you thought of all the p_____ies? Is there any p_____y of his coming here next week? There is no p_____y of getting the price reduced any further.

artificial A thing is *artificial* when it is made or produced not by nature but by people. But when we compare artificial things with **natural** things we often think of artificial things which have some features which are like features of natural things.

> *Examples:* All units of measurement are a_____l, because space, time, weight, and other dimensions are not naturally divided into units. (But we can count units just as we can count things.) She wore a hat with a_____l flowers around the edge. A_____l wood can now be made which looks just like real wood. A_____l silk looks and feels very much like natural silk, but natural silk threads come from silkworms.

(the) final = the last, at the end.

> *Examples:* The f____l chapter in the book is very long, but it is the most interesting. In the f_____ operation of the war 2,000 prisoners were taken. When will you give him your f_____ answer? In his _____ statement the senator promised to give a million dollars for new university buildings.

unlikely = improbable, not probable. This adjective is more commonly used than "improbable."

> *Examples:* It is *unlikely* that he has kept records of all his students' names and addresses. A change in the political situation in the near future is un_____ly.

7.2 WORD STUDY

Exercise: The following sentences are incomplete. Complete them by writing "unlikely" in the right place. Rewrite each sentence.

1. It is that he will approach the President directly.

   _____

   _____ .

2. It is that life exists on Mars.

   _____

   _____ .

3. An agreement between the two groups is a possibility, but it is.

   _____

   _____ .

4. It is that all the powder will dissolve at once.

   _____

   _____ .

5. It is that Canada will send us much grain this year.

   _____

   _____ .

6. The existence of any earlier records is.

   _____

   _____ .

7. It is that the price of potatoes will fall until the end of the season.

   _____

   _____ .

express
express
= show in words, looks, or actions or **in** a special form, e.g., express in feet, express in grams, express in a formula.

Examples: It is difficult to *express* one's feelings. It is difficult to ex_____ one's feelings in words. In her letter she ex_____ed her interest in our work. The relation between the radius of a circle and its circumference is ex_____d in a formula.

Exercise: Do the following problems.

1. Express the following words in figures:

   forty-two _____ a million _____ three hundred _____

   two hundred thousand _____

7.2 WORD STUDY

2. Express the following fractions in decimals:

$\dfrac{256}{100}$ _____ $\dfrac{2}{10,000}$ _____ $\dfrac{4}{10}$ _____

$\dfrac{58,962}{100,000}$ _____ $\dfrac{6}{20}$ _____ $\dfrac{2}{25}$ _____

$\dfrac{1}{2}$ _____

3. Express the following lengths in meters:

365 centimeters _____   2 yards _____

2½ yards _____   1,000 centimeters _____

25 feet _____

rely on = trust (a person), always expect that a person will give help, believe that (a thing) will do its job well and not break down, believe that (a person) will keep his or her promises, or do what he or she has promised to do.

We *rely on* a person when we can always expect help when we need it; or when we believe that a person's promises will be kept. We r___ __ a thing (e.g., a car) when we believe that it will do its own kind of work well without stopping or breaking down. We r___ __ a statement, an estimate, a story when we believe that we can base our actions on its truth or accuracy.

Make sensible sentences from the following tables:

I	II	III
This clock	can be relied on	to get you there in time.
This book		to keep correct time.
Miss Smith	cannot be relied on	to finish the work in time.
The factory		to give the facts.
Politicians		to use safe methods.
A D.C. 8		to give value for money.

We cannot	rely on	his statement.
No one can		this car.
You can		her promises.
Everyone can		this washing machine.
		the government.
		the army.

suitable = right for the purpose, the weather, etc.
unsuitable = wrong for the purpose, the weather, etc.

Examples: Your dress is not *suitable* for a wedding. A scale with very small units is un_____le for weighing coal. We must find a more s_____ place for the meeting.

Exercise: Write the word "suitable" **in a suitable place** in the following sentences.

1. This kind of paper is for most purposes.

_____.

2. You should use more examples in your essays.

_____.

7.2 WORD STUDY

3. There are gas stations at intervals along the route.

   _____ .

4. These definitions are not for such a short book.

   _____ .

5. This kind of wire is for an electric heater.

   _____ .

6. These diagrams are obviously for a children's book.

   _____ .

7. These bars are not of a width for your purpose.

   _____ .

8. Divide this passage into paragraphs of a length.

   _____ .

about = approximately
over = more than
under = less than

Note: "Over" and "under" can be used with lengths of time but not with points of time.

Exercise: Write these words, where they are suitable, in the blank spaces in the following sentences.

1. Children _____ sixteen are not allowed in this movie.
2. In England a policeman must be _____ 5 feet 10 inches tall.
3. If you come at _____ six o'clock it will be convenient.
4. It is _____ two hours since the plane arrived, but he has not come.
5. If the table is _____ four feet wide it will not go through the door.
6. I don't know how much sugar there is here, but I guess it is _____ three pounds.
7. It is difficult to teach a class which has _____ 150 students.
8. Your temperature is now _____ 98.4 degrees; so you can go home.
9. It happened at _____ four o'clock in the morning.
10. It takes _____ four hours to reach my uncle's house, even when the roads are dry.

devise = to think of a way of making (a machine, a plan, a tool, etc.) or a way of doing (an operation, an experiment, etc.)

Make sensible sentences from the following table:

I	II	III	IV
He	devised	an operation	for lengthening a muscle.
Mr. Field		a plan	for stretching metals.
The doctor		a machine	for lifting tree trunks.
The engineers		an instrument	for the development of science teaching.
The scientists		a classification	for measuring the distances between stars.
The principal			for historical records.

7.2 WORD STUDY

discuss = to talk about (a subject), often with the hope of reaching an agreement or solving a problem.

Examples: Scientists often dis__ss standards of measurement, but they do not always reach an agreement. Yesterday we dis_____ed the definition of "pressure." Yesterday this group of economists spent two hours dis_____ing ways of expanding trade. This problem has been dis_____ed for two centuries, but no one has solved it yet.

a quarter

The space inside this circle is divided into four equal parts. It is divided into *quarters*.

Divide this square into quarters.

A quarter of this square is black. Which quarter is black? The top _____ quarter is black.

This is a clock. When the long hand points to **three** we say it is a qu_____ past three.

When the long hand points to **nine** we say it is a qu__ter to or of three. On a clock, the figure three represents a qu_____ of the distance around the clock. The figure nine also represents a qu_____ of the distance around the clock.

lift = to move something from the ground or move something to a higher position (usually something heavy).

drop = to let something fall.

I've *dropped* my glasses! I hope they are not broken.

He dropped a stone into the water.

7.2 WORD STUDY

continue
continue (to)
continuously
continuous
several
finally

Yesterday it rained without stopping for six hours; it rained *continuously* for six hours. My son and I were in the sitting room. He was reading a book called "Customs and Conventions in Modern Europe."

"Do you think this rain will *continue*?" I asked him. He did not even hear my question. He *continued to* read. I spoke to him *several* (= three or more) times, but he did not answer. He c_____ed to read. *Finally* (= in the end) I said, "Yesterday I bought a new record for you." He jumped up, dropped his book on the floor, took the record from me, and put it on the record player.

If a student tries to read or study c_____ly for s_____l hours, he will get tired. He will not remember very much. C_____s reading is not good for the eyes. It is better to stop reading at intervals of 30 or 40 minutes and do something else for several minutes.

Look closely at a small area of a picture by Cezanne, Pissarro, or Van Gogh. Choose part of the picture which represents the sky. At a distance it may look blue, but if you look closely you will see that the surface is not painted c_____ly with the same color. At a distance you may see only one color, but if you look more closely you will see that there are actually s_____l colors painted on the surface in very small patches (= small, irregular parts of a surface).

Van Gogh was a great painter, though he was not famous during his lifetime. Nothing could stop him painting. When he was poor and had no money in his pocket he c_____ed __ paint. When he was ill he _____ __ paint. (He painted c_____ly.) When he was mad and had to be shut up in a house by his friends he _____ __ paint. He never sold a picture in his lifetime but now his pictures are sold for millions of dollars. There are s_____ pictures by Van Gogh in American museums.

develop
(a) development
industry
lead to
continue to

It is interesting to study the historical *development* (= the growth) of the City of London. In the beginning there was only a small village on the banks of the river Thames. This village grew and *developed* through the centuries, and now London is one of the largest cities and busiest ports (= towns or cities with a harbor) in the world.

What *led to* (= caused, resulted in) this d_____nt? What were its causes? The most important cause was the d_____ of trade between London and other cities in England and Europe. Trade d_____d when farmers could produce more grain than they needed for themselves and could sell grain to other people. These people were then left free to d_____p (= cause something to develop) better methods of doing their own work, and this l__ __ a division between different kinds of workers doing different kinds of work.

Later, in the sixteenth century, America was discovered and trade routes between the West and the East were d_____ed. This l__ __ a further d_____nt of trade between London and other countries.

In the eighteenth century something else happened which had an important effect on the d_____ of London as a city. A machine was devised which could use the power of steam instead of the power of human bodies. The use of the steam engine in factories l__ __ the d_____ of London as a center of *industry*. Hundreds of factories were built in London and other British cities. In the nineteenth century the number of people living and working in London multiplied by ten. This was a direct result of the d_____ of British in_____y and of the growing volume of London's trade with other countries, where in_____y was not so highly d_____ed.

Throughout the nineteenth century London c_____ed to d_____p as a port, as an industrial center, and also as a center for the newer activities* of banking and money exchange. It also became a center of scientific ac_____ty and educational d_____. It was already the home of the Royal Society (of scientists) and it now became a university city.

Note: * An activity is not a single action, but a **kind of** work (or play) that takes time and keeps people busy.

7.2 WORD STUDY

imitate
(an) imitation
suppose
experience
(an) ability
experienced
inexperienced
repeat
(a) repetition
practice
   (uncountable)

People learn how to do things: how to fry eggs, how to ride a bicycle, how to drive a car, how to clean a refrigerator, how to speak another language without making any mistakes. How do they learn?

Suppose (= imagine) that you want to learn to fry an egg. The first step is to copy what another person does; copying what another person does is *imitation*. You will probably ask a friend to fry an egg and after watching her you will *imitate* her. You saw her switch on the electricity; you will do the same. You saw her put oil into a frying pan; you will i_____e this action. You will i_____ each of her actions. When you want to learn how to say an English word you will listen to somebody saying the word and try to i_____ the sound.

When we learn through i_____n, we learn from other people's *experience*. People's experience is the knowledge or *ability* (= power to do things) which they have as a result of their past learning and past act_____s. When you learn to fry an egg you should not i_____te an *inexperienced* cook; you should i_____ an *experienced* cook, a cook who has had a lot of ex_____ce. An ex_____ced cook is one who has fried eggs many times before and who knows what oil is best, how hot the oil should be, how long the cooking takes, what mistakes you are likely to make, and so on.

You can learn from the e_____ce of a friend or a teacher. You can also learn much from your own e_____ce, which means that you try to do things yourself and succeed or make mistakes. (The word "experience" comes from a Latin word which means "to try.") An in_____ced cook is one who has not often tried to cook things.

After i_____n, the next requirement for learning how to do a thing is *repetition*. S____ose you are learning English and you want to learn the word "experience." First you will i_____ your teacher when she says the word until you can say it correctly, and then write the word with the correct spelling, by i_____ing it as you see it on the blackboard or in a book. Then you must *repeat* the word; you must say it again and again in suitable sentences and suitable situations.

This workbook will help you to do this, because it asks you to r_____t words many times in various situations. A single r_____ion is not enough. Many r_____s are necessary before a word is learned.

R_____n for the purpose of learning is called *practice*. To learn things well, to develop our various abilities (= powers to do different things) we need a lot of pr_____ce. Not all r_____ion is pr_____ce, of course. Most machines (for example, clocks) r_____t their movements again and again, but this r_____ion is not pr_____ce. A machine does not **learn** anything, or want to learn anything. It simply does the same thing again and again. P_____e is necessary for learning, whether we want to learn to speak English, ride a bicycle, or sing well. P_____ helps us to form good habits. (It can help us to form bad habits too, if we continue to repeat a word incorrectly or an action in the wrong way.)

a practice
   (countable)

A practice is a way of doing something that is commonly done, or something that is done regularly.

Mrs. Brown is a very hard-working woman. It is her usual pr_____ce to clean four rooms before breakfast. She makes a pr_____ce of washing up the dishes as soon as breakfast is finished. She does not believe in the pr_____ce of lying in bed in the mornings. If other housewives imitated her pr_____ces, this would be a good thing.

Mr. Smith, our senator, wants to put an end to some of the pr_____ces which limit the freedom of shoppers. He wants to end the pr_____ce of closing stores on Sunday, and also the pr_____ce of limiting beer stores to certain city districts. Although they are enforced by law in this country, these pr_____ces do not exist in many European countries.

The pr_____ce of calling one's parents by their first names has not yet become a custom in England and America, but it is expected to become a custom within the next twenty years.

7.2 WORD STUDY

safe
dangerous
possibility
expect
guess
estimate
practical

Human beings are animals who live by learning. People must learn to do what is *safe* for them to do. They must eat what is s____ for them to eat, not things which will kill them or make them ill. They must learn to keep away from places which are not s___, like the middle of the road when there is a lot of t_____c. They must learn not to do *dangerous* things, not to eat things which are d_____us for their health. They must keep away from places which are _____, places which are not _____.

The difficulty about this is that we can't know everything or learn everything. In life we often meet new situations; so we do not always know what to ex____t. In a new situation we do not always know what will be _____ and what will be _____s.

Suppose a man wants to climb a high rock. He does not know exactly how high it is and he has no way of measuring it.

He must *estimate* (= *guess*) its height, and think of the places where he will put his hands and feet as he climbs. He sees several sharp edges of rock which, he hopes, will be suitable to step on to or hold on to. He does not know if they are s__e, because he does not know how strong they are. He must es_____e their strength. He must make an e_____e of their strength before he begins to climb the rock. If he makes a mistake in his _____, it may be d_____s for him.

Experienced climbers have no fear because they have learned from ex_____ how to use their eyes as measuring instruments and how to balance the weight of their bodies in various positions.

We are sure about many things which happened in the past. We cannot be so sure about the future. We usually base our plans for the future on what has happened in the past; our past ex_____ce teaches us what to e_____t in the future. But there are no facts in the future, only *possibilities*. We must choose among various p_____ies.

One reason why people like going on vacations is that they can do what they choose. They can choose between different places to visit and various act_____ies. When they are working they have some choice, but they cannot choose many things. Many of their ac_____ies are chosen for them. But when they are on vacation they can choose between safe ac_____ies, like lying on the seashore, and d_____ ac_____s, like climbing high mountains. They can wear conventional clothes or unconventional clothes.

On a vacation each new day brings something new and unexpected. It is not necessary to spend much time on *practical* activities (= activities which are useful for the ordinary purposes of life, such as getting enough food to live on). Climbing mountains is not a pr_____l activity because it is not useful for the ordinary purposes of life. Looking at the beautiful colors of the forests in autumn is not a p_____ a_____y. Reading poetry and listening to music serve no p_____ p_____se and are not p_____ a_____. Practical people are either people whose actions and activities have a practical purpose or those who know how to do ordinary things or plan ordinary activities in the easiest, best, and quickest way.

precise
precisely
precision
devise
suitable
(an) error
reduce

A measurement can be more *precise* or less p_____e. Suppose you are asked to measure the length of a table. If your measurement is correct only to the nearest half inch it is not very pre_____. If it is correct to the nearest tenth of an inch it is more pre_____, and if it is correct to the nearest hundredth of an inch it is very p_____. It does not matter how *precisely* you measure something, you can still *reduce* the *error** (make the error smaller) by making a more p_____ measurement. All measurement is approximate because its accuracy depends on the scale of units used and the *precision* of the measuring instrument. Instruments which measure with great p_____on are called p_____n instruments. P_____ inst_____s are necessary for some purposes but not necessary or *suitable* for others. A thing is s_____ble when it is right for its purpose.

Note: * Error here means the difference between a less approximate result and a more approximate one.

7.2 WORD STUDY

A balance used for weighing drugs (= medicines) or jewels must be a pre_____n instr_____, but this would be quite unsu___ble for weighing coal, sand, or blocks of stone. It would take too much time to weigh such things on a small, carefully made balance, and it might be bad for the balance.

Wooden rulers are u_____able for many scientific purposes, though they are s_____le for ordinary practical purposes. Scientists require very pre____ data, and in modern times s_____l p_____n instruments have been dev____d (like the micrometer) which can give results correct to the nearest thousandth of an inch or even to the nearest millionth.

reduce

Mr. Jones is a grocer. He sells fruit and vegetables. At the end of February he sells apples for 12 cents a pound. At the beginning of March he *reduces* the price and sells his apples for 10 cents a pound.

Mrs. Smith weighs 160 pounds. She wants to r_____e her weight (to make it less); so she begins to eat fruit for breakfast instead of bread and butter, eggs and bacon. At the end of the week her weight is only 150. She has r_____ed her weight by ten pounds.

Mr. Smith is the principal of a school. In the lowest class there are 40 children. The superintendent comes around and says that this class is too large; he asks Mr. Smith to _____ the size of the class. In some cities there is not always enough water for every purpose; so people are asked to _____ the amount of water they use in their gardens.

Note: Reduce usually means make the size or number or amount of something smaller *on purpose.*

Unit VII

7.3 DICTATION EXERCISES AND DICTATION PASSAGES

A   1. The passage *Sentence Patterns* will now be read to you. Write the articles (if any) which precede the following words and the nouns which follow them.

   (a) _____ regular _____

   (b) _____ large _____

   (c) _____ sentence _____

   (d) _____ many _____

   (e) _____ many _____

   (f) _____ certain _____

   (g) _____ longer _____

   2. Number the following words in the order in which you hear them.

features	intervals	purposes

   practice   set   pattern

   numerous   impossible   certain

   3. When you hear the passage again, give the prepositions which *precede* the following phrases.

   (a) _____ a large number   (d) _____ many purposes

   (b) _____ features   (e) _____ many situations

   (c) _____ this kind   (f) _____ short intervals

   4. The passage *Sentence Patterns* will now be given as dictation.

B   1. Listen to the passage *Precision Instruments* and give the correct forms of the following verbs.

   (a)   use   (d)   enable

   (b)   make   (e)   measure

   (c)   divide   (f)   obtain

   2. Number the following words in the order in which you hear them.

   instruments   factories   dimensions

   artificial   continuous   slight   error

   scale   volume   figures

   3. Listen to the passage *Precision Instruments* again, and cross out the word in each of the following pairs which is incorrect.

   (a)   model - modern   (e)   indivisible - invisible
   (b)   instrument - instruments   (f)   finely - fine
   (c)   measurement - measurements (g)   figures - figure
   (d)   unit - units   (h)   result - results

   4. When the teacher tells you to begin, underline the words given below in the passage *Precision Instruments*. This is a **race**.

   separate   precision   approximate   accurately
   distinct   units   indivisible   finely
   modern   engineers   compared to   ordinary

   5. The passage *Precision Instruments* will now be given as dictation.

117

7.3 DICTATION PASSAGES

(a) Sentence Patterns

When a sentence has regular features, features which are found in a large number of sentences, we call this set of features a sentence pattern. Patterns of this kind are numerous, and it is impossible to learn all of them. We should learn those which can be used for many purposes and in many situations. After learning a certain pattern, we should practice writing it, first at short intervals and then at longer intervals.

(b) Precision Instruments

Engineers who work in modern factories use precision instruments when they measure things. It is true that every measurement is approximate, because our measuring units make an artificial division of something which is actually indivisible. Length, volume, and weight are not separate distinct things but continuous dimensions. But precision instruments have a finely divided scale which enables us to measure more accurately. When we measure with these instruments there will be a slight error in our figures, but it will be small compared to the error in results obtained by using ordinary instruments.

UNIT 7

Unit VII
7.4 READING PASSAGES

(a) Approximation

In ordinary life we often use the phrases "exact measurement," "exact copy," "exact repetition," or we make statements like "This table is exactly six feet long." These phrases and statements are useful for some practical purposes. But if "exact" means "without any possibility of error," they cannot describe reality (= what is real). Counting and calculation *can* give exact results. Measurement and imitation *cannot* give exact results.

All measurements are approximate, for two reasons. First, the activity of measuring requires human sight and judgment, which differ in different people. Secondly, no scale of measurement is final. It is always possible to obtain a more precise measurement by using a more precise scale. It does not matter how many divisions you put on a scale; between those divisions it is always possible to mark smaller divisions which will give greater precision to the measurement. It is not practical (= useful for the ordinary purposes of people) to go on dividing units and dividing units forever. There is always the possibility of error in our measurements. But we must *fix the limits* of the possible error, if we wish to be accurate. If we speak carefully about measurement, we will not say "The length of this table is exactly six feet," but "The length is six feet to the nearest quarter of an inch" or "The length is six feet to the nearest tenth of an inch." Both of these statements may be accurate, but the second states a more precise measurement. Accuracy depends on using a scale with standard units suitable for the purpose, using it carefully, and stating the limits of possible error. Precision depends on the size of the units. The smaller the units, the more precise your measurement will be.

(b) Estimates

To make an estimate means to guess the number of things in a group, or guess a measurement of some kind. It sometimes means to make a calculation about the future which is based not on exact data (because no one has exact data about the future) but on past experience. This kind of estimate has some basis, but it generally has to be revised and corrected later.

When you estimate a number, a size, a temperature, or a weight you do not count things one by one or use a measuring instrument. You look at a group of things without counting them and try to get a rough, general idea of their number, or you try to weigh something in your hand instead of on a balance. You feel hot and say "My temperature must be 100 degrees" or you look at a room and say that you estimate its area as 10 x 8 feet.

Now look at the room you are sitting in and make an estimate of its floor area. Take a book in your hand and make an estimate of its weight. Probably your estimate will be inaccurate and unreliable (you will not be able to rely on it) unless you are lucky or you have had practice in guessing lengths and weights.

But in many situations in ordinary life we do not have time to measure things and must rely on estimates. Drivers do not have time to measure the distance between their own car and an approaching car. They must guess it; the guess or estimate will be based on their past experience. Experienced cooks do not trouble to measure the amount of salt they put into the soup, or the sugar they mix with the flour. We often say things like this: "Don't lift that box, it's too heavy," or "The water hasn't boiled yet." We don't put the box on a weighing machine and weigh it before we make the first statement, or put a thermometer into the water before we make the second one.

Suppose a man comes into the house and says "There are two inches of snow on the road." It is unlikely that he has taken a ruler and measured the level of the snow above the surface of the road. His statement is only an estimate, but we rely on it because we believe that it is approximately correct. We put our boots on before we go out into the snow.

For practical purposes in some situations it is safe to make estimates of quantity, but in other situations it is obviously dangerous. If it is your job to weigh drugs or make airplanes, do not rely on guessing but use a precision instrument.

(c) Planning a House

Building a house is an operation which costs quite a lot of money. Suppose you plan to build a house. Your first step will be to find a suitable piece of land. Your choice will depend on various things. You will probably try to find a sunny place, in a pleasant situation, near stores and bus stops, not too far from your friends and the place where you work.

7.4 READING PASSAGES

Next you will find an experienced builder, and together with the builder you will work out a plan. The builder will draw the plan. It will show the number of rooms, their position and size, and other features such as windows, doors, the bath, the stove, and electric outlets. The builder will work out an estimate of the cost of your house, estimating the cost of the wood (or bricks), the glass, and everything else that must be used in building the house. Later on, when the builder starts to build, this estimate must be corrected and revised. The estimate is based on existing prices, but prices may change, the value of money may change, and many other things may happen between the time when the estimate is made and the time when the builder builds the house.

When the builder gives you the estimate, you may wish to change your plan. (You may also wish to change your builder, if the estimate is too high!) You may find that some of the features you wanted at first cost too much, or that you can spend a little more and add something to your original plan. The builder's estimate depends on the plan, but the final plan also depends on the builder's estimate.

(d) Measurement

When a measurement is made by directly comparing an object to be measured with the units on a measuring instrument, we have direct measurement. When we use a ruler to measure the length of a sheet of paper, or a measuring cup to measure the amount of sugar in a bag, we are using an instrument to get direct measurement. When we cannot directly compare a measurement with the object or the dimension to be measured, we must use indirect measurement.

Results which are obtained by using a measuring instrument like a ruler are called *continuous data*. Such measures, giving us continuous data, are never exact.

You can measure your weight in pounds and fractions of a pound. Suppose you have a weighing machine with 1/16 pound as its smallest unit. You weigh yourself and find that your weight is 105 5/16 pounds. Then you go to a different weighing machine which has 1/32 pound as its smallest unit. This scale is more precise, and when you weigh yourself on this machine you find that you weigh 105 9/32 pounds. A scale of still finer precision will probably give a slightly different result. It does not matter how precise your measuring scale is, it is possible, though not always practical, to devise one which will be still more precise. The limits of precision are fixed only by the difficulty experienced by engineers in devising instruments and machines which will record very, very small differences.

(e) Revision Passage: A Conference on International Standards of Measurement

A c_____ce was held in Djakarta on int_____al st_____ds of mea_____t. Ag_____ent was reached on the use of cer_____ sy____ls for un_ts of l___th and w___ht in the m_____c sy____m. The m____ers of the c_____ce also ag____d to set up a committee to cl____ify the u____s of l___th, w___ht, and v_____e used in v_____s countries. It was ag____d to rem__e the central offices of the Inter_____ Standards Association from London to New York. The President st__ed that in the future one c_____ce would be held in the E___t every two years and one in the W__t.

There was disag_____ent on the sy___ls used to ex_____ss dec____l fr_____s. Some me_____rs thought that a period should be used before a dec____l fr_____, but other me____rs wanted a comma to be used. The French sc_____ists thought that the use of a comma in this pos____on was sl____tly more co__on, but others did not acc_pt this. There was also a certain am___nt of disag_____ent on the sy___ls for math_____al op_____ns, esp_____lly for mult_____ion and div_____n. The sy_____s for add_____n and subt_____ion (plus and minus) were acc_____ed by most members.

It was agr__d at the meeting that a list of standardized abbr_____ions for w____hts and mea_____es should be prepared and disc_____ed at the next c_____ce, and that a book should be pub_____ed giving def_____ons of all u____s acc____ed as st_____ds at an off_____al or government l____l.

Sev____l other su_____ts were dis___ssed. One of the su_____ts dis___ssed was the poss_____ity of dev____ng a s___gle inter_____ sy___m of nu_____cal sy____ls. A meeting lim____d to European me_____rs

7.4 READING PASSAGES

dis_____ed the u____s used for three dim_____ns, esp_____lly the u____s for l_____d v___me.

Fin___y, letters rec____ed from absent me____rs were read out, and the conference closed. The f____l speech at the conference was made by the Pr___dent of Indonesia, who thanked the me____rs for vi___ing his c___try.

Unit VII

7.5 VOCABULARY TEST

To test yourself on the vocabulary of this section, fill in the missing letters in the incomplete words.

N____ays rich people often pay a qu___er of a m____on dollars for a famous painting. N_____ly, there are a number of dish_____t people who d___se methods of getting this money without giving anything in r_____n for it. The most ob_____s way of doing this is to s___l a picture, but most pictures of great v___e are locked up and looked after c___fully; so it is very un_____ly that a theft will s_____d. Though s_____al paintings are st___n every year, in most s_____ons theft is not a pr_____al po_____ty. It is also difficult to find a s_____ble buyer for a st___n picture.

Another way of o_____ing the money dish_____ly is to paint an im_____on or copy of a famous painting or to i_____te the m_____ds of painting used by a famous painter so that people will believe that a ce_____n picture is his work when a_____ly it is not. The pr_____on of i_____ons of this kind needs sp___al ab_____y and a lot of p_____ce. In m_____n times, however, it has become quite c____on and is almost a special in_____y.

It is d_____rous for a man who sells a lot of pictures to r__y co_____tely on his judgment about the or___n of a painting. An inex_____ced man will often g___s wrong. And even men who have years of ex_____ce in judging paintings and naming the artists are sometimes guilty of an e___r of judgment.

The only way to r___ce the number of i_____ns on the market is to o_____n and p____sh pr___se sc_____ic d__a about each picture that is going to be sold. Famous painters ex____ss themselves partly through the re_____on of very small f_____res of paintwork that are almost im_____ble to i_____te. Sc_____ic in_____ts e___le us to di___ver whether a painting has these f_____res or not. There are other d__a which are equ___y im_____t. Paint which was made in a c_____n country at a c_____ time is made of a mixture of ch___cal su_____ces which can be pr_____ly de_____ed and which cannot be ob_____ed in the same mixture by a modern painter. Even the age of the paint used can be dis_____ed by sc_____ic m_____ds.

Unit VIII

8.1 VOCABULARY

These are the words you will practice in this unit:

VERBS

cost		(+ noun of price)
exchange	(ex·change')	(+ plural noun)
exchange		(+ noun + for + noun)
pay for		(+ noun)
purify	(pu'ri·fy)	(+ noun)
receive	(re·ceive')	(+ noun)
supply	(sup·ply')	(+ noun)
supply		(+ noun + to + noun)
supply		(+ noun + with + noun)
value	(val'ue)	

NOUNS

(the) average	(av'er·age)	mathematics	(math·e·mat'ics)
a customer	(cus'tom·er)	oxygen	(ox'y·gen)
(a) demand (for)	(de·mand')	a physicist	(phys'i·cist)
a diamond	(di'amond)	physics	(phys'ics)
a district	(dis'trict)	plenty (of)	(plen'ty)
economics	(e·co·nom'ics)	research	(re·search')
an economist	(e·con'o·mist)	scarcity	(scar'ci·ty)
an engineer	(en·gi·neer')	a supply	(sup·ply')
engineering	(en·gi·neer'ing)	(a) training	(train'ing)
goods		vegetables	(veg'e·ta·ble)
a mathematician	(math·e·ma·ti'cian)		

ADJECTIVES

average	(av'er·age)
cheap	
expensive	(ex·pen'sive)
insufficient	(in·suf·fi'cient)
limited	(lim'it·ed)
local	(lo'cal)
monetary	(mon'e·tar·y)
original	(o·rig'i·nal)
physical	(phys'i·cal)
plentiful	(plen'ti·ful)
research (worker)	(re·search')
scarce	
scientific	(sci·en·tif'ic)
situated (in, on, at, etc.)	(sit'u·at·ed)
trained	
untrained	(un·trained')
valuable	(val'u·a·ble)
worth	

ADVERB

artificially	(ar·ti·fi'cial·ly)

Unit VIII

8.2 WORD STUDY

INSTRUCTIONS: Study the following words and the uses of them:

purify

A substance is *purified* when it is made pure. In nature, most substances are not pure. They must be artificially p_____ed. Distilled water is p_____d by the method of distillation.

Note: The ending "-ify" usually means "to make," e.g., "magnify" = to make large, "simplify" = to make simple, "solidify" = to make or become solid, "unify" = to unite or make into a unity.

artificially

= by the work of people, not by nature

If we want pure oxygen, we must buy oxygen that has been p_____d *artificially*. He devised a cheap method of producing the substance a_____lly. At present, because of the government's action, prices are a_____lly low.

receive

When you *receive* a gift, a letter, or money from someone, you get it from that person, often by mail or from a distance. You r_____ve a letter; this means that it has been sent, it arrives, and comes into your hands.

Examples: The letter was sent but I did not r_____e it. Yesterday he r_____d a check for $200. Did you r_____ the book I sent you last week? He has not yet r_____d permission from the university to continue his studies.

original

= (a) the first, the earliest
  (b) not imitated but produced by a person's own brains or imagination

Examples: (a) The original building (the building which first stood in this place) was made of wood. His o_____l purpose was to study economics in an American university.

(b) He has no o_____ ideas. This method of calculating is not _____; it was discovered by Newton. He never does anything _____; he always im_____s other people.

local

= (a) belonging to a certain district or a limited area
  (b) belonging to one's own district

Examples: (a) The money for our schools comes from the central government, not from the l_____ government. When we go to another country, we should learn something about the l_____ customs.

(b) He generally goes to the l_____ movie. Why don't you visit a _____ doctor? We can't buy rice in the _____ stores, but you can get some in the city.

oxygen

Oxygen is a gas which is necessary for life and which exists in large quantities in the atmosphere.

Living things breathe o_____ and depend on it for their life. There is enough o_____ in the air at low levels for us to breathe easily, but at greater heights there is less air pressure and therefore less _____. Airplanes and mountain climbers carry supplies of oxygen which have been a_____lly p_____ed.

a district

A district is a part of a town or a country. A district can be a political unit. Most cities and large towns are divided into d_____s. London, for example, is divided into postal d_____s, represented by abbreviations such as N., N.E., S.W. (What do you think these abbreviations represent?) Postal d_____s are not always the same as local government d_____s.

a diamond

A diamond is a jewel that has great value because it is so scarce. Natural d_____s are very valuable. D_____s can be produced art_____lly; d_____s produced in this way are less v_____le than natural d_____s, but they are also v_____ because they are difficult to produce. D_____s can be used for cutting glass and for certain other industrial operations. Some rich women like to wear them.

8.2 WORD STUDY

plenty of   = a lot of, more than enough

Note: In your own writing it is safer to use **a lot of**, which can be used more often than **plenty of**.

Examples: Please stay and have tea with us; we have *plenty of* food. Our country has p_____y of meat and does not have to buy it from other countries. The movie doesn't start till eight; so you have p_____y of time to finish your essay. These exercises are long and will give you p_____ of practice. We have p_____ of vegetables already; so please don't buy any more.

situated   *Note:* You should understand this word, but **do not** use it yourself. Use only the preposition.

This town is *situated* in a valley near the sea. The church is s_____ed on the hillside, about a mile from the town.

New York City is situated on the Hudson River where it enters the Atlantic Ocean. Washington, D.C., is situated on the Potomac River.

London is s_____d on the River Thames. Portsmouth is situated on the coast about 60 miles southwest of London. Montreal is s_____d on the St. Lawrence River.

goods   = things made or produced to be sold. Used in the plural form only.

Examples: Japanese *goods* can be bought in most Asian countries. This store sells only leather g____s. Most of the g_____ we produce are sent overseas. If we reduce the price of our g_____ other stores will do the same.

cost   Past tense **cost**. No **is + -ed** form.

When you buy a thing, it *costs* a certain amount of money (i.e., the price of the thing).

Examples: How much did your car cost? It c_____ $5000. It c_____s $50 to fly from Boston to New York City. Her daughter's wedding c____ more than she expected; so she did not have a vacation that year.

Exercise: Complete the following sentences by adding the word **cost** (in its correct form and in the right place in the sentence). Rewrite each sentence.

1.   Last week potatoes ten cents a pound.

    _____.

2.   How much does this instrument?

    _____?

3.   How much will it you to go by air?

    _____?

4.   Nowadays a package of cigarettes often more than a dollar.

    _____.

5.   It will not much to have your watch repaired.

    _____.

6.   Electricity probably more than it did last year.

    _____.

7.   A taxi (ride) too much money.

    _____.

125

8.2 WORD STUDY

8.   In 1941 a pound of rice only fifteen cents.

_____.

9.   When I was young, most things less than they do now.

_____.

10.   It will you less than you thought.

_____.

exchange   When two people (or countries, etc.) *exchange* things, they give something to each other and get something else in its place. When a man exchanges one thing **for** another, he gives the first thing and gets the second in its place (instead of the thing he gave).

Examples: The two countries ex_____ed prisoners. He ex_____ed the red shirt for a blue one.

Exercise: Use the verb **exchange** in its correct form to complete the following sentences. Rewrite each sentence in the space provided.

1.   When two countries trade with each other, they goods.

_____.

2.   He went back to the shop and his wooden ruler for a metal one.

_____.

3.   Sometimes universities in different countries teachers.

_____.

4.   Two students sitting in the front row places.

_____.

5.   The economists will meet and ideas.

_____.

6.   Buying means money for things.

_____.

7.   He his old car for a new one.

_____.

8.   The students their notebooks and corrected each other's work.

_____.

_____.

for (in exchange)   One thing can be exchanged *for* another; things can be exchanged for money (we pay money for them); work can be exchanged for money (we work or do work for money); money can be exchanged for things or for work (we buy things for money or we buy people's work for money).

When there is an exchange, the preposition "for" is used before the thing (or money, or work) which is given or received in exchange.

Exercise: Complete the following sentences, using **for** and naming the thing or price given in exchange.

1.   He bought this house _____.

2.   He sold his house _____.

3.   I want to exchange my first-class ticket ____ a _____.

8.2 WORD STUDY

4. She says she will type the exercises ___ _____ _____ a page.

5. He will pay you a dollar an hour ___ __ing his housework.

6. She says she will not work ___ less than _____ _____ a day.

7. He gave the man fifty cents ___ _____ing his luggage.

8. He works as a gardener ___ _____ a week.

9. In Thailand you can employ a servant ___ _____ _____ a month.

10. He paid $1,000 ___ _____ .

a training
an engineer
engineering
mathematics
a mathematician
economics
an economist
physics
a physicist
research

Study these definitions and then do the exercise which follows.

A course of *training* is a course of teaching, practical work, etc., which brings a person to a certain standard in a subject, a game, or a special activity.

An engineer is a person who makes machines or who makes machines work or who plans the building of bridges, roads, etc. He is a man with a training in *engineering*.

Engineering is the subject studied by engineers, or the work that they do.

Mathematics is the science of number, measurement, and calculation or the work done by people when they calculate.

A mathematician is a person with a training in mathematics.

Economics is the study or science of economic relations.

An economist is a person with a training in economics.

Physics is a group of sciences or a system of laws relating to heat, light, sound, electricity, movement, and all forms of energy.

A physicist is a person who has much knowledge of physics.

Research (uncountable noun) is the work done by a trained person to find out new facts about a subject.

Note: Mathematics, economics, and physics are **uncountable** nouns ending in -s.

Exercise: Use **one** of the words in the list above to complete each of the following sentences. Use the word **in its correct form** and write it in the right place. Rewrite each sentence. Be **very careful** to spell the words correctly.

1. Most cannot understand the present rise in the cost of living.

_____

_____ .

2. The who made this bridge has become famous.

_____ .

3. He never studied at school so he can neither add nor subtract.

_____

_____ .

4. Your study of should teach you that a higher level of production cannot be reached until industry is more highly developed.

_____

_____ .

8.2 WORD STUDY

5.   When you study you will study the laws of heat and electricity.

_____

_____.

6.   To develop industry in our country we must build more factories and train more.

_____

_____.

7.   The country cannot solve its economic problems without the help of trained.

_____

_____.

8.   To understand about radio and television you must learn something about the laws of electricity which form part of.

_____

_____.

9.   Nowadays every politician should have a in economics.

_____

_____.

10.   Sometimes use calculating machines to help them to solve problems.

_____

_____.

11.   Mathematics and physics usually form part of a course in.

_____

_____.

12.   Isaac Newton was both a and a mathematician.

_____.

13.   He does in chemistry at Columbia University.

_____.

14.   A knowledge of is necessary for a person who wants to do research into the trade relations between underdeveloped countries.

_____

_____.

limited   (a)   A quantity or a supply of something is _limited_ when it is not very large and when it cannot be made larger.

(b)   A limited purpose, plan, problem, etc. , is one which does not go beyond a certain limit, which is within certain stated or defined limits.

8.2 WORD STUDY

Exercise: In each of the sentences in this exercise, use **limited** in one of the blank spaces and **one** of the words given here in the other blank spaces.

supplies	amount	speed	knowledge
quantity	agreement	height	number
capacity	value	estimate	time
purposes	space	areas	interest
	trade	weight	

1. At present _____ of coal are _____ but we may receive more next month.

2. He has only a _____ _____ of physics.

3. Fortunately the _____ where the disease exists are still _____ .

4. This _____ is based on a very _____ number of facts.

5. The actual _____ of students admitted is _____ by the size of the classrooms.

6. The work must be finished in a _____ _____ .

7. America and Russia have reached a _____ _____ on the question of supplies of grain to Israel and Egypt.

8. It is difficult to build playgrounds in large cities because _____ is so _____ .

9. He has only a _____ _____ in this subject.

10. _____ between countries is _____ by the level of production.

11. Universities have an entrance examination because their _____ is _____ .

12. The _____ of industrialization in an underdeveloped country is _____ by the supply of trained workers.

13. The room is so small that it can only be used for a _____ number of _____ .

14. The _____ that passengers are allowed to carry is _____ .

15. The _____ of money we can spend abroad is _____ by law.

16. The _____ at which an airplane can travel is partly _____ by its supplies of oxygen.

17. The _____ of food a man can eat is _____ by the capacity of his stomach.

18. I am afraid these books are of very _____ _____ .

the average
average

A _____ B   C _____ D   E _____ F

Here are three lines. Measure them. What is the length of AB? What is the length of CD? What is the length of EF?

What is the *average* length of these three lines?

Here are five numbers: 6, 8, 21, 4, 11.
What is the average of these numbers?

It is _____ .

When we want to find the a_____e of several measurements or the a_____e of several numbers, what must we do?

We must a___ the numbers or the measurements and find the t___l; then we must di_____ this t_____ by the number of measurements or of numbers which we have a___ed. This will give us ____

_____ .

An average man likes a quiet home, good health, good friends, and a peaceful life. Who is this a_____ge man? Actually he does not exist. He is an imaginary man. We think of him as an ordinary man whose ways, ideas, feelings, and standards are like those of most people. He is neither very stupid nor very clever. He is n_____r very rich n__ very _____. He is n_____ very hard-working ___ very

8.2 WORD STUDY

_____. He is n_____ very friendly ____ very unf_____y. He is n_____ tall ____ sh____. He is _____ fat ____ ____. His weight is neither above average nor below average. It is a_____e. If he happens to be an engineer, he is _____ a good engineer ____ a bad one. He is an _____ engineer. If you put him in a group of people and make comparisons of any kind, he will always be somewhere in the middle. The average man (or woman) is only an idea in our minds. He (or she) does not actually exist.

When we want to find (or think about) the average, we c_____re things of the same kind. When we compare things we have a st_____rd in mind. What we say d____nds on the standard we choose. Some people may say that the average man or woman is stupid. If they say this, it means that their standard is not based on ordinary men and women but on the better brains in their society. Many people will say that the average village in India is hot, or that the average village in England is clean. When they say these things, it shows that their standards (of heat or of cleanliness) are not based only on Indian villages or on English villages.

plenty of
plentiful
scarce
scarcity
value
valuable
be worth
expensive
pay for

This year the farmers have grown a lot of rice. There is a lot of rice in the country, more than enough for people's needs. There is *plenty of* rice. Rice is *plentiful*.

Sometimes the farmers do not grow enough rice for everybody. Then rice is not pl_____ul. If they grow very little rice, it is difficult to buy rice or obtain it. Rice is *scarce*. Food is sc_____ when there is not much of it, when it is grown or produced only in small qu_____ies.

Sometimes a certain kind of food becomes sc____ because only a little of it is pr____ced or gr__n; it is pr_____ed or gr__n only in small qu_____ies. The weather may be a cause of this. Suppose that one year the weather is not suitable for apples. It is a bad year for apples. Then apples will become sc_____. Next year the weather may change and apples will be pl_____l again. There will be pl____y of apples on the trees and in the stores.

But some things are always sc____e, because nature is not rich in these things. Gold, for example, is a s_____ metal. Diamonds are always s_____. They are not pl_____l at any time. The *scarcity* of natural diamonds does not depend on the weather or on the ease or difficulty we may have in removing diamonds from the earth. Their s_____ty is simply a fact about the world we live in; the earth does not contain many d_____ds.

When natural things or substances are sc_____, they usually have great *value*. They are *valuable*. They are va_____le because a small number of these sc_____ things or a small quantity of these sc_____ sub_____ces can be exchanged for a large number of other things (which are not so scarce) or a large quantity of other substances (which are not so scarce).

They are v_____le because many people want them but only a few people can get them. Some people value things which are difficult to obtain more than things which are easy to obtain. We v____e diamonds more than we v____ coal. Many people v____e difficult activities like climbing mountains or doing higher mathematics more than they v_____ easy activities like walking or reading light novels.

Why do we value things, or substances, or activities? We v_____ them because they are *worth* something. What does this mean? When a thing is w__th something, this means that we want it enough to give something else in exchange for it. When an activity is w____ something, this means that we are ready to give a lot of time to it, to exchange other activities (which also take time) for it. Everything we v____ must be *paid for* or has been paid for in work, in energy, in training, in money, or in some part of our lives. A thing, or an activity, or the result of an activity is w__th the time, energy, work, or the other things that we are ready to give in exchange for it.

Diamonds are valuable, and they are usually very *expensive*. Not everything which is v_____le is also ex_____ve. Suppose your teacher says "This essay contains some valuable ideas." He does not mean that he is ready to pay you $1,000 or even $100 for your ideas, or that anyone will pay you a lot of money for them. A thing is expensive when it costs a lot of money, when its price is high. When a teacher says that your ideas are valuable, he means that they are worth something—not money but something else. He means that they are worth studying (which takes time), they are worth thinking about (which takes time), or perhaps that they are worth developing, which means that you should spend some more time and brain power working them out.

8.2 WORD STUDY

If a man says "I found my experience as a teacher in a primary school very valuable," he does not mean that he was paid a lot for this. He means that his experience is w_____ something to him; he would not like to exchange it for other ex_____nces.

valuable
expensive
cheap
a customer
physical

When we say that a thing is *valuable*, we mean that it has value, it is w__th something, that people will be ready to give money, work, or other things for it. When we say that a *physical* thing (an object which can be touched and seen) is valuable, we usually mean that people will be ready to give a lot of money for it. Money **represents** value because it can buy almost anything; it can be exchanged for most kinds of work. (But, as we know, there are some things, activities, and ideas which cannot be bought for money.)

When we say that a physical thing like a picture, a house, or a carpet is v_____le, we us___lly mean that people will be ready to give _ ___ __ money for it. The v_____ of a car or a house is the money that can be obtained for it when everyone knows what it is and when a careful estimate has been made of what it is worth.

It is obvious that the value of a physical thing does not always stay the same, because prices of the same thing (for example, a pound of apples) may differ from one store to another. When the price of a thing is higher than it ought to be, we say that it is *expensive*, and when it is lower than it ought to be, we say that it is *cheap*. Read the following dialogue:

Mr. A. Yesterday I was very lucky. I bought a valuable picture, probably worth about $1,000.
Mr. B. Was it expensive? What was its price?
Mr. A. No, as I told you, I was lucky. It was not at all ex_____ve. It was very ch__p. I bought it for only $20.
Mr. B. Didn't the dealer know its value?
Mr. A. No, he didn't know that it was so v_____ble. That's why I bought it so cheaply.

The **price** of a thing is the money that is asked for, paid, and received for that thing **at a given time**. It is obvious that the price of a thing may be more or less than its value. If the price is too high, the thing is e_____ve. If it is lower than the real value, the thing is ch___. When *a customer* (a buyer) goes into a store to buy something, he will not buy it if he thinks it is ex_____ve. Suppose he wants to buy a certain kind of carpet. He will compare the prices in different stores. Stores which sell things cheaply generally have more c_____ers than stores which sell things at high prices.

a supply
supply
a customer
scarce
scarcity
vegetables
insufficient

Mrs. Brown lives in Mayfield. The local grocer *supplies* her **with** flour, eggs, tea, sugar, and other groceries. The local fruit and vegetable store s_____s her ____ apples, oranges, tomatoes, potatoes, and other fruit and *vegetables*. The butcher's shop s_____s her ____ meat. All the food she needs can be obtained from these stores. These stores s_____y her with food. She is a c_____er at these stores.

Sometimes, when tomatoes are *scarce*, the fruit and vegetable store cannot s_____y them. When eggs are s_____e, the grocer cannot su____y them to everybody. When there is a *scarcity* of long grained rice, the grocer cannot s_____ it, or can only s_____y it in limited quantities.

When there is a good s_____y of rice, the grocer can s_____y it to everyone. When there is not enough for everyone, he may s_____y it only to his old c_____mers.

When supplies are *insufficient* (= not enough), grain becomes sc___cer and its value rises. Its price r____ too; it becomes more ex_____ve. When there are plentiful s_____s of gr__n, the p____ of gr__n falls. It becomes ch__per.

scientific
research
research
trained
untrained
a training

Tom Fielding is a scientist. He has had a sc_____c education. He has had *a training* in sc_____c methods. He reads sc_____c books. He is interested in s_____ problems. He works in a chemistry laboratory, and uses s_____ methods to discover new facts: in other words, he does *research*. He is a *research* worker. He d___ r_____ **into** changes in certain substances produced by changes in temperature.

Tom is a *trained* research worker. Nowadays t_____d r_____ch workers are scarce. The s__ply of t_____ed workers is insufficient (= not enough) for the needs of science and industry; so t_____ed

8.2 WORD STUDY

r_____ch workers are valuable and ex_____ve. Their work and their abilities are w__th a lot of money.

Tom's brother Jack is not a scientist. He has had no sc_____ training. He is a cook in a big hotel. He has had no special training as a cook. He is *untrained*. But Jack is not a bad cook; he does not make many mistakes. Though he is unt_____ed, he is not inexperienced. He has worked in several hotels and has learned a lot from his ex_____ce.

Their sister Mary is an economist. She has had (a) training in ec_____ics. She teaches in the local university (where Tom works) and d___ r_____ch into trade relations between countries in southeast Asia. Last year she published a book on this subject. Next month she is going to Japan to continue her r_____, and last week there was a paragraph about her in the local newspaper. She will work at a r_____ institute situated north of Tokyo.

increase
an increase
decrease
a decrease

A number of things (or people) *increases* when the number becomes greater. The size of a thing in_____s when its size becomes greater. We in_____se a number when we add to it or make it greater. We i_____ the size of a thing when we make it greater. A driver in_____s his speed when he drives more quickly. Intensity i_____s when it becomes greater. A number of things (or people) *decreases* when the number becomes smaller. The size of a thing d_____s when its size becomes smaller. We d_____e a number when we subtract from it or make it smaller. We d_____ the size of a thing when we make it smaller. When a driver drives more slowly he reduces or d_____s his speed. Intensity d_____s when it becomes less.

When a number becomes larger there is an in_____e in that number. When a thing becomes larger there is an in_____e in its size. When a number becomes smaller there is a d_____ in that number. When a thing becomes smaller there is a d_____ in its size.

Examples: Supplies of potatoes will soon in_____e. The value of land has i_____ed in the last few years. You have in_____ed your kn_____dge of human nature. We decided to in_____e the membership (i.e., the number of members) of the club. If you think your pay is insufficient, why don't you ask for an in_____? There has been an in_____ in the demand for wool.

The numbers of science students have rapidly d_____ed. The area of countryside open to the public is d_____ing. A d_____se in the traffic on the roads is very unlikely. He is trying to d_____ his weight. There has been an in_____ in office floor space and a d_____se in the amount of space used for private housing. This medicine will d_____ the pain.

Unit VIII

8.3 DICTATION EXERCISES AND DICTATION PASSAGES

A   1. The passage *The Scarcity of Diamonds* will now be read to you. When you hear the following adjectives, write the articles (if any) which precede them and the nouns which follow them.

(a) _____ any natural _____

(b) _____ special _____

(c) _____ common _____

(d) _____ large _____

(e) _____ million _____

(f) _____ large _____

2. Number the following words in the order in which you hear them.

experience	artificially	diamonds	scarce
devised	required	succeeded	
knowledge	valuable	worth	

3. Listen to the passage *The Scarcity of Diamonds* once more, and write the **uncountable** nouns that you hear. There are only three.

4. When you are asked to do so, underline the following words in the dictation passage *The Scarcity of Diamonds*. This is a race.

natural	operations	training	devised
common	diamonds	substance	likely
special	economics	a quarter	producing

5. The passage *The Scarcity of Diamonds* will now be given as dictation.

B   1. The dictation passage *Heavy Industry and Industrialization* will now be read to you at an ordinary reading speed. Number the following words in the order in which you hear them in the passage.

development	industrial	industrialization	
objects	Western	supplies	
industrialists	supplied	developed	

2. When you are asked to do so, underline the following words in the dictation passage *Heavy Industry and Industrialization*. This is a race.

expensive	regularly	based on
local	highly	rely on
economic	usually	depends on
likely	conveniently	level

3. Listen to the passage again. In the following pairs, cross out the word which is incorrect (following the order of the passage).

(a) country - countries   (h) Nigeria - a given area
(b) distinction - distinctions   (i) supply - supplies
(c) goods - good   (j) operations - operation
(d) lighter - light   (k) situation - situated
(e) smaller - small   (l) convenient - conveniently
(f) growth - grow   (m) customer - customers
(g) label - level   (n) regularly - regular

8.3 DICTATION EXERCISES AND DICTATION PASSAGES

4. The first paragraph of the passage *Heavy Industry and Industrialization* will be read to you again two or three times at intervals of about five minutes. After hearing it, fill in the gaps in the framework given to you below. Work in pairs. The words required to complete the paragraph are given below it, but not in the order in which you must use them.

In _____ _____ _____ , heavy _____ _____

_____ developed. The _____ between _____ _____

and _____ _____ is _____ on _____ _____ _____ ___ _____

_____ produced. Heavy _____ _____ _____ ,

while _____ _____ uses _____ to _____ _____

_____ _____ required _____ _____ purposes _____ _____

_____ _____ offices.

the	countries	heavy	based
the	distinction	light	is
the	goods	light	produce
of	homes	many	produces
for	industry	our	highly
in	industry	smaller	
and	industry	various	
	industry	Western	
	industry		
	machines		
	machines		
	nature		
	objects		

5. The passage *Heavy Industry and Industrialization* will now be given to you as dictation.

8.3   DICTATION PASSAGES

(a)   The Scarcity of Diamonds

We know from experience that any natural substance which is scarce is likely to be valuable. No special training in economics is required in order to learn this. It is common knowledge, for example, that a large diamond may be worth as much as a quarter of a million dollars. Operations have been devised for making diamonds artificially, but so far no one has succeeded in producing them in large quantities.

(b)   Heavy Industry and Industrialization

In many Western countries heavy industry is highly developed. The distinction between heavy industry and light industry is based on the nature of the goods produced. Heavy industry produces machines, while light industry uses machines to produce the smaller objects required for various purposes in our homes and offices.

The growth of industry in a country depends on the general level of economic and industrial development. In its beginnings industrialization is likely to be expensive. To reduce costs, industrialists in a given area usually rely on local supplies of coal or electric power for their operations. Factories are usually situated in places which can be conveniently reached by road or railroad, so that customers can be supplied regularly.

Unit VIII
8.4 READING PASSAGES

(a) Value and Price

1. Units of money are units of measurement. Like units of weight or length, money units are conventional; they are fixed by people, not by nature; they differ in different countries.

2. But when we measure with money, what do we measure? A ruler marked in inches can measure a table or a wall. A dollar is also divided into smaller parts, called cents. What do we measure with a dollar? What do we compare with it?

3. It is true that two kilograms of salt cost more than one kilogram of salt. But money does not measure weight; if it measured weight, one kilogram of tea would cost the same as one kilogram of salt. But obviously the tea costs more; and a kilogram of gold costs much more. Then what does money measure?

4. Money measures different things. It measures flour, milk, and vegetables. It measures houses, dresses, fountain pens, and university courses. It measures, in fact, everything that is bought and sold in the world.

5. If you look through the price list of a big store, you can see and compare the prices of various things. But what do you compare? A diamond ring is much smaller than an egg, but its price is much greater. A good egg may cost six cents, but a good diamond may cost 6,000 dollars or more. What does money measure?

6. Money measures *value*. The price of a thing measures its value. A diamond is more valuable than an egg; a doctor's time is generally more valuable than an ordinary gardener's time; an hour and a half of a gardener's time may have the same value as a few dozen eggs. This makes value very difficult to understand. It is not as easy to compare values as it is to compare weights, lengths, and temperatures.

7. An egg has some value, but a real diamond has much more. Why? The air around us has no monetary value. Though we cannot live without it, it cannot be bought or sold. Air is not a scarce substance. It covers every part of the earth's surface; so there is plenty of it. There is also plenty of oxygen all around us, because air has a lot of oxygen in it. But oxygen is not free like the air. If we want pure oxygen we must buy it, and in fact it is bought by hospitals, mountain climbers, space travelers, and others.

8. Are there many diamonds in the world, or only a few? There are not very many. The quantity of diamonds in the world is quite limited. Diamonds are scarce. Is there a lot of gold in the world or only a little? There is only a little. Gold is not found in very large quantities like coal or wood. Gold is *scarce*. Is there a lot of salt in the world or only a little? In many parts of the world salt is found in l___e qu_____ies. There is p____y of salt in the world. Salt is not sc___e. It is pl_____l. Which costs more money (per gram), gold or salt? The answer to this question is obvious. Gold costs more. Why does it cost more? Because it is sc___e.

9. In general, which has more value, a scarce thing or a plentiful thing? A sc__ce thing has more value. So scarcity is part of the meaning of value.

10. Which has more value, a very good picture (an original picture, not a copy) or a bad picture? A very good picture is more valuable, because there are not many good pictures in the world. The number of good pictures in the world is limited. We sometimes read in the newspapers that a picture has been sold for 20,000 or even 100,000 dollars.

11. Which has more value, a doctor's time or an untrained worker's time? A doctor's time is more valuable, because doctors are scarcer than untrained workers.

12. Money is a measure of value. You will remember that when we measure length, we use a ruler which itself has length. When we measure weights, we use weights on a balance, or the effect of weight on a spring balance.

13. In the same way, if money is a measure of value, and if scarcity is part of the meaning of value, we must use something which is scarce itself as money. If money is to be a useful measure of value, it must itself be a scarce thing. This is obviously true, isn't it? If money were plentiful, if governments did not limit the amount of money in a country, if people could make as much money as they liked and use it, what would the result be? If this happened, could money be a measure of value? No, it could not, because it would have very little value itself, and its value could not be fixed.

8.4 READING PASSAGES

14. Originally, money was made of scarce, valuable metals like gold and silver. Because it was scarce and could easily be shaped into coins (small pieces of money), gold was originally chosen as the standard of value. It is still used as a standard. But most countries nowadays also use paper money, which is made by governments. Only a limited amount of paper money is made, but sometimes governments make too much and then the value of this money falls.

15. Scarcity is part of the meaning of value, but it is not the whole meaning. There is plenty of oxygen in the air, but we have to pay for purified oxygen. There is plenty of salt in the sea, but we have to pay for the salt we use. If we live near the sea and we require a small quantity of sand, we can get it without paying anything, but if we want a large quantity of sand for any purpose, we must pay for it. If we live in a district where there is no sand, we may have to pay a higher price.

16. There is plenty of oxygen in the air, but it is not easy to obtain. Not everybody knows how to get it out of the air. To purify oxygen requires time and work, special machines and instruments, trained engineers and scientific knowledge. Sand is less difficult to obtain, but it cannot be moved in large quantities without hard work and a car or a truck or a train. A thing may be difficult to get because it is far away, or because hard work is required to move it, or because special training is required to produce it in its pure form. Beautiful pictures are valuable not only because they are scarce but because they are difficult for ordinary people to paint. I cannot sit down and paint a beautiful picture for myself, just as I cannot get salt to eat or even wood to make a table without going to a store.

17. Money measures the value of a thing. It measures the scarcity of that thing, the research and work that goes into making it, the difficulty of that work or research, the training required by the people who do it. It also measures work itself, and the scarcity of different kinds of workers. When engineers are scarce, they will be highly paid, but they are generally paid well, because nobody can become an engineer without a long training.

18. The price of a thing, which is a fixed amount of money, is a measure of its value. It is not always an accurate measure of value. Sometimes expensive things are not very valuable and sometimes valuable things are not very expensive. People who buy and sell do not always know how to measure value accurately. People who sell generally try to get as much money as possible, and people who buy generally try to give as little as possible. The monetary value of a thing is the money that can be obtained for it *in general*, when everyone knows what it is and when a careful estimate has been made of what the thing is worth. But sometimes sellers do not know the real value of what they sell; sometimes buyers do not know the real value of what they buy. Sometimes traders find ways of raising prices *artificially*, for example, by joining together and forming a group to limit the quantity of a thing so that it becomes scarce.

19. The value of things which are bought and sold also depends on what the economists call "demand." When you go out shopping you may sometimes notice a store window full of dresses that nobody wants to buy, or another store window full of good dresses or coats at greatly reduced prices. When only a few people want to buy things of a certain kind, we say that there is not much *demand* for things of this kind. When dresses are no longer in fashion, there is not much d_____d for them and their v___e falls. Nowadays there is not much d_____d for furniture which was made twenty or thirty years ago, while there is a greater d_____d for furniture made a hundred years ago. Furniture which is a hundred years old is therefore more v_____e than furniture only twenty years old.

20. We have now seen that the monetary value of a thing depends on three factors*: its scarcity (natural or artificial), the work or training required to produce it, and the demand which exists for things of that kind.

21. In this passage we have talked about monetary value, or the value of money and of the things which money can buy. This is not the only meaning of "value," but it is the one which is important to economists. There is another meaning which is important to mathematicians. The value of x or y in mathematics, or the value of a symbol, is the number or quantity which the symbol represents.

---

* a factor = a fact (usually a *general* fact) which helps to produce a certain result, or a certain kind of result.

8.4 READING PASSAGES

(b)   Economics

During the nineteenth century England became an industrial country. Many factories were built, and large quantities of cheap goods were produced. At first people thought that this development would result in a better life for everybody. They believed that the new factories could supply everybody's needs and that most English people would get rich. But this did not happen. A few people became richer, but many people became poorer; even rich industrialists sometimes lost their money when their factories produced goods which people did not want or could not buy. The value of goods and even the value of money itself rose and fell in a way that was difficult to understand.

To study these new problems and try to solve them a new science arose—the science of economics. Earlier thinkers had noticed that there was something wrong with their country's economic life. They wished for a better society, and to express their wishes they wrote books describing perfect societies or "utopias." The systems of society which they described in these books were not based on historical facts or even on historical possibilities. They were imaginary social systems, expressing only the writers' wishes and feelings. An idea which exists only in a person's head, which does not represent anything that actually exists, cannot be expected to change a historical situation.

In the nineteenth century, however, a group of thinkers began to develop new methods of studying the economic life of society. Instead of looking into the future and dreaming of utopias, these thinkers (whom we now call "economists") turned their attention to existing societies and actual economic relations. They believed that by looking at the facts it would be possible to discover the laws governing social and economic situations and changes, just as Sir Isaac Newton had discovered the laws governing the movements of the earth, the sun, and other physical bodies in space. Two economists of that time whose ideas were original and who left their mark on later thought and action were an Englishman called Adam Smith and a German called Karl Marx.

(c)   Industrialization

At the beginning of the Industrial Revolution* (about 1800 A.D.) England led the world in trade. British merchants (traders) were rich and powerful. They supplied the money to set up factories because they wanted to produce goods which they could sell all over the world.

In Russia industrialization came later. At the beginning of the twentieth century only a few Russians lived in towns or worked in industry. Most people worked on the land. After the 1917 Communist Revolution, the industrial workers in the few industries which then existed formed a government and became the masters of their own factories. Their government set up new industries and planned what the farms and factories should produce for the next five years, to meet the country's needs. This was called the First Five-Year Plan, and other plans followed it.

Many countries are still underdeveloped, and this means that they are not yet industrialized, or only partly industrialized. Most of them are in Asia, Africa, and Latin America, and these are the poorest parts of the world.

Every country nowadays wants to industrialize itself in order to increase its wealth. For this purpose factories must be built, workers must be trained, and power must be supplied. To pay for all this, an underdeveloped country must have something to trade with, like oil or gold or grain. It must also develop better methods of working on the land.

Nigeria is an example of an underdeveloped country which has plans for expansion. The Nigerian government has a plan for industrialization. Oil has been discovered in certain districts in Nigeria but refined (= purified) oil is expensive to produce. For this, special operations are necessary which require trained engineers. The Nigerian government hopes to meet the cost by obtaining help from other, more highly developed countries.

Oil and electricity can supply Nigerian industry with power to make machines and other steel goods. Nigerian oil can also be sold to other countries. At present Nigeria obtains most of its money by selling cocoa. But cocoa is unreliable (= cannot be relied on) because its price keeps changing. Nigeria is not the only country which produces cocoa, and supplies of cocoa are not controlled in relation to the existing demand. Nigeria would be in a safer position if it could sell a variety of goods instead of only one kind.

When a country produces a variety of goods, it is usually able to sell some of them. At any given time there will probably be a demand for some of them, even if the others are difficult to sell. So its trade with foreign countries will be more regular and continuous than trade carried on by a country which sells only one or two kinds of goods.

8.4 READING PASSAGES

Like most modern developing countries, Nigeria has only a limited supply of suitably educated people. Most of these people are not trained at home. More engineers and scientists are required. Self-government and industrialization in Nigeria have made it possible for Nigerians to enter their local industries. But they cannot do the kind of work required of them without suitable training.

In modern times most countries on the road to industrialization need help from outside. If they do not receive this help, their development will be slow.

---

* a revolution = a change in society which has a far-reaching effect on all social and economic relations.

Unit VIII
8.5 VOCABULARY TEST

To test yourself on the vocabulary of this section, fill in the missing letters in the incomplete words.

Students of e_____ics study relations between pr_____ers, tr__ers, and cu_____ers, those who s__l and those who buy. They also study the laws of s_____y and d_____d. R_____ch into the d_____d for g__ds of a c_____n kind in a di_____t is called market r_____ch. It is r_____ch into l___l d_____d for things which are (or which can be) pr____ced to be sold.

C_____n things, like di_____ds or v_____ble pictures, are always in d_____d because of their sc_____ty and because they can be kept in good condition for a very long time. Because they only ex___t in l___ted qu_____ties they are very ex_____ve.

But there is also a d_____d for many other things which are pl_____l and which do not c__t much. There is a r_____ar d_____d for things which are n_____ry for life, like bread. Sometimes, however, there is a d_____d which c_____ues only for a short time and is not repeated. This happens when a fashion changes or when a thing is d__ven off the m_____t by another thing of the same kind which is ch____er or b____er in one way or another.

A few things, like ve_____bles of different kinds, are much ch____er at c_____n times of the year than at others. There is a seasonal d_____d for such things. The price d_____ds on the su__ly. But they do not keep or in_____se their v___e like di_____ds. So, if they are very e_____ve, few people will buy them.

When money is p_____l people often choose to ex_____ge their money for l__d, di_____ds, works of art, or other o_____ts which can be r____ed on to keep or in_____se their v__ue.

Unit IX

9.1 VOCABULARY

These are the words you will practice in this unit:

VERBS

acquire	(ac·quire')	
appear	(ap·pear')	(= to be present)
control	(con·trol')	
decide (to)	(de·cide')	
decide that		
disappear	(dis·ap·pear')	
enable	(en·a'ble)	(+ noun + to)
face		
improve	(im·prove')	
listen to	(lis'ten)	
observe	(ob·serve')	
occur	(oc·cur')	
predict	(pre·dict')	
revise	(re·vise')	
spin		(= rotate)
turn		(left, right, around, south, etc.)
wait for		

NOUNS

(an) accident	(ac'ci·dent)	(an) observation	(ob·ser·va'tion)
appearance	(ap·pear'ance)	an occurrence	(oc·cur'rence)
an axis	(ax'is)	(an) order (= sequence)	(or'der)
control	(con·trol')	a prediction	(pre·dic'tion)
a compass	(com'pass)	a sign	
a crisis	(cri'sis)	a signal	(sig'nal)
a decision	(de·ci'sion)	(a) skill	
a direction	(di·rec'tion)	(a) speed	
disappearance	(dis·ap·pear'ance)	a turn	
an event	(e·vent')	weather	(weath'er)
(an) improvement	(im·prove'ment)		

ADJECTIVES

facing	(fac'ing)	rapid	(rap'id)
foreign	(for'eign)	reliable	(re·li'a·ble)
insufficient	(in·suf·fi'cient)	responsible (for)	(re·spon'si·ble)
international	(in·ter·na'tion·al)	skilled	
opposite	(op'po·site)	spherical	(spher'i·cal)
particular	(par·tic'u·lar)	sufficient	(suf·fi'cient)

ADVERBS

especially	(es·pe'cial·ly)
rapidly	(rap'id·ly)
sufficiently	(suf·fi'cient·ly)

PREPOSITION

toward	(to·ward')

CONJUNCTION

unless	(un·less')

PHRASE

according to	(ac·cord'ing)

Unit IX

9.2 WORD STUDY

INSTRUCTIONS: Study the following words and the uses of them:

foreign = in, of, or from another country (not one's own country).

A *foreign* country is a country which is not one's own. A foreign language is not one's own language, but the language of another society.

Examples: When you visit f_____n countries, you should try to understand their customs. It is interesting to learn about f_____ customs. Our country will not become rich until it increases its f_____ trade. My friend knows five _____ languages.

skill (a) = ability to do something well, or in the best and quickest way. (uncountable)
a skill (b) = a special kind of skill. (countable)
skilled (c) = having skill (as a result of training or experience) or requiring skill. A skilled worker has skill. Skilled work requires skill.

Examples:

(a) Great s_____ is required to drive a car in this part of the city. You do not need much s_____ to look after a house like this. S_____ is usually the result of practice.

(b) Typing is a s_____ which can be learned at home. When we learn a f_____n language, we learn new s_____s. Looking after children requires a number of practical s_____s.

(c) S_____ed workers are scarce in Nigeria. Cleaning floors is not highly s_____ed work. Removing a tooth neatly is a s_____ operation.

particular A *particular* thing or place or time or person is one thing or place or time or person thought of as distinct from others. A teacher who is interested in a particular student has a special interest in **this** student as distinct from others. If you do **not** study at any particular time, this means that you do not have a special time (a time distinct from others) for studying. "The way in which a particular country is industrialized" means the way in which one country, distinguished from others, is industrialized.

Examples: The way in which a p_____lar country is industrialized and the time when this happens depend on the facts of its social history. The value of a p_____lar object depends partly on its scarcity and partly on the work required to produce it. She does not get up at any p_____r time. Must the shirt be of a p_____ color?

Exercise: Rewrite each sentence, using **particular** before the most suitable noun.

1. This substance will dissolve in water only at a temperature.

   _____

   _____ .

2. You must stand at a distance from an object before you can photograph it.

   _____

   _____ .

3. The jug need not be of any color, but it must have a capacity of two pints.

   _____

   _____ .

9.2 WORD STUDY

4.   The choice of a unit as a standard depends partly on its convenience for a variety of purposes.

_____

_____ .

5.   I have no reason for going out today.

_____ .

6.   Our future trade with any country will depend on its willingness to have trade agreements with us.

_____

_____ .

7.   Why are you so interested in this problem?

_____ ?

8.   In this situation no one can give you any useful advice.

_____ .

9.   Do you have in mind any publisher for your book?

_____ ?

10. I do not wish to join any political party.

_____ .

improve	(a) = become better
	(b) = make (something) better
an improvement	(c) = becoming or making better, or its result

Examples:

(a)   Your health will *improve* if you smoke less. Skill i_____s with practice. As he grows older his handwriting does not im_____. The political situation has i_____.

(b)   You should try to im____e your spelling. The soup will not be im_____ by putting more salt in it. You can i_____ this paragraph by making it shorter.

(c)   There is no i_____ment in her health. Your new hair style is not an i_____ment. Do you notice any i_____t in this room?

weather	= features of the atmosphere such as temperature, sunshine, rain, wind, clouds in a **particular area** at a
(uncountable)	**particular time.**

Examples: What will the *weather* be like today? He does not go out in cold wea___r. We will not start building until the wea___r improves. Farmers depend for their success on the right kind of w_____r. We must wait for warmer w_____ before we go on our vacation.

acquire	= get something (often something valuable or useful) for oneself by skill or ability or by one's own actions or activities.

Examples: He soon *acquired* a good knowledge of English. Skill can only be acqu__ed by practice and experience. In the eighteenth and nineteenth centuries Britain ac_____d an Empire. He ac____ed all this land during the last five years. You will not ac____e a knowledge of human nature by reading books. If you continue to spend your time like this, you will ac____e a bad name.

9.2 WORD STUDY

revise

(a) = read or learn something again, in order to know it better.

(b) = write something again, making corrections and improving it, or change something to improve it.

Note: This verb can only be used about something that can be planned, learned, read, written, or thought.

Examples:

(a)   Today we will *revise* the grammar of the past tense. For homework you can revise the first three chapters of your textbook.

(b)   Before the book is published, the index and the last chapter must be re____ed. After staying in the town for a week, he completely r_____ed his ideas about it.

rapid

(a) = quick; often used about **a change, an increase, an advance, a growth, a development, an improvement**, etc.

rapidly

(b) = quickly; often used with verbs like **change, develop, improve, increase, grow**, etc., also **speak**.

Examples:

(a)   He was surprised at the *rapid* growth of the city. When he left the hospital his health showed a rapid improvement. In the last few years there has been a r_____ advance in medical science.

(b)   If you practice half an hour every day your pronunciation will r_____ly improve. He spoke so r_____ly that no one could understand him. His skill has developed r_____ly since he started driving lessons. The demand for trained engineers has rapidly increased.

especially

= particularly

Especially is used when we want to point out the special importance of certain members of a group in comparison with others, or the special importance of certain times, places, etc., in comparison with others.

Examples: There has been an improvement in trade relations this year, especially between European countries. People using the roads, especially drivers, should be more careful in wet weather. People using the roads should be more careful in wet weather, es_____lly at night. People using the roads should be more careful in wet weather, es_____lly in the crowded city districts. He is interested in several subjects, es_____lly European history and anthropology.

(a) speed

The *speed* of a moving object is measured by the time it takes to travel a certain distance. My car can go **at a speed** of 60 miles an hour. A car which travels a long distance in a short time goes **at a high speed**; a car which takes a long time to travel a short distance goes **at a low speed**. A car traveling at a high s____d goes quickly; a car traveling at a low s_____ goes slowly. A car goes **at top speed** when it travels as quickly as its engine will allow it to travel.

Examples: In towns the s_____ of traffic is usually limited to 30 miles an hour. He was traveling at a s_____ of 100 miles an hour when he suddenly noticed a cat in the middle of the road. He tried to reduce his s_____, but could not do so in time. When going around corners it is safer to drive at a low s_____. She has increased her s_____, and can now type 40 words a minute.

a crisis
pl. crises

A crisis is a point reached in life, history, an illness, etc., when the situation can no longer continue as it is, and there must be important changes. A crisis may also be a time (or point in time) of great difficulty or danger.

Examples: As a result of the political crisis in Poland, a new government was formed. During the economic crisis of 1929-1933, thousands of people lost their jobs. Sometimes there is a c_____s in family life, when children do not agree to their parents' plans. Last year there was a bank c_____, and Britain was forced to devalue the pound. The danger of an international c_____ has decreased in the last few months.

9.2 WORD STUDY

international   = existing between nations (e.g., an *international* agreement, international trade); used by people of different nations (e.g., an international hotel, an international system of measurement); or having an effect on several different nations (e.g., an international crisis).

Examples: An international council was formed to supply information about weather. The metric system of measurement has become an in___national system. The i_____national cr___s was caused by the rapid rise in the price of gold.

control   noun = power to govern or to keep something within limits or to make (someone or something) follow rules or follow a certain path, direction, or course of action.

control   verb = to have *control* of something or someone (e.g., a horse, a boat, a child, oneself, or one's feelings). A man who controls his horse keeps it on the road and makes it go where he wants it to go. A man who can control his own feelings can keep them within limits, govern them, and rule them.

Note: Notice the spelling of the forms of the verb: **control, controls, controlled, controlling.**

Exercise: Rewrite each sentence, using the **correct form** of the verb **control** or the noun **control** in **one** blank space and one of the following words in the other.

horse	students	prices	situation
traffic	weather	amount	speed
level	pressure	error	supplies

1. He lost _____ of his _____ , which began running around and around the field and tried to throw him off.

   _____

   _____ .

2. The dam _____ the _____ of the water in the lake.

   _____

   _____ .

3. It is difficult to _____ _____ who do not live in the hostels.

   _____

   _____ .

4. Because of the war, _____ of grain and oil to ordinary customers must be _____ .

   _____

   _____ .

5. The President stated that the political _____ was no longer under his _____ .

   _____

   _____ .

6. A policeman stands in the middle of the road and _____ the _____ .

   _____

   _____ .

9.2 WORD STUDY

7. You cannot give exact figures, but you can _____ the _____ by stating its limits.

    _____

    _____.

8. Men have won great power over nature, but they do not yet have _____ of the _____ .

    _____

    _____.

9. The government hopes to keep the cost of living as it is by _____ _____ .

    _____

    _____.

10. Inside airplanes the _____ of the air is _____ by special methods.

    _____

    _____.

11. This is used to _____ the _____ of the car.

    _____

    _____.

12. If she does not _____ the _____ of food she eats, she will get very fat.

    _____

    _____.

sufficient   = enough
insufficient   = not enough

Examples: Is there s_____ient food for the journey? When supplies of grain are in_____ient, we must buy grain from foreign countries. In underdeveloped countries the supply of trained engineers is usually in_____t.

**a direction
toward
turn
opposite**

9.2 WORD STUDY

In this map the names of a few towns are given. A represents a ship; B represents a car; C represents a bicycle; D represents a horse; E represents another car.

The ship, A, is sailing in a certain *direction*. In which direction is it going? It is going in the direction of Napier. It is going *toward* Napier. It is going west. From this map, we cannot be sure that the steamer is going **to** Napier. We can only see its d_____n. We cannot say where it is going to. It might *turn* north and go to Gisborne. We can only say that **now** it is going toward Napier.

Look at the car, B. Where is it going to? The map does not tell us. It might be going to T_____ or R_____ or H_____ or M_____. In what di_____n is this car going? It is going in the d_____ of T___o. It is going northwest.

Perhaps this car is going to Rotorua. If it is going to Rotorua, it must t__n right after leaving Taupo. Perhaps it is going to Mangakino. If it is going to Mangakino, it must t____ l___ after leaving Taupo. In what d_____n must this car t__n if the driver wants to go to Tauranga? It must ____ r____.

Look at the car, E. Is it going in **the same direction** as B? No, it is not going in the same d_____. It is going in the *opposite* direction. It is going t_____s N_____r. It is going southeast. B is going northwest and E is going s____e___. E is going in the o_____e d_____n from B.

In what d_____n is the bicycle, C, going? It is going n____e___ t_____s G_____e.

In what d_____ is the horse, D, going?

turn
facing
face

Here is a teacher *facing* a row of students. The students *face* the teacher. The teacher tells them to *turn* right.

Now the students are not f_____g the teacher. They have t____ed right.

Here is a car on a mountain road. It is coming to a corner. It must t____ around the corner.

Here is a car on a mountain road. It cannot turn around the corner, because there is a tree across the road. The car must t____ around (on the road) and go back. It must t____ ar____d and go in the o_____e d_____n.

a turn
an axis
pl. axes
spin
spherical

When a round object like a top or a *spherical* object like a ball makes **several complete turns**, we say that it *spins*. It spins around the imaginary line which goes through its center.

The line around which it s____s is called its *axis*. When a top s____s on its a___, it does not fall. Here are some other things which can s__n on their axes.

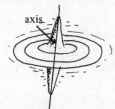

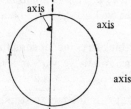

A top spins on its axis.

The earth spins on its axis.

A dancer spins.

9.2 WORD STUDY

enable
a compass

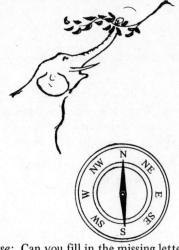

The elephant has a trunk. Because of its long trunk, the elephant can reach branches of trees and pull them down. The elephant's trunk *enables* the elephant to reach branches and **pull** them down.

Some birds and animals have very long legs. Their long legs en_____ them to run fast and cover great distances.

A compass en_____s the captain of a ship to find the d_____n and keep in the right d_____.

Exercise: Can you fill in the missing letters in the following sentences? (Use the correct form of the verb **enable** + noun + to.)

1. A kn_____ge of ec_____cs en_____ politicians to understand the ec_____c s_____n in their country.

2. A s___ly of ox____n e_____s airmen and mountain climbers to br__the at great h__ghts.

3. The dec____l system of numbers e_____s us __ add, su_____ct, mu_____ly, and di_____ fractions.

4. Money values are sym____ic v____es which en_____ people __ ex_____ge a great variety of g__ds and services without meeting each other.

5. The rules of the University Staff Club e_____ its mem___s (but not others) to buy drinks in the club building between 10 a.m. and 6 p.m.

6. Prec_____n inst_____ en_____ eng_____s __ make measurements correct to a thou_____th of an inch.

7. The conv_____s of language en_____ people __ u_____d each other.

8. When a word has sev___l meanings, the context often en_____ us __ dist_____h between them.

9. The use of para_____hs en_____ us __ dis_____h between the different steps or changes in a writer's thought.

10. A mach____ called the Hovercraft has been dev__ed which e_____s passengers to tr___l close to the su____ce of the land or the sea without touching it.

11. This information will e_____ us __ make an appr_____te est___te of the cost of the house.

12. A gift of 500 dollars will _____ him __ cont_____ his studies.

listen to

= give attention to a sound or noise

Tom went for a walk beside the river. He *listened to* the sound of the flowing river. He l_____ed __ the birds singing. He l_____ __ a shepherd singing on the top of the hill. He l_____ __ the sheep calling on the hillside.

In the evenings we l____n __ the radio. Sometimes we l_____ __ music, sometimes we l_____ __ plays, and sometimes we l_____ __ radio lectures.

wait for

When we *wait for* something to come, or something to happen, we stay where we are and wait until it comes or until it happens. When we wait for a friends, we stay in the same place until they come (because we expect them to come).

Examples: We will w__t f__ the rain to stop before we go out. He is w___ing ___ the car. W___ ___ the bell before you go into the class. Don't _____ ___ him; he may be late. They w___ed for the bus for two hours, but it did not come. I w____d ___ him to finish speaking.

148

9.2 WORD STUDY

unless   = if . . . not

Exercise: Rewrite the following sentences, using **unless** in each sentence to make it meaningful.

1.   *Example:* One country cannot trade with another it has goods to sell.

     Rewritten: One country cannot trade with another unless it has goods to sell.

2.   I will telephone you this evening I am too busy.

     _____.

3.   You can probably buy this land it belongs to the university.

     _____.

4.   His English will not improve he attends his classes regularly.

     _____.

5.   We cannot rely on these calculations they are checked by someone else.

     _____

     _____.

6.   He agrees to the plan it will have to be changed.

     _____.

7.   I cannot buy the car the price is reduced.

     _____.

8.   The cause of his disease is discovered, he will die.

     _____.

9.   We should choose another date this date is really convenient for everyone.

     _____

     _____.

10. He takes the direct route he will not arrive until Saturday.

     _____.

11. They cannot start new industries they have sufficient trained workers.

     _____

     _____.

12. India continues to receive supplies of grain from America, she cannot feed her people.

     _____

     _____.

according to   *According to* the Bible, God made the world and everything in it in seven days. This means: The Bible **says that** God made the world and everything in it in seven days.

According to the radio, it will rain tomorrow. This means: **Someone speaking officially on the radio says** that it will rain tomorrow.

9.2 WORD STUDY

Examples: According to our teacher, the past tense is very common in English. Acc____ing to the dictionary, **control** is spelled with only one l. Acc_____ __ the President, the economic situation has improved in the last three months. Acc_____ __ the newspaper, more than twenty houses were destroyed in the storm. Acc_____ __ my watch, it is nearly six o'clock. Acc_____ __ the published results of his research, some insects can live for two or three days without oxygen.

Note: The phrase "according to" gives the **origin** or **authorship** of a statement, a piece of information, or a rule, so that we know whether to rely on it or not.

Exercise: Find a sentence in the **second** column which goes with a phrase in the **first** column and give it the number of the phrase it goes with.

1.	According to my watch	it will be fine tomorrow.
2.	According to the newspaper	it is eight-thirty.
3.	According to the Bible	the course of true love never runs smoothly.
4.	According to Shakespeare	Professor Jones lectures on Wednesday and Friday.
5.	According to the radio weather forecast	trade relations with Europe have slightly improved.
6.	According to the scientist Sir Bernard Lovell	coffee tastes better with a pinch of salt in it.
7.	According to the university timetable	students must return books after two weeks.
8.	According to some people	there was shooting across the Jordanian river yesterday.
9.	According to the President	there are probably many other planets where life exists.
10.	According to the library rules	it is better to give than to receive.

decide to
decide that
a decision

Tom had four weeks' vacation at Christmas. At first he was not sure whether to stay at home or to go away, but finally he *decided to* go away for at least two weeks. Should he travel in the North Island or go to the South Island? It took him some time to *decide*, but in the end he d_____d to go to the South Island. His friend Jack d_____d to go with him, and the two boys then d_____ that they would go by boat to Christchurch and from there take the train to Ashburton. From Ashburton they d_____ that they would walk in the dir_____ of Lake Pukaki. They agreed not to make any more *decisions* or plans before they left, because they wanted to feel free to walk where they liked and stay where they liked after they left the train.

A decision is an interesting act of the human mind. When I decide to do something I say that I will do it; perhaps I do not tell another person, I only **tell myself** that I am going to do it. So a decision is like a promise which I make to myself. When I decide to do something and afterward do not do it, this is like breaking a promise which I have made to myself.

When two people d_____e something together, they **agree** to it. An agreement, which requires a decision by two people or more, or by two or more groups of people, is a kind of promise. When a man tells you that he has decided to do something (for example, to buy a new car) you expect him to do it, unless he tells you later that he has changed his mind.

observe
(an) observation
an event
(an) order
predict
a prediction
a sign

When scientists *observe* a group of stars, or a particular star, or the habits of a particular animal, or the results of an experiment, this means that they look at them carefully. They usually record their *observations*; they write down what they have ob_____ed.

Sometimes scientists ob_____ an object and its features, for example, a star or a mountain or a bird; sometimes they o_____ an *event*, which is something which happens at a particular time. A weather scientist, for example, will o_____ the movements of clouds, changes in the atmosphere, thunder and lightning. These are not things or objects but ev___s. A scientist who is interested in birds may o_____ how a particular bird builds its nest or catches insects or how it flies. These are also e_____s. When scientists o_____ a large number of ev___s of the same kind, they may notice that these ev___s form a pattern. They notice, as a result of their ob_____tions, that certain ev___s often or always follow each other in the same way, in the same *order*. Not only scientists, but ordinary

9.2 WORD STUDY

people notice certain patterns of e____ts in nature, as a result of their ob_____tions in the past. For example, when we see lightning in the sky we expect that this will be followed by thunder. We have experienced this order of events, **lightning — thunder**, and we expect these e____ts to happen in the same or__r; first lightning running across the sky, then the noise of thunder, then rain. After seeing lightning we are sure that thunder will follow. Because of this we can take lightning as a *sign* of thunder.

When we see smoke rising among the trees or from a chimney, we take it as a s__n of a fire. We know that where there is smoke there must be a fire, so smoke is a s____ of fire. When you hear your mother's footsteps on the stairs they are a s____ of your mother or of her presence in the house. When you hear the distinctive song of the cuckoo, it is a s__n that the bird is near; you may not be able to see the bird, but the song is a s__n of the bird's presence in the trees above your head.

Some signs enable us to *predict* events; they enable us to know or say that other events will happen. Lightning is a s__n of thunder and enables us to pre____t thunder. "Pre" is a Latin word which means "before" and "dict" comes from "dicere" which means "say." When we predict an event, we say (before it happens) that it will happen. When I say that it is going to rain tomorrow, I pre_____ this ev__t, I make a *prediction*. When economists say that the price of grain will fall next month, they make a pre_____ion. When politicians say that the war will end in the next few months, they pre_____ this happy e___t. People pre_____ ev___s when they expect them to happen. They base their pre_____ns on certain s__ns, but, unfortunately, pre_____s about human e_____s or changes in human situations are often mistaken, because human actions do not always follow a pattern.

(an) order

In nature some events always happen in the same *order*, because the earlier events are the causes of the ones which follow; first lightning appears, then thunder is heard. The order is (1) lightning, (2) thunder. This is an or___ in time. Other kinds of o_____ are possible. I can place my books on the shelf in o_____ of size; first the big ones, then the middle-sized ones, then the smaller ones. This is an o_____ in space. The words in the dictionary follow the o_____ of the alphabet; first words beginning with A, then words beginning with ____ , then words beginning with ____ , and so on.

1. Write the following in order of **size** (the largest first): the moon; the earth; the sun.

_____

2. Write the following words in **alphabetical order**: stretch; multiple; equivalent; angle; season; solar.

_____

3. Write the following dates **in their historical order**: 1968; 1001; 304; 1666; 1850; 1780.

_____

(an) accident
occur
an occurrence
a signal
control
responsible for

The general meaning of *an accident* is something which happens without a purpose. An accident cannot be predicted and is therefore unexpected. Suppose you go out shopping and suddenly meet your brother. This meeting is not the result of any agreement or decision; so you meet him by accident. The meeting is only an accident. This acc____nt is probably pleasant, but many acc_____ts are unfortunate events. You may, for example, drop a plate and hit the cat or break the plate. This is also an a_____ (an unfortunate one) because you neither wished nor decided to drop the plate. The word accident is used about human ev__ts, not natural ones. We believe that everything in nature has a cause (or causes); we do not believe that every human event or action has a purpose.

Accidents often occur (= happen) when people cannot *control* the **order** of events for some reason. On April 10, 1968, there was a great storm in my home town and many accidents *occurred*. (Please notice the spelling of this past tense form! **occurred**.) Roofs blew off houses, drivers lost control of their cars, which were pushed over or pushed off the road by the wind, and a ship went in the wrong direction, struck some rocks in the harbor, and later overturned.

This brings us to the more limited meaning of accident. In its more limited sense an accident is an unfortunate, unexpected *occurrence*, especially on the roads or railroads or airlines, for example, when one car hits another, or a car hits a man and kills him, or when a train leaves the line and overturns, or

9.2 WORD STUDY

when a plane falls. We also speak of accidents in factories and homes.

We will think about this kind of acc_____t. Suppose a car turns around a corner and hits a man on a bicycle, who falls off his bicycle and breaks his leg. This event does not oc___ as the result of a human purpose or a human dec_____n. The driver of the car does not dec____ to break the cyclist's leg, and the cyclist does not d_____ __ fall off the bicycle. But the a_____t may be the result of carelessness. Perhaps the driver is driving too quickly, or perhaps he does not look at the traffic *signal*. In this case the acc_____t is the driver's fault. It is the result of his mistake. He is *responsible for* the acc_____t. But perhaps it is not the driver who makes the mistake. Perhaps he is not careless in any way. Perhaps the cyclist is riding on the wrong side of the road, or does not give a sig___l to the driver, by putting her hand out to show the direction in which she wishes to go. In this case the mistake is the cyclist's mistake; she is resp_____ble f__ the acc_____, and the driver is not r_____ble f__ it.

A person is responsible for anything which needs care because of its effect on life or on other human beings. Every grown-up person (except a mad person) is res_____ble for his or her own actions, because most of our actions can have an effect on other people. If an accident occurs because a man is careless in his actions, he is res_____ble f__ that accident. A teacher or a factory worker, an engineer or a policeman or the captain of a ship is r_____ble for the work that he or she does. A builder who does not fix a roof properly is res_____ble for the acc_____t when the roof blows off in a storm.

People are also res_____ble f__ things or people under their care or control. Parents are r_____le for their young children. People who keep animals like cats or dogs are r_____le f__ them. A principal is r_____e f__ the school. A captain of a ship is r_____ f__ the ship. A person who has a car is r_____ f__ the car; he or she must keep it **in good order** (this means that all the parts of the car should be there in the car, in their right positions, ready for use, and that nothing should be broken or too old or too weak to be safe).

When drivers do not notice a traffic sig___ and there is an acc_____t, they are r_____e f__ that acc_____t. If a man dies as a result, the driver is partly r_____e f__ that man's death. The doctor and nurses may also be partly r_____, if they do not look after the man properly while he is in the hospital.

We are not r_____ f__ natural e____ts like storms or heavy winds or earthquakes or floods. But we may be r_____ f__ accidents caused by natural e_____s, if we do not try to learn from past experience and if we do not build houses, cars, bridges, roads, and ships strong enough to stand against the forces of nature. Responsibility means **taking care** in our actions and in the things we make; it therefore means learning from exp_____ce and trying to pre_____ what will happen in the future. The meaning of responsibility is partly social; we are r_____le **to other people** f__ our actions and f__ the people or things under our care. A principal, for example, is held r_____le by the parents of the pupils and by the local government f__ the pupils' education. A r_____le person is one whom other people can trust or rely on.

The word responsible is derived from **respond**, which means "answer." People who are responsible for their actions are expected to answer, when they are questioned by people who hold them responsible. Responsible people are expected to know **why they do something**. A small child or a mad person is not expected to know this.

appear
appear
appearance
disappear
disappearance

(a) When a thing arrives at a place or comes near a place and can be seen by those present, or when it was there before but can only now be seen because of changes in the light, or when it comes into existence and is seen for the first time, we say that it *appears*. In this sense appear can also be used about people or animals. The *appearance* of a thing or a person, in this sense, is the event of the thing or the person appearing.

Examples: Suddenly Mary appeared at the window. Your friends did not a_____r at the meeting. We waited for three hours but the plane did not a_____r. One by one the stars a_____r in the sky. The

9.2 WORD STUDY

speaker was late, and we waited anxiously for his a_____ce. The a_____e of the police quieted the crowd. The a_____e of the ship in the distance was the signal for a lot of activity. After a few days the first leaves a_____ on both sides of the plant.

(b) Especially with a plural subject, appear may mean "exist" or "occur," if the occurrences can be seen.

Examples: These insects a_____r in large numbers in the central forests. The figures which a_____r on the clock face represent hours. In the word "extreme" the letter "e" a_____s three times. This kind of behavior only a_____ in small tribal societies.

(c) appear followed by an adjective or by to + stem

In this construction appear is equivalent to **seem**. A thing appears to have certain qualities or features when it seems to have them, i.e., when it shows signs of having them although we cannot be sure whether it really has them or not. In this sense **appears to have** is in contrast with **really has**. A thing appears to do something when it seems to do so. Appearance may also have the same sense, and both verb and noun can be used of people, animals, and things.

Examples: This book a_____s interesting. She a_____red tired (i.e., she looked or seemed tired). He a_____s to be a kind father. She does not a_____r to understand what is said to her. He a_____s to have many friends. The box a_____ed to be empty. We should not judge people by their a_____ce (i.e., by the way they look or by what they seem to be).

(d) As distinct from sense (c), the appearance of a thing or a person may mean simply the way it looks, features of a thing, or a person which can be seen, without any idea that it (or he or she) may not really have the character it seems to have.

Examples: I was asked to describe the appearance of the thief. The a_____e of the food which you cook is very important.

(e) *disappear, disappearance*: One meaning of these words is related to (a), the first meaning of appear, appearance. A thing or a person disappears when it (or he or she) leaves a place or can no longer be seen there. But we use disappear, disappearance only when we do not know how the thing or person left the place, or where it (or he or she) went to, or what happened to it (or to him or her) afterward. We also say that things disappear or speak of their disappearance when, while we are actually looking at them, they stop existing or can no longer be seen.

Examples: Last week a famous scientist dis_____ed from his home. My fountain pen has d_____d. The two men d_____ into the darkness. Her family are worried about her d_____. If you use this chemical to clean your shirt, the marks will d_____ immediately. The stars d_____d and the sun came out. Some memories d_____ quickly; others have a long life.

(f) The second meaning of disappear, disappearance follows (b), the second meaning of appear. In this sense things or people disappear when they no longer exist or occur.

Examples: By 1940 many of the old customs had d_____d. Many of the original New Zealand birds have d_____. If family life d_____ from the world, people will be more like machines. One feature of modern society is the rapid d_____e of many conventions.

Unit IX
9.3 DICTATION EXERCISES AND DICTATION PASSAGES

A   1. The passage *A Political Speech* will now be read to you. When you hear the following adjectives, write the articles (if any) which precede them and the nouns which follow them.

    (a) _____ present economic _____

    (b) _____ political _____

    (c) _____ northeastern _____

    (d) _____ skilled _____

    (e) _____ dangerously high _____

    (f) _____ few _____

  2. Number the following words in the order in which you hear them.

directions	developments	neighbors
especially	dangerously	already
predicted	risen	occurred

  3. When you are asked to do so, underline the following words in the dictation passage. This is a race.

foreign	occurred	control	reduce
untrained	allowed	level	face
responsible for	expanded	crisis	choose

  4. The passage *A Political Speech* will now be given as dictation.

B   1. The passage *Traffic Accidents in the City* will be read to you at ordinary reading speed. Number the following words (given here in a different order) in **the order in which you hear them in the passage.**

occur	occurrences	occurred
especially	unusually	approximately
insufficient	average	acquire
control	observe	activities

  2. The passage *Traffic Accidents in the City* will be read again. In the following pairs, cross out the word which is incorrect.

    (a) reports - report   (f) single - signals

    (b) occured - occurred   (g) estimated - estimate

    (c) figures - figure   (h) control - controlled

    (d) currencies - occurrences   (i) acquire - quiet

    (e) observe - serves   (j) activity - activities

  3. The passage *Traffic Accidents in the City* will now be given as a dictation.

C   1. The teacher will read the passage *Man and the Forces of Nature* two or three times at intervals of about five minutes. Work in pairs, and try to fill in the missing words, which are given below in a different order.

are	not	natural	accidents
be	not	natural	events
to build	and	responsible	events
do	for	strong	earthquakes

9.3 DICTATION EXERCISES AND DICTATION PASSAGES

learn	by	the	floods
may	of	and	forces
to stand	from		roads
			ships
			storms
			houses

We _____ _____ responsible _____ _____ _____ _____ like _____ ,

_____ _____ , and _____ . But we _____ _____ _____ for

_____ caused _____ _____ _____ if we _____ _____

_____ _____ experience _____ try _____ _____ _____ ,

_____ , _____ _____ _____ enough _____ _____ against

_____ _____ _____ nature.

9.3   DICTATION PASSAGES

(a)   A Political Speech

The government, especially the President, must be held responsible for the present economic crisis. Though the events leading to this situation were predicted months ago by our economists, the President did not listen to them but allowed developments to pass beyond his control. If he had improved political relations with his northeastern neighbors, made trade agreements with them, and expanded foreign trade in other directions, the crisis would not have occurred. Now thousands of skilled workers in addition to untrained workers have lost their jobs. Steps must be taken at once to reduce the cost of living, which has already risen to a dangerously high level. In a few weeks we may be faced with a revolution, and we must choose a government which will enable us to face it.

(b)   Traffic Accidents in the City

According to reports on television, an unusually large number of traffic accidents have occurred during the last six months. The average monthly figure has been well over 1,500. It is stated by the police that many of these occurrences were due to the failure of drivers to observe local traffic signals, especially in the crowded city districts. It is estimated that approximately eighty percent of all traffic accidents occur within the city limits, where there are insufficient police to control the dangerous crossings. There will be no improvement until we acquire a police force sufficiently large, well-trained, and well-paid for all the important activities required of it. Unless we have a bigger and better police force, accidents will not decrease but increase.

(c)   Man and the Forces of Nature

We are not responsible for natural events like storms, earthquakes, and floods. But we may be responsible for accidents caused by natural events if we do not learn from experience and try to build houses, roads, and ships strong enough to stand against the forces of nature.

Unit IX

9.4 READING PASSAGES

(a) Predicting the Weather

In many cities and large towns there are weather observatories, suitably situated. The local observatory is probably familiar to most geography students. Here scientists make observations and collect and classify facts about the weather, either recorded from their own observations or recorded by special instruments which can also "observe" more accurately than any human eye. An observatory of this kind belongs to the people of the town where it is situated; its purposes are both scientific and practical.

Weather scientists, or weathermen as they are often called, are not only interested in recording features of the weather at the time when they occur. They are also interested in future occurrences, for example, in tomorrow's rain and next week's sunshine. It is their job not only to observe and describe the weather but to predict it. They must tell people what kind of weather to expect in the future.

It is obviously important to a farmer, a fisherman, an airplane pilot, and a ship's captain to know what the weather will be like. Unless they know what weather to expect, they cannot plan their activities or operations. Farmers may wait for the weather to improve before they sow their grain; airplane pilots may wait for the weather to improve before they climb into a plane and begin a journey. The meaning of the word "improve" may, of course, differ for the farmer and the pilot. For the farmer "better weather" may mean "wetter weather" and for the pilot "better weather" may mean "drier weather."

But farmers, pilots, and captains are not the only people who are interested in the weather. Almost everyone at some time listens to weather reports on the radio. Outdoor games cannot be played unless the weather is suitable. Housewives listen to the weathermen's predictions (which are generally called weather forecasts) and wait for the weather to improve before they wash a lot of clothes. Business people driving to work or driving home after office hours need information about the surfaces of the roads and any other information which will enable them to avoid (= keep away from, keep free from) accidents. Even school children may want to know if it will be warm enough to go out without a coat.

How can scientific workers predict rain or sunshine, cold weather or hot weather? They keep records of a very large number of occurrences—rainfall, clouds of various kinds, winds, temperatures. They observe the exact time and place of each occurrence, and also the order and connection of the occurrences. They observe how weather changes, how clouds and winds travel from one place to another, how a "cold front" displaces a "warm front." These facts enable them to form a map or chart of the weather.

They notice that weather changes often follow the same pattern, and so they are able to take certain events as *signs* that others will follow. When scientists make a prediction, this is because their knowledge of weather patterns and of causes and effects has enabled them to take certain events as signs of others.

We all know that dark, heavy clouds are often a sign of rain. This means that when we see such clouds we can predict that it will rain after a short time. A barometer recording air pressure also enables us to predict rain in the near future. But a weatherman can obtain reliable information from distant places by radio and use this information to predict rain two or three days before it actually arrives.

It is true that weathermen do not always predict correctly. Their estimates of future occurrences are often slightly inaccurate and sometimes completely wrong. This is not because they are careless or irresponsible but because the weather at a particular place and time is not the result of a single cause but the result of several causes operating together. For this reason future weather events cannot be predicted without some error. The weatherman is never in a position to know all the facts or all their possible patterns.

(b) The Solar System

The sun and the nine planets which move around it are called the solar system. The planets have different sizes, but they are all smaller than the sun. The length of the sun's diameter is approximately 864,000 miles, over a hundred times the diameter of the earth.

Suppose the earth had the size of a tennis ball. Then, by comparison, the sun would be a sphere about 22 feet in diameter—about the length of a large bus. And on this scale the two bodies would be separated by nearly half a mile.

9.4 READING PASSAGES

(The actual distance between them is just under 93 million miles.)

The sun is a sphere of intensely hot gas. It is made up of hydrogen, a light gas, and smaller amounts of various other gases. The temperature of the sun's edge (which can be safely looked at through dark glasses) is approximately 5000 degrees Celsius, but the temperature at its center is estimated at 20,000,000 degrees.

The planets move in regular orbits (= circular or curved paths) around the sun. Two of them—Mercury and Venus—are closer to the sun than we are. The nearest planet to the sun is Mercury. It is so close to the sun that it is impossible for any form of life to exist there. It is not much larger than the moon, and probably has no atmosphere. Every time Mercury goes around the sun it spins once on its axis. This means that half the planet always faces the sun (just as half the moon always faces the earth), while the other half is continuously dark. The heat of the sunlit side must be intense—strong enough to melt metals. The darker side must be very cold, so cold that any air would rapidly be converted into ice.

Venus is slightly smaller than the earth. Its atmosphere is so thick that no one has seen its actual surface. We can only guess what its surface is like. Probably it is very hot, with a temperature about 300 degrees Celsius. Scientists know that carbon dioxide gas is present in the atmosphere of Venus. They are less sure about the presence of water, though there are some signs of it. Spaceships have entered the atmosphere of Venus and signaled back important information.

Mars has a thin atmosphere so that its surface can be seen through a telescope. It looks red, and the redness is probably due to the presence of red dust. There are interesting lines and marks on the surface, which at one time were thought to be canals (= artificial rivers). For a long time people thought that life or even people existed on Mars, but in modern times scientists have discovered more about its atmosphere and temperature which, they believe, are unsuitable for living things.

Jupiter is the largest of all the planets. It is more than 1,300 times as large as the earth. Its atmosphere contains gases poisonous enough to kill all forms of life as we know it.

Saturn is also covered with clouds of poisonous gas. It has a system of beautiful rings which can be observed through a powerful telescope. They look solid, but are probably made up of millions of tiny (= very small) bodies spinning around Saturn. Both Jupiter and Saturn are intensely cold, and most of their gases must be liquid or frozen solid.

Uranus, which cannot be seen without a telescope, was first observed in 1781 by Herschel. Neptune and Pluto are also so far away that they cannot be seen without a telescope. Before they were observed, their existence and positions were discovered indirectly, by mathematical calculation.

Pluto was not actually observed until 1930. It is the most distant planet yet observed, and travels at a speed of three miles a second. On the average, Pluto is nearly forty times as far from the sun as the earth is; it goes around the sun once in 248 years, if we take the earth's year as a standard.

Each planet is separated from its neighbors by millions of miles. Compared with the great distances between them, the planets are therefore very small. The solar system contains a lot of empty space and only very few solid bodies.

(c)   Effects of the Division of Labor

A hundred years ago there was much less division of labor (= work) than there is today. One carpenter made the whole of a table—perhaps he made all the furniture necessary for a house—and he worked in a simple workshop, probably with hand tools. He was usually a skilled workman, and the furniture he made was often good, sometimes beautiful. But it took him a long time to make it. By modern standards the quantity of furniture he could produce in a given time was small, and the cost was high. Only rich people were able to acquire a lot of furniture.

Most modern furniture is made in factories by machines. Nowadays a man working in a furniture factory may spend his whole time looking after one machine which can perform (= do) only a single operation, for example, shaping the legs of a certain kind of table. A large number of people will work on other parts of the table, each performing a single operation, and by this division of labor a great many tables can be completed in a comparatively short time. An experienced worker may understand all the operations which are necessary to make the table, even if still do only one of them.

9.4 READING PASSAGES

But when a factory produces automobiles or electrical machines that require a great variety of parts, even this is not possible. Even an experienced worker will not understand all the operations required to make the car or the machine. It is very likely that different factories will be responsible for making different parts.

In modern life, therefore, all people depend on everyone else's work in addition to their own. The danger of this is that workers may begin to think that their own particular job is not important, that it does not matter very much how they do it. In the old days, when one, or even two or three people were responsible for the whole of a piece of work (for example, making a cart to be pulled by a horse), it was easy to say who was responsible if the cart was badly made or if it met with an accident because one part was not properly made.

But nowadays, if a car has an accident because one of its parts was not properly made or finished, or because certain parts were not properly joined together, it is difficult to discover who was responsible for this. Suppose a man has the job of joining together two parts of a car wheel; suppose he never touches a complete car or even a complete wheel. It will not be easy for him to feel responsible for the success or reliability of the car as a whole. Actually, of course, workers are quite as important as they were in earlier times, even if they only make a small part of an object or a machine. The automobile cannot be made without the people whose particular job is to join parts of the wheel together, and unless they do their job well the automobile industry cannot produce safe automobiles. Their skill and care are necessary. If a large number of workers are careless the loss to the industry, being multiplied many times, will obviously be great.

In the present century this problem, the problem of human responsibility for work done, may be solved or at least changed by a new development. In very modern factories machines are not controlled by people but by other machines. Some of these "controlling" machines give signals which can start a particular operation or stop it. Others have the job of checking the results of each operation, so that every part (of an automobile, for example) or every set of connected parts must reach a certain standard. Finally there are calculating machines called computers which control all the other machines. One might almost say that in these factories machines are responsible for the finished object and for every part of it. Actually, of course, there are still human beings—highly skilled and highly trained human beings—who are responsible. They are the engineers who designed (= made the plans for) the automobile; the people who designed the computer and other controlling machines and made them; and the people who operate the computer itself. The people who operate the computer must understand how it works, know its language, give it instructions, and be able to control it.

Unit IX
9.5 VOCABULARY TEST

To test yourself on the vocabulary of this section, fill in the missing letters in the incomplete words.

A man who wants to be happy in a f_____n city must learn not only a f_____n language but also f_____n customs and c_____ns. This means that he must ac_____e new habits. Driving or walking in an unf_____r city, for example, is often a pr_____m for a traveler. It is un_____ly that the s_____m of traffic s_____ls will be f_____r to him, and if he does not take the trouble to learn the new s_____m he may be r_____le for a_____ts.

In the first few weeks of his stay he really needs a r_____ble friend who can take him around the city and advise him about his de_____ns. In a strange city it is not easy to pr____ct the w_____er, and u_____s he has a friend to a_____e him a f_____er may not wear s_____nt clothes, or he may wear too many. He will also need to know what to wear for p_____ar purposes and e____ts, for example, an evening party at which he is a guest. He will need the ex_____ce of his friend when he goes shopping, es_____ly ad____e about a_____ge prices and r_____le stores.

A happy and su_____l tr____ler is never worried by unex_____ed oc_____ces. He is always ready to c_____l his feelings, l_____n to advice, r___se his opinions, change his h___ts, and i_____ve his pronunciation.

Unit X
10.1 VOCABULARY

These are the words you will practice in this unit:

VERBS

design	(de·sign')
invent	(in·vent')
last	
lose	
possess	(pos·sess')
prevent	(pre·vent') (+ noun)
prevent	(+ noun + from + -ing)
regulate	(reg'u·late)
rotate	(ro'tate)
swing	
unwind	(un·wind')
wind (up)	

NOUNS

an astronomer	(as·tron'o·mer)	(a) material	(ma·te'ri·al)
astronomy	(as·tron'o·my)	(a) movement	(move'ment)
a calendar	(cal'en·dar)	a pendulum	(pen'du·lum)
a chain		a period	(pe'ri·od)
a coil		a process	(proc'ess)
(a) connection	(con·nec'tion)	(a) rhythm	(rhyth'm)
a curve		a rod	
a date		(a) rotation	(ro·ta'tion)
a design	(de·sign')	a second	(sec'ond)
a dial	(di'al)	a sequence	(se'quence)
a face	(of a clock, etc.)	a shadow	(shad'ow)
a hand	(of a clock)	a spring	(of a watch, etc.)
an invention	(in·ven'tion)	a swing	
an inventor	(in·ven'tor)	a telescope	(tel'e·scope)

ADJECTIVES

ancient	(an'cient)
chief	
coiled	
complicated	(com'pli·cat·ed)
connected (to, with, by)	(con·nect'ed)
curved	
fast	
flat	
wound (up)	

ADVERBS

backward	(back'ward)
fast	
forward	(for'ward)

CONJUNCTION

whenever	(when·ev'er)

PREPOSITION

during	(dur'ing)

PHRASE

in connection with or in this connection	(con·nec'tion)

Unit X

10.2 WORD STUDY

INSTRUCTIONS: Study the following words and the uses of them:

ancient   = of or belonging to very early times

Examples: In *ancient* times, people thought that the earth was flat. There are many a_____t buildings in Rome. He is taking a course in a_____ history. There are some a_____ clocks in the museum. The pyramids of Egypt are very a_____.

a curve
curved

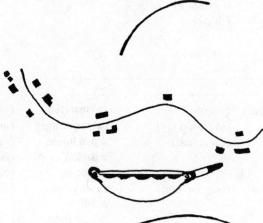

A line with this shape is *a curve.*
This is a *curved* line.

This road is c_____d. In this section of it there are three c_____s.

This pan has a c_____d bottom.

This house has a c_____d roof.

The sun's path across the sky is c_____d.

flat   A surface is *flat* when it is not curved, when it does not rise or fall; it is flat when it is at the same level everywhere.

Examples: In ancient times people thought that the earth was flat. He generally goes out in a flat-bottomed boat. The country around Christchurch is mostly f___; there are not many hills. The best place for an airfield is a perfectly f___ field. Some of these hills have f___ tops, like table tops.

A hill with a flat top.

This pan has a flat bottom.

a rod
a pendulum

A rod is a long, thin, straight piece of metal or wood.

A pendulum is a rod with a weight at one end; it hangs from a fixed point so that the weighted end can move freely.

In pendulum clocks there is a c_____d metal bar at the top of the pendulum rod.

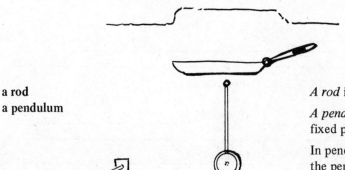

In some bathrooms there are metal rods for towels.

10.2 WORD STUDY

a chain

This is part of *a chain*. A chain is made of a number of rings passing through one another in a line. Chains are used for various purposes, such as tying up wild animals or keeping keys together. Ch____s are often made of metal.

A ch____ of events is a number of events which follow each other and are connected together.

a spring

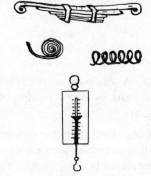

A spring is a piece of metal which will return to its original shape or position when pulled or pushed or pressed.

A watch has a very small sp_____. All automobiles have sp_____s. A spring balance contains a sp_____ which stretches when a weight is hung on it. When the sp_____ stretches, it moves a pointer downward.

This is a spring balance.

a coil
coiled

This is an electric *coil*.

This is a coil of rope.

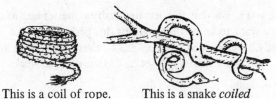

This is a snake *coiled* around a tree.

This metal spring is coiled.

Now it is tightly coiled.

wind up
wound up
unwind

We *wind up* a length of wool or cotton or a thread of any material when we give it the shape of a coil by turning it around and around.

We w____ a watch up when we turn a little screw which coils the watch spring tightly, so that the spring can afterward *unwind* and move the hands of the watch. Certain clocks need to be *wound up*. We wind a clock up by turning a key.

We can get water from a well by turning a handle and w____ing a rope up.

Note: Wind is pronounced to rhyme with find or mind. Wound is pronounced to rhyme with found or sound or ground.

(a) material

A material is a substance of which something is made. The m_____ials used in making airplanes must be strong and light. This coat is made of warm material. In the last few years industrial research workers have invented several new m_____ls. Some of the m_____ls needed by our factories must be bought from other countries. Suitcases can be made of leather, plastic, and other m_____ls. Leather is a hard-wearing m_____l.

a calendar
a date
a period
a second

		SEPTEMBER				
S	M	T	W	T	F	Sa
–	–	1	2	3	4	5
6	7	8	9	10	11	12
13	14	15	16	17	18	19
20	21	22	23	24	25	26
27	28	29	30	–	–	–

Here is one page of *a calendar*. A calendar shows us the months of a particular year, the days of each month in that year, and the days of each week in their correct order. A c_____ar helps us to find *dates* and calculate *periods* of time. A date is a particular day of the month (September 25th, for example) or the day on which a particular event occurs.

10.2 WORD STUDY

What is the d____ of your birthday? _____

What was the d___ of your arrival in this country? _____

What is the d___ of your next test or examination? _____

How does a c_____r help us to find dates? Suppose you know that your next test will be on Saturday. Today is Tuesday, September the 8th. You can look at the c_____ and find the d___ of your next test. This is easy. And if your tests are always on Saturday, you can make a list of all their d___s without counting the days, by looking at the c_____r. Look at the c_____r and give the dates of the other tests in September.

_____ _____ and _____ _____ .

A c_____r can also help us to calculate periods of time. A period is a length of time, which may be measured in seconds, minutes, hours, days, weeks, months, years, or even centuries. *A second* is the shortest period of time. There are sixty s_____ds in a minute.

A calendar does not help us to calculate periods measured in seconds, minutes, or hours. It does not help us to cal_____e p_____ds measured in years or centuries (unless we use a very special kind of c_____r). But it helps us to c_____e per__ds measured in days, weeks, or months.

Suppose you know that the first university semester begins on September 4th and ends on December 4th. You want to know the length of this period in weeks. You can find the length of this p_____d very easily by looking at a c_____r. Every week is on a separate line of the c_____ar; so it will not take you more than a few sec__ds to count the weeks.

Periods of Time

Questions:

1. How many days are there in April?*

    _____ days.

2. How many seconds are there in an hour?

    _____ seconds.

3. How many years are there in a century?

    _____ years.

4. How many days are there in a year?

    _____ days.

5. How many months are there in a year?

    _____ months.

6. How many hours are there in a day? (i.e., in a day as given on the calendar)

    _____ hours.

7. How many minutes are there in a day?

    _____ minutes.

8. How many days are there in October?

    _____ days.

9. How many weeks are there in a year?

    _____ weeks.

10.2 WORD STUDY

*Learn this short poem.

> Thirty days go past
>   In April and September.
> Thirty days go past
>   In June and in November.
> Twenty-eight in February,
>   February has to hurry.
> Seven months have thirty-one,
>   And so the earth goes around the sun.

a design
design
designed by

A design is a plan of a thing which will be (or may be) made or produced, for example, a building, an automobile, a table, or a dress. When engineers *design* an automobile they make a design or a plan of it.

Examples: Have you seen the de____ns of the new school? Do you think it is well de____ned? It is de_____ed by the architect who de_____ed the Town Hall.

She is a dress designer. She de_____s dresses for the president's wife. The dresses worn by the president's wife in France were d_____d by her.

This is an unusual kind of stove. It is d_____d to use the sun's heat to boil water and cook food.

invent
an invention
an inventor

To *invent* something is to think of or make something **completely new,** or design something which did not exist before. *An inventor* is a person who invents something, and the *invention* is the new thing which is made or designed, or the original idea of that thing. The inventor of the first pendulum clock was probably Galileo. He did not make it himself, but drew a diagram of a clock which would work with a pendulum. The pendulum clock was his inven____. Since Galileo's time many people have de_____ed pendulum clocks and many factories have produced them, but Galileo was the inv_____r because the original idea was his. In our century many engineers have de_____ed airplanes and hundreds of airplanes have been built, but the men responsible for the in_____ of airplanes were two Americans, Orville and Wilbur Wright. These brothers were the first men who designed a flying machine with an engine, which could actually fly. So we can say that they in_____ed the airplane.

An in_____r is a person with original ideas and also a practical person. The object which inventors design does what they they say it will do. When the steam engine was invented, for example, it was not just an idea in someone's head. It was the design of an engine which actually worked and moved when steam pushed the piston.

chief

= most important.

Examples: The *chief* industrial cities in England are Manchester, Birmingham, and Liverpool. What are the ch____ rivers in the United States? The ch____ value of his inv____ion was its usefulness to doctors. His ch____ purpose in coming here was to observe local customs. The ch____ date to remember in the history of the airplane is 1903.

fast
fast

adjective = having a speed greater than (or much greater than) the average or standard speed.
adverb = (going) at a speed greater than (or much greater than) the average or standard speed, or at a great speed.

Examples: This is a *fast* train. He is a f____ runner. Your watch is f____. Nothing is f____er than the speed of light. He runs f_____. She is not a f____ worker. I cannot understand you when you speak so _____.

Note: The adjective **fast** and the adverb **fast** have the same form. These words are used about continuous activities, not single movements or events, because the first means "having a high speed" and the second means "at a high speed."

10.2 WORD STUDY

a sequence   A *sequence* of happenings or events is a number of happenings or events which follow one another; or the order in which things follow one another.

Examples: He lost money because of a se_____ce of bad harvests. A story represents a se_____ce of events. Though many people observed the accident which occurred in the center of the city, they were not sure about the exact se_____ce of events. In this book the actions and battles of the war are not described in historical se_____ce. The cards in your hand are not in numerical s_____e.

a process   A *process* is a connected sequence (in time) of changes, developments, methods, or operations which form a pattern. Natural processes are often repeated, and an artificial process can usually be repeated.

Examples: Scientists have studied the process of growth in many animals, for example, frogs and rats. Scientists have now discovered more about the pr___sses of sleep and dreaming. The development of human thought and language must have been a long pr___ss. Bessemer invented a p_____ss for making steel. People who try to reduce their weight usually find that it is a slow p_____. Printing p_____es are much faster than they used to be. Engineers must study various industrial p_____es. Sociologists study the p_____es by which societies are formed and develop or change.

Note: When **a process** is used to name a sequence of events in nature or society, it is generally used for a **regular pattern** of events which happen according to scientific laws or which are found **repeated** elsewhere. For this reason we do not speak of **a process** when we speak of a sequence of events which depend on human decisions, e.g., a battle or the story of a particular man's life. This kind of sequence **can happen only once**, and cannot be understood as a pattern depending on scientific laws.

But we also use **a process** for a sequence of methods or operations (designed by people) which **can be repeated or imitated.**

possess   = have

Examples: He *possesses* two shirts and a pair of shoes. The local authorities po___ss some land on the other side of the university. The office does not p_____ an electric typewriter.

Note: Do **not** use this word yourself. "Have" is the word used most often, and you should use this instead.

connected by   = joined together, or related, or related by ideas or purposes (used with a plural subject only).

Examples: The two towns are *connected by* a railway. These two wires are not connected. The two families are connected by marriage. The two paragraphs are not connected. This word has two connected meanings. The topics discussed in these two essays are closely connected. These two problems are probably connected.

connected to   physical senses = joined to

Examples: The wheel is *connected to* the top of a pendulum. The gas stove is not yet connected to the supply. The island is connected to the mainland by a long bridge. All the machines are separately connected to the electricity supply.

connected with   = having a social connection with

Examples: I am not *connected with* him in any way. Miss Y is connected with the Smiths by marriage. Mr. X is not connected with this school.

connected with   = related to something by ideas or purposes

Examples: The first paragraph is not really *connected with* the second. In many people's minds Malaya is connected with rubber and tin, and New Zealand is connected with meat and butter. The students' demonstration was not connected with the workers' demands. The President's visit to France is not connected with the peace talks.

10.2 WORD STUDY

connection The senses of this noun follow the various meanings of "connected."

Examples: There is no *connection* between the kitchen water pipes and the bathroom water pipes. I need a new bicycle pump connection. What is your connection with the school? There must be some connection between these events. He decided to end his connection with the socialist party.

**in connection
with
in this
   connection**

Examples: The President is visiting New York *in connection with* the trade talks. A course of lectures will be given in connection with the National Geophysical year. A meeting will be held in connection with the students' demands.

Mr. Smith, who is now 70, is the oldest teacher in our school. *In this connection* I would like to remind you that he was the first teacher to drive to school in a car.

rotate = spin around on axis
a rotation = one complete spin or turn (e.g., by an object on its axis)
rotation = the activity or process of rotating, or starting from one point and coming around again to the same
   (uncountable)   point

Examples: The earth *rotates* on its axis. Its *rotation* is regular. A single ro_____n of the moon takes about 27½ days, and the moon takes the same time to go around the earth. R_____n of crops is practiced by good farmers; they grow corn in their fields one year, oats the next year, and grass the third year; then they begin the sequence again and repeat it. During Mr. A's absence, Mr. X, Miss Y, and Mrs. Z will take his classes in rotation.

regulate We *regulate* something, for example, a machine or a movement or a moving object, when we control it systematically or cause it to obey a rule.

Examples: The movement of this clock is reg_____ed by a pendulum. The policeman stands in the middle of the road and r_____tes the traffic. Some machines are self-reg_____ing. The temperature of the oven is reg_____ed by this dial.

**prevent
prevent** We *prevent* an accident when we act in such a way that the accident does not happen. We prevent a marriage when we act in such a way that the marriage does not occur. The government pre_____s an economic crisis when it acts in such a way that the situation does not become critical, does not become a crisis. We pre_____ an event or a situation when we act in such a way that the event or situation does not occur.

We pre____t someone **from** entering the room when we lock the door or do something which makes it impossible for him to enter the room (though he wants or tries to do so). We p_____t a friend f___ lifting a box by making it impossible for him to do this, or by telling him not to do it, although he wants or tries to lift it. We p_____ someone f___ sleeping if we make it impossible for him to sleep. We p_____ someone f___ doing something when we make it impossible for him to do it, although he wants or tries to do it. We p_____ something from happening, if we act in such a way that it does not happen.

Exercise I: Substitution Table

I	II	III	IV	V
How	can you	prevent	an accident	?
	can they		a crisis	
	can we		a war	
	will you		a repetition of the mistake	
	will they		his action	
	will we		her marriage	

10.2 WORD STUDY

Exercise II: Substitution Table

I	II	III	IV	V	VI	VII
We	could not	prevent	her	from	marrying	
You			him		sleeping	
I			them		eating	
					falling	
					practicing	
					removing the furniture	
					listening to the radio	
					waiting for me	
					making the statement	
					choosing that route	
					acquiring the land	
					noticing the errors	
					stealing the diamond	

Exercise III: Find a phrase in the **second** column which goes with a sentence in the **first** column and give it the number of the sentence it goes with.

1.	You can prevent him from smoking	by buying it ourselves.
2.	We can prevent them from entering the room	by keeping quiet about it.
3.	You can prevent this material from stretching	by stopping supplies of materials.
4.	They can prevent the level of the river from rising	by changing the rules of the club.
5.	They can prevent him from becoming a member	by making an artificial lake.
6.	They can prevent our industries from developing	by reducing his pocket money.
7.	We can prevent him from selling the invention to America	by locking the door.
8.	We can prevent them from discovering the process	by keeping it flat.

whenever (a) = at any time
(b) = every time, as often as

Exercise I: Substitution Table

I	II	III	IV
Come and see us	whenever	you like	
You can talk to me		you have time	
He is ready to help you		you are free	
		you have a problem	
		it is necessary	

Exercise II: Substitution Table

I	II	III	IV	V
Whenever	there is a crisis	,	he runs away	
	the situation gets difficult		he asks my advice	
	he is in difficulties		he goes to sleep	
	he has to make a decision		he consults his wife	
	he has a problem to face		he consults the Bible	
	he does not know what to do		he gets angry	
	his children argue with him		he starts drinking	
	his children are naughty			

10.2 WORD STUDY

Exercise III: Substitution Table

I	II	III	IV	V
Whenever	money is worth less	,	prices rise	
	the value of money falls		the cost of living rises	
	food becomes scarce		the standard of living falls	
	goods become scarce		the government faces problems	
	there is scarcity of food		the government becomes unpopular	
			workers demand higher wages	

lose pronounced to rhyme with **shoes, choose, whose.**
lost past tense.
lost participle; pronounced to rhyme with **cost.**

When a man no longer has what he had before, though he still wishes he had it, he has *lost* it; it is lost. We *lose* things for various reasons; because of an accident, because of carelessness or forgetfulness, or for other reasons. We lose people because of separation or death. When you put your pen down somewhere and do not remember where you put it, you lose it. When a man's wife dies, he loses his wife. Sometimes a man l__es his hair; sometimes he l___s his job; sometimes he l____ his memory. In an economic crisis many people l___ their money. Sometimes there is an accident because the driver l____ control of his car. A country may l___ some of its trade if it cannot pro__ce goods cheaply enough. We can l___ bad habits; we can also l___ good ones. Students can l___ their interest in a certain subject, if the teaching is bad or if their old interests are displaced by new ones. A watch l___s time when it goes more slowly than it did before. Time is l__t, in general, when it is spent on unnecessary activities instead of those which are necessary for a particular purpose.

Exercise: Each of the following sentences requires some form of the verb **lose** to complete its meaning. Rewrite each sentence, using the correct form of the verb (**lose, loses,** or **lost**) in the right place.

1. He two sons in the war.

   _____ .

2. If you do not keep your money in a safe place, you may it.

   _____ .

3. The diamonds are; I can't find them anywhere.

   _____ .

4. If you want your health to improve you must try to weight.

   _____ .

5. In 1950 a ship was at sea, and all the passengers were drowned.

   _____ .

6. Because of the bad weather, some of the harvest was last year.

   _____ .

7. When a hot object is placed in cold water it will some of its heat.

   _____ .

8. The factory has four of its best engineers.

   _____ .

10.2 WORD STUDY

9. The little boy who was was found three miles from his home.

     _____.

10. When a substance is burned it some of its weight.

     _____.

11. When goods are very plentiful they some of their value.

     _____.

12. He all his money in the last economic crisis.

     _____.

13. Gold does not its value because it is limited in quantity.

     _____.

during	(preposition of time) (a) = as long as (a period) continues (b) = at some point or points of time in (a period) *Examples:* (a) The sun gives light *during* the day. During the war no one could leave the country. (b) He came to see me during my absence. During the war many people lost their homes. *Note:* Unless you know English well, it is safer to use "in." **During** cannot be used in certain contexts.
last **lasted** **has lasted**	*Note:* This verb has **no** "is + -ed" form. (a) = continue for (a period of time) (b) = be enough for (a period of time) *Examples:* (a) The meeting *lasted* three hours. The journey lasted two days. How long will this weather l____? (b) We have enough grain to l___ two years. This quantity of coal will only l___ two weeks. We have sufficient food to l___ us for some time. *Note:* This is another word which you should understand but **not use** in your own writing. Use **continue** or **continue for** for meaning (a) and **be enough for** for meaning (b).
a pendulum **a swing** **a period** **a rhythm** **swing** **regulate** **a movement** **complicated** **backward** **forward**	*A pendulum* is a rope or a rod, usually made of metal, which has a weight at one end and is fixed at the other end. If you give the weighted end a push, it will move first in one dir__tion and then in the opp____te d_____tion. It will move *forward* and *backward*, and then again f_____d and back____d. It will *swing*. When you push the weighted end of a p_____m, it begins to sw__g. A child likes to sw__g. This child is part of a pendulum! When a p_____m s_____s, it moves backward and f_____, and then repeats these *movements*. It moves first in one dir_____n and then in the opp_____e di_____n. Each of these movements is called *a swing*. The *period* of each s__ng is the time it takes. When a p_____um is of a given length, the period of each swing is the same. If you make the pendulum longer, the p_____d of its sw___ will be longer; but every swing of this longer pendulum will have the same p_____d. The p_____d of the swing, therefore, depends on the l___th of the pendulum.

10.2 WORD STUDY

Backward and forward, backward and forward, b_____d and f_____, the pendulum swings. It swings with a regular *rhythm*. It has a rhythm. You can feel it and hear it as the pendulum moves through the air. What do we mean by a rhythm? A rhythm (notice the spelling!) is a pattern of movements or of sounds. It is a pattern in time. You will remember that in a p_____rn there is always repetition; a p_____rn repeats itself or is rep___ted. A rhythm is a kind of pattern, and so a rhythm must be something which re____ts itself or is r_____ted. What is repeated in a rh____m?

Take a ruler and hit the table with it. First hit it three times quickly (making the periods between these actions the same), then wait for exactly one second. Now repeat all this. Repeat it again and continue to repeat it. You will hear the rhythm. It will be like this:

___ / ___ / ___ / ___ / ___ /

What is repeated in this rhythm? A sequence of movements is repeated and a sequence of times is repeated.

The rhythm of a pendulum is a very simple one. There are only two different movements (a movement backward and a movement forward), and there is only one interval or period of time.

Some rhythms are not simple, but very *complicated*. Here is a diagram of two lines of a song, "Ding-dong-bell, Pussy's in the well."

Ding dong bell	Pussy's in the well.
Who pulled her out?	Little Tommy Stout.

The rhythm of this song is not very c_____cated, but it is more c_____ted than the rhythm of a p_____um. You probably have records, which you play on your record player, of pieces of music which have much more co_____cated r_____ms than this song.

We say that a thing is complicated when it is not simple, when it has many parts and many different kinds of parts.

A pair of scissors is a simple machine because it has only _____ parts and they are both of the same kind. An airplane is a very complicated m____ine and so is a computer, because they both have many p__ts of many d_____ent kinds.

When we say that something is complicated, we often mean, in addition, that it is difficult to understand or learn or solve. A complicated machine is not easy to understand; a complicated rhythm is not easy to learn (for example, the rhythm of a dance, a song, or a poem); a c_____ed problem is not easy to solve.

It is easier to write simple sentences than to write c_____ed sentences. A c_____d sentence has many words and many clauses* in it, and the clauses may be of different kinds. If you want to write correct English it is much safer to write simple sentences, sentences which have only one clause.

Note: * A sentence or a part of a sentence is called a clause if it contains a finite verb.

regulate
a hand
 (of a clock)
a dial
a face
 (of a clock)
ancient
a shadow

A clock has two *hands*, a long hand and a short hand. The short hand shows the hours and the long hand shows the minutes. The hands move around the *dial* of the clock, which is the surface on which the numbers appear. Sometimes the dial of a clock is called the *face* of the clock. Other instruments on which numbers appear and which have hands or pointers which move around, pointing to the numbers, also have dials. A speedometer (which measures speed) also has a d___. Certain weighing machines have d____s. A sundial was an *ancient* clock. A sundial had a pointer, but the pointer itself did not move; its *shadow* moved, pointing to different numbers as the sun changed its position in the sky and made the shadow change its direction.

10.2 WORD STUDY

The hands of a clock move around its dial with a regular rhythm, tick-tock, tick-tock. A clock measures time. The units of time are standard units, like the other units we use to measure things. An hour must not be longer or shorter than the standard hour, whose length is fixed by instruments kept at the Government Observatory.

A minute must not be sh_____r or l_____r than 1/60th of a standard hour, and a second must not be sh_____r or l_____r than 1/60th of a standard minute.

To keep the movements of a clock regular, and to prevent them from getting too long or too short, they must be *regulated*. When movements, activities, or processes are r_____ed they are made to follow or obey a rule or standard. What r_____s a clock? Sometimes a clock is r_____ed by a pen_____m. A p_____m is fixed to a wheel which turns the hands of the clock, and the movements of the hands are r_____ed by the movement of the p_____m.

A face. The drawings below will give you some meanings of "face."

The face of a girl.

The face of a clock.

A cube has six faces. How many of them can you see in the picture?

A shadow is the area of darkness made on the ground, on a wall, etc., by an object which cuts off the direct light of the sun by standing in the path of the light.

a telescope
an astronomer
astronomy

Here is *an astronomer* looking through *a telescope*. He is observing the stars. A t_____pe is an instrument which enables us to observe objects in space, i.e., stars and planets. An astronomer is a person who studies the stars. *Astronomy* is the study or science of the stars. These two words are derived from the Greek word "aster," which means "a star."

-able
-ible

Notice the use of these endings to form words which mean *can be + -ed* and *cannot be + -ed*. A *reliable* person or thing is one which can be *relied on*. An *unacceptable* gift is a gift which cannot be ac_____ed.

Finish the following sentences:

1. A noticeable improvement is an im_____ment which can be n_____ed.
2. An event is predictable, when it can _____ .
3. A plant is unclassifiable when it cannot _____.
4. An uneatable meal is a m _____ which _____.
5. A measurable amount is an a_____t which _____.
6. A washable material is one which _____ .
7. An enjoyable vacation is a v_____ which _____ .
8. An inadvisable action is one which cannot _____.

Unit X

10.3 DICTATION EXERCISES AND DICTATION PASSAGES

A 1. The passage *Calendars* will now be read to you. In the following pairs, cross out the word or phrase which is incorrect (i.e., the word you do not hear).

   (a)   movement - movements   (f)   Tuesday - Thursday
   (b)   earth's - earth   (g)   enables - enable
   (c)   convenient - convenience   (h)   occurs - occurred
   (d)   seeker - sequence   (i)   activities - activity
   (e)   divided - divide

   2. Number the following words in the order in which you hear them. (The teacher will read them in a different order from the one below.)

   event   sequence   record   based on
            certain   particular   ancient
   calendar   calendars   enables

   3. When the teacher gives you a signal, underline the following words in the dictation passage *Calendars*. This is a race.

   dates   convenience   ancient   February
   activities   journey   regulate   sequence
   calendars   Saturday   possesses   modern

   4. The passage *Calendars* will now be given as dictation.

B 1. The passage *Changes in the Value of Money* will now be read to you. Number the following words in the order in which you hear them.

   especially   received   accepted   control
            economists   level   skilled
   complicated   worth   acquired

   2. The passage *Changes in the Value of Money* will now be read to you. Write the articles (if any) which precede and the nouns which follow the adjectives given below.

   (a)   _____   international monetary   _____
   (b)   _____   American   _____
   (c)   _____   reliable   _____
   (d)   _____   large   _____
   (e)   _____   present   _____
   (f)   _____   last   _____
   (g)   _____   foreign   _____
   (h)   _____   official   _____
   (i)   _____   government   _____
   (j)   _____   less valuable   _____
   (k)   _____   economic   _____
   (l)   _____   skilled and unskilled   _____

   3. When the teacher gives a signal, underline the following words in the dictation passage *Changes in the Value of Money*. This is a race.

   reliable   official   prevent   received
   international   foreign   lead to   system
   valuable   monetary   continue to   materials

   4. The passage *Changes in the Value of Money* will now be given as dictation.

10.3 DICTATION PASSAGES

(a) Calendars

Every home possesses at least one calendar. Ancient calendars were based on the movements of the moon, but modern calendars are based on the earth's journey around the sun. For convenience, the days of the week are given a sequence of seven names, and the months into which the year is divided are given a sequence of twelve names. The second day of the week is Tuesday, and the sixth day is Saturday. The second month of the year is February and the eighth is August. A date is a certain day in a certain month in a certain year. A calendar enables us to find and record the date on which a particular event occurs, and to plan and regulate our activities in relation to important dates.

(b) Changes in the Value of Money

The international monetary system is so complicated that even economists do not always understand it. Its operations are therefore difficult to control. In general, a unit of money can only continue to be a reliable standard if the amount of gold it is worth does not change. For some time the American dollar was widely accepted as a standard. The Americans acquired large amounts of gold during the present century, especially in the World War of 1940 to 1945, when they received gold as payment for goods and materials supplied to foreign armies.

The British unit of money is called the pound. The American unit of money is called the dollar. In the last ten years both these units have been devalued, that is to say, their value in gold (and in the amount of goods they can buy) has fallen. When the price of goods rises and the value of money falls, we call this process inflation. Inflation leads to economic crisis, factories are unable to sell their goods; skilled and unskilled workers are thrown out of work. Governments should do everything possible to prevent this unfortunate situation from occurring.

Unit X

10.4 READING PASSAGES

(a) The Measurement of Time

Distance, weight, and temperature are measured by counting units, and time is also measured by counting units. To serve as units of time, we must use occurrences which have the same period and which are repeated one after the other in a continuous chain. We find such a continuous repetition of equal units whenever there is a regular movement which repeats itself again and again without stopping and without change of speed. A regular movement of this kind can be used as a unit of time; a sequence of such movements can form a time scale.

The first movements used as standards of time were those of the earth and the moon. It takes the earth one day to make a complete turn on its axis; in other words, "a day" is the name we give to one complete rotation of the earth, when we think of it as a unit of time. It takes the earth one year to encircle (= go around) the sun. The year and the day form the bases of our system of time measurement.

In a calendar we also find months and weeks. Though the words "month" and "moon" are related in their origin, a month in our calendar is a purely conventional division of the year and does not have the same period as the moon's rotation, which lasts only 28½ days. Calendar months are not even equal to one another. Some people believe that we could improve the calendar by dividing the year into months of more equal lengths. A week, of course, is simply a sequence of seven days.

The units which are shorter than the day are the hour, the minute, and the second. These units are very important for our practical activities, but they are not directly derived from natural processes. They are artificial divisions of a day. It is only accidentally that people chose to divide the day into 24 hours. They could have divided it into 10, or 20, or 60 or any other convenient number of units.

After agreeing on the number of hours in a day, people designed many different kinds of clocks to produce or mark movements which could be counted as hours. The chief clocks of ancient history were water clocks and sundials. In a water clock, the unit of time was artificially produced. The water in a special container was allowed to flow out of it, and the flow was carefully regulated so that it did not change its speed. The unit of time was the amount of time it took for the water to flow out.

On a sundial, the passage (= passing) of time was shown by the movement of the shadow of a fixed object placed in the sunlight. This object, a stick or a pointer, was usually fixed to a flat stone and lines were drawn on the stone to mark the hours. The shadow, of course, was produced by the sun but lines drawn by people represented the conventional units of a time system. Time passes; the passage of time is a movement, whether natural or artificial, whether it is the journey of the earth, the movement of a shadow, the flow of a certain quantity of water, or the swing of a pendulum.

One of the greatest inventions of the clock makers was the pendulum clock. A pendulum used for a clock is a metal rod; one end is fixed and the other end is weighted. The weighted end of the rod swings backward and forward with a regular rhythm. This pendulum is connected to a set of wheels and regulates them. The wheels have teeth around their edges so that they cannot move without following the "tick-tock" intervals of the moving pendulum. One of these wheels is connected to the hands of the clock. The clock hands must also follow the "tick-tock" intervals of the swinging pendulum, and as they go around the clock face they count the swings of the pendulum.

The swinging movements of a pendulum are regular; the intervals of time marked by the traveling clock hands are equal or approximately equal. British standards of time are fixed at Greenwich Observatory, where astronomers observe the movements of the sun, moon, and stars, and use their observations to regulate clocks which are designed to measure time with great precision. Government offices and radio and television stations check their own clocks by signals received from the observatory, and we can check our clocks and watches by listening to the time signals on the radio. We say that a watch is "fast" when its hands move fast by the official standard, and we say that it is "slow" when its hands move too slowly. When a watch is fast its hour hand reaches each number on the dial too soon and when it is slow the hour hand reaches each number too late.

10.4 READING PASSAGES

(b) Sundials

The first clock used by people still exists, and all human time systems still depend on it. It is the sun. Like us, people of ancient times said it was morning when the sun appeared and night when it disappeared. When the sun stood highest in the sky they knew it was the middle of the day. We still use the sun as a clock unless we need to fix times more precisely.

As a time marker, however, the sun itself was of limited value. It looked very small compared with the sky, and it was difficult to guess with any accuracy how far it had traveled at any point in its journey. Measurement requires a scale. Obviously a scale could not be drawn on the sky itself to mark divisions of the sun's passage. Then how could a scale be made?

For a long time people knew that shadows moved. Then one day someone noticed that shadows changed their length and position as the sun moved through the sky. This clever person discovered a relation between a shadow and the sun's journey. So the idea of a sundial was born.

It is possible that a tree in an open space was first used as a sundial, because a tree had some of the features of a sundial. Its position was fixed and it threw long shadows which changed their length and position in a regular way. Later the idea must have occurred to someone that a stick or rod or spear could be used in the same way as a tree, and he or she made the first sundial. A man could cut two poles (= thick wooden sticks) of the same length, one for himself and one for his wife. He could then go out hunting and tell his wife "When the shadow is as long as my arm, I will come home."

The word "dial" is derived from a Latin word meaning "day." A sundial's shadow measures the sun's day. Sundials are still used in some countries. In certain parts of Africa, only a few years ago, a small sundial was made by placing two crossed sticks over an empty pot. In Egypt the trunk of a palm tree is still used. It is planted vertically* in the ground and a circle is drawn around it for the dial, with stones placed in the circle to mark the hours.

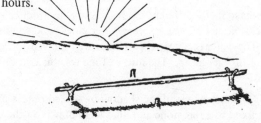

Another kind of sundial was a long rod placed over two forked sticks. A short stick was driven into the ground on the western side of the rod and another on the eastern side. When the moving shadow of the rod left the short stick on the western side, the working day began. When the evening shadow reached the little stick on the other side, it was time to stop work.

An interesting fact about the earliest Egyptian sundials has been discovered. The "hours" they measured were *not equal*; they were periods of different lengths. We can understand how this happened. When the Egyptians made their first sundials they marked the lines on them at equal intervals, just as if they were marking equal units on a ruler. But the sun's effect on shadows is not regular. Morning shadows and evening shadows travel faster than shadows thrown by an object in the middle of the day. To allow for this, the intervals marking the earlier and later hours on a sundial should be made wider than those marking the midday hours. In the ancient Egyptian time system this was not done, and so in this system morning and evening hours were actually shorter than midday hours. Since the Egyptians regulated the length of the day by sunrise and sunset, summer hours were also longer than winter hours.

To correct these irregularities, later sundials were marked with a suitable scale, like the one below.

1st hour	2nd	3rd	4th	5th	6th	7th	8th	9th	10th	11th
(sunrise)					(noon)					

Seasonal changes in the length of the day were also allowed for.

It is impossible to measure anything accurately unless you know exactly what it is that you are measuring. We speak of the moving sun, but it is actually the earth which moves on its axis when day passes into night. The ancient Egyptians did not know that day and night, as people experience them in any particular locality, are an effect of the earth's rotation on its own axis. The axis of the earth is an imaginary line through its center. The ends of this line are the North and South Poles. Above the North Pole there is a star called Polaris. The final discovery about sundials was that the vertical part of a sundial should point to Polaris to give an accurate shadow.

---

* vertically = at right angles to the earth's surface (adverb).

Unit X

10.5 VOCABULARY TEST

To test yourself on the vocabulary of this section, fill in the missing letters in the incomplete words.

An in_____n is usually the end result of a long s_____ce of ideas, experiments, and im_____ments. The in_____n of the clock shows this clearly. The original idea of a clock was the idea of standardizing a movement or a pr_____s so that it would always take the same p_____d of time and could therefore be used to reg_____e another p_____s, such as cooking a meal. This was the b____s of the hour glass, an a_____nt in_____t.

Later two more requirements were a__ed; first, the r_____t that a movement having a certain p_____d should be con_____sly re____ted, and secondly that it should be po_____e to ob_____e and count the re_____ns. A machine with these f_____es en____ed people to measure the p_____ge of time and give a time di_____n to all pr_____ses and ac_____es.

Though these b____c ideas seem s____le, modern clocks are in fact co_____ted in_____ts. They depend for their de____n on the ex_____ce of special m_____als, highly developed ind_____l p_____ses, and en_____rs with specialized s___ll and tr____ing.

In a pe_____m clock the sw____ing p_____m is co_____ted to a wheel which ro_____s when driven by the force of the p_____m. The ro_____n of the wheel is co_____lled by metal teeth cut in the edge of the wheel at equal in_____ls. A small modern clock or a watch has a slowly unw____ing sp____g which takes the place of the p_____m. We r__y on our clocks and watches as pr_____n in_____ts and d_____d from them a high degree of ac_____y.

In a_____t times farmers in the fields worked ac_____ing to their own na_____l rh____ms and often sang while they worked. They only worked fa__er than usual in a c_____s, for example when they knew a storm was coming. Perhaps the in_____n of clocks has led people to v__ue time in a wrong way. The r_____ms of factory work are de_____ned by the requirements of machines, not by h____n needs. In a factory an hour is d____ded into minutes; each minute has the same l____th and is w__th an e____l amount of money. Perhaps our ab_____y to measure time in this way has made us f____et that a man has only one life, which cannot be counted as a s_____ce of equal u__ts of equal v___e. The fact that time can be measured in this way sometimes pr_____ts us from seeing that life is not measurable; in other words it is not a di_____n.

abbreviation 5
ability 7
about 7
accept 6
accident 9
according to 9
accuracy 1
accurate 1
acquire 9
action 4
activity 7
actual 5
actually 5
add 1
addition 1
agree 6
agreement 6
alcohol 6
alike 3
allow 1
almost 6
American ton 3
amount 2
ancient 10
angle 2
appear 9
appearance 9
approximate 6
approximately 6
Arabic 3
area 2
artificial 7
artificially 8
astronomer 10
astronomy 10
at sea 4
atmosphere 2
average (n., adj.) 8
axis 9

backward 10
balance 3
bar (n.) 1
barometer 2
based on 1
basic 1
basis 1
belong to 4
block (n.) 1
brightness 6
British ton 3
by air 3
by land 3
by sea 3

calculate 4
calculation 4
calendar 10
capacity
 (of a container) 2

Celsius 2
center 4
century 1
certain (particular) 4
chain 10
chapter 6
cheap 8
check (v.) 3
chemical 4
chief 10
choose 2
chose 2
chosen 2
circle 4
circumference 4
class 4
classify 5
coil 10
coiled 10
common
 (occurring often) 5
compare 3
comparison 3
compass (n.) 9
complete (adj.) 1
complicated 10
cone 5
connected 10
connection 10
contain 2
container 2
continue 7
continuous 7
continuously 7
control (v., n.) 9
convenience 3
convenient 3
conveniently 4
convention 6
conventional 6
convert 2
cool (v., adj.) 1
correct (adj.) 3
correctly 5
cost (v., n.) 8
countable 6
crisis 9
cube 4
cubic 2
curve 10
curved 10
custom 6
customer 8

dangerous 7
date 10
datum 7
decide 9
decimal (n., adj.) 6
decision 9

define 2
definition 2
degree
 (of heat, etc.) 2
demand (n.) 8
depend on 5
depth 1
derived from 2
design (v., n.) 10
determine 4
develop 7
development 7
devise 7
diagram 2
dial 10
diameter 4
diamond 8
dimension 3
direct (adj.) 4
direction
 (toward a place) 9
directly 4
disagree 6
disagreement 6
disappear 9
disappearance 9
discover 3
discuss 7
displace 4
dissolve 4
distance 1
distinction
 (difference) 6
distinctly 6
distinguish 6
district 8
divide 1
division 1
drop (v.) 7
during 10

the East 3
economic 5
economics 5
economist 8
edge 4
effect 5
empire 3
enable 9
engineer 8
engineering 8
enter 5
equal (to) 1
equator 2
equivalent (to) 2
error 7
especially 7
estimate (v., n.) 7
Europe 3
European 3

event 9
exact (adj.) 6
exactly 6
example 5
exchange (v., n.) 8
exist 5
existence 5
expand 1
expansion 1
expect 6
expensive 8
experience 7
experienced 7
express (v.) 7

face (n.)
 (of a clock, etc.) 10
face (v.) 9
facing 9
fact 1
Fahrenheit 2
fall 5
familiar with 1
fast (adj., adv.) 10
feature 5
final 7
finally 7
flat 10
flow 4
fluid 4
for example 1
foreign 9
form 1
formula 4
fortunately 4
forward 10
fraction 6

general 6
generally 4
goods 8
grain 3
guess (v., n.) 6

hand
 (of a clock) 10
happen 4
harbor 5
heat (v.) 1
height 1
hundredth 6

imaginary 2
imagine 2
imitate 7
imitation 7
important 4
improve 9
improvement 9

in connection with 10
in this connection 10
inconvenience 3
inconvenient 3
incorrect 3
indirect 4
indirectly 4
industry 7
inexperienced 7
instead of 1
instrument 2
insufficient 5
intensity 5
international 9
interval 4
invade 3
invasion 3
invent 10
invention 10
inventor 10
irregular 4

kind (of) 3
knowledge 5

last (v.) 10
lead to 7
length 1
letter
 (of alphabet) 3
level 5
lift (v.) 7
limit (v., n.) 5
limited 5
liquid (n., adj.) 2
liquid volume 2
listen to 9
local 8
lose 10

material (n.) 10
mathematician 8
mathematics 8
matter (v.) 7
member (of) 6
mercury 5
method 2
metric 1
metric ton 3
million 1
minus (sign) 6
monetary 8
movement 10
multiple 1
multiplication 1
multiply 1

narrow 5
natural 3
nearly 1
necessary 1
North Pole 2
notice (v.) 4
nowadays 1
numerous 5

object 4
observation 9
observe 9
obtain 4
obviously 2
occur 9
occurrence 9
official 1
operation 6
opposite (adj.) 9
order
  (sequence) (n.) 9
ordinary 6
origin 2
original 8
originally 2
over (more than) 7
oxygen 8

paragraph 6
particular 9
pattern 4
pay for 8
pendulum 10
perfect 1
period 10
physicist 8
physics 8
planet 3
plenty 8
plentiful 8
plural 2
plus (sign) 6
the Poles 2
political 5
politician 5
position 3
possess 10
possibility 7
possible 4
practical 7
practice (v.) 5
practice (n.) 7
precede 6
precise 7
precisely 7
precision 7
predict 9
prediction 9
prefix 6

pressure 2
prevent 10
price 5
probably 1
problem 3
process 10
produce 5
prove 5
purify 8
purpose 5

quantity 1
quarter 6
quite (completely) 6

radius 4
rapid 9
rapidly 9
receive 8
record (v., n.) 4
rectangle 4
rectangular 4
reduce 7
refer to 4
regular 4
regularly 5
regulate 10
related (to) 5
relation (general) 5
relationship 5
reliable 9
rely on 7
remove 6
repeat 4
repetition 4
represent 4
require 5
research 8
responsible 9
revise 9
rhythm 10
right angle 2
right angled 5
rise 5
rod 6
Roman 3
rotate 10
rotation 10
route 4
row (n.) 3
ruler 2

safe 7
scale (n.)
(of units) 4
scarce 8
scarcity 8
scientific 8
sealed 5

season 3
second (n.) 10
sentence (n.) 5
separate 3
separately 3
sequence 10
set (n.) 1
several 7
shadow 10
sign (n.) 9
signal 9
simple 3
singular 2
situated 8
situation 5
size 3
skill 9
skilled 9
slightly 5
social 6
society 2
solar 3
solid (n.,adj.) 2
solve 5
South Pole 2
special 1
speed 9
speedometer 6
sphere 2
spherical 9
spin 9
spring (metal) 10
standard (n., adj.) 1
state (v.) 6
statement 4
stretch 5
subject (n.) 6
substance 6
subtract 3
subtraction 3
sufficient 9
sufficiently 9
suitable 7
sum 3
supply (v., n.) 8
suppose 5
sure 1
surface 2
swing (v., n.) 10
symbol 4
system 1

telescope 10
temperature 1
tenth 6
thermometer 5
thousandth 6
to the nearest
  (inch, etc.) 6

total (n., adj.) 3
toward 9
trade (v., n.) 3
traffic 6
train 8
trained 8
training 8
travel 3
traveled 3
triangle 3
tribe 3
tube 5
turn (v., n.) 9

unconventional 6
uncountable 6
under (less than) 7
unit 1
unless 9
unlikely 7
unsuitable 7
untrained 8
unwind 10
usually 2

valuable 8
value (n.) 1
value (v.) 8
various 5
vegetables 8
volume 2

wait for 9
weather 9
weight 2
the West 3
Western 2
whenever 10
width 1
willing 6
wind (v.) 10
without 4
worth 8
wound (up) 10